The ARRL
Introduction to Emergency Communication Course

This is a transcript of the online course (#EC-001), offered through ARRL's Continuing Education Program.

For more information about ARRL online courses and emergency communications training visit: www.arrl.org/courses-training.

Copyright 2011 American Radio Relay League, Inc. All material included herein, whether visual, textual or aural, is the property of The American Radio Relay League and its licensors. No part may be reproduced, recorded or otherwise copied by any visual, aural or other means. Printing of course text for personal use only is permitted. Specific permission is required to use this material in any training or product.

ISBN: 978-0-087259-730-3

Fourth Edition, Second Printing

ARRL Introduction to Emergency Communication Course Transcript
Table of Contents

	Preface	1
	How to Complete this Course	3
Section 1	**The Framework: How You Fit In**	
Topic 1	Introduction to Emergency Communication	4
Topic 2	Amateurs as Professionals	13
Topic 3	Network Theory and Design	22
Topic 4	Emergency Communication Organizations and Systems	34
Topic 5a	Served Agency Communication Systems	46
Topic 5b	Working Directly with the Public	56
Section 2	**The Networks for Messages**	
Topic 6	Basic Communication Skills	64
Topic 7a	Basic Net Operations	74
Topic 7b	Introduction to Emergency Nets	81
Topic 7c	Net Operating Guidelines	91
Topic 7d	The FCC Ruling on Drills and Employees	100
Topic 8	The Net Control Station	104
Topic 9	Net Control Station Operator Practices	112
Topic 10	The Net Manager	124
Topic 11	Introduction to the National Traffic System	132
Topic 12	Specialized Nets and Their Operations	147
Topic 13	Severe Weather Nets	155
Section 3	**Message Handling**	
Topic 14	Basic Message Handling – Part 1	165
Topic 15	Basic Message Handling – Part 2	177
Section 4	**What Happens When Called**	
Topic 16	The Incident Command System	188
Topic 17	Preparing for Deployment	197
Topic 18	Equipment Choices for Emergency Communication	207
Topic 19	Emergency Activation	223
Topic 20	Setting Up, Initial Operations and Shutdown	229
Section 5	**Considerations**	
Topic 21	Operations & Logistics	238
Topic 22	Safety & Survival	250
Topic 23	ARES PIO: The Right Stuff	261
Topic 24	Alternative Communication Methods	268
Topic 25	What to Expect in Large Scale Disasters	277
Topic 26	Hazardous Materials Awareness	285
Topic 27	Marine Communications	292
Section 6	**Alternatives and Opportunities**	
Topic 28	Modes, Methods and Applications	300
Topic 29	Other Learning Opportunities	310
	Answers to Topic Knowledge Review Questions	316
	Appendix	

For error corrections, updates and supplementary material, and to download audio and video files referenced in this course, please refer to the product notes page on the ARRL website at: http://www.arrl.org/product-notes.

About ARRL and the Amateur Radio Emergency Service (ARES®)

The ARRL Amateur Radio Emergency Service consists of licensed amateurs who have voluntarily registered their qualifications and equipment for communications duty in the public service when disaster strikes. ARES members learn more about emergency operations and practice regularly by providing aid for non-emergency events like parades, marathons and drills.

Amateur Radio, often called "ham radio," has consistently been the most reliable means of communication in emergencies when other systems failed or were overloaded.

ARES has formal, national agreements to provide emergency communications aid for FEMA, DHS, the American Red Cross, the Salvation Army, the National Weather Service and many other response organizations.

To learn more go to www.arrl.org/ares.

What is the ARRL?

Founded in 1914, the American Radio Relay League is the 156,000-member national association for Amateur Radio in the USA. Its purpose is to promote and advance the art, science and enjoyment of Amateur Radio.

ARRL is the primary source of information about what is going on in ham radio. It provides books, news, support and information for individuals and clubs, sponsors special events, publishes an informative monthly magazine and topical newsletters for specialized interests as well as other services for members. ARRL is ham radio's advocate in Washington acting to preserve and protect Amateur Radio frequencies and privileges.

Learn more about ARRL at www.arrl.org/about-arrl.

To join ARES you must have a ham radio license. To find out more about getting an Amateur Radio license, go to www.arrl.org/new-to-ham-radio.

For more information about ARRL member benefits, refer to the outline of member benefits at the back of this book, or go to www.arrl.org/join.

Welcome to the ARRL Amateur Radio Introduction to Emergency Communication Course

Preface

Amateur Radio Emergency Communications (AREC) is provided by several different types of emergency communications organizations. ARES, RACES, ACS, SKYWARN, SATERN, REACT, etc. all play an important part in serving their communities. It is not the intent of this course or the management level course to promote any specific group over another.

At the same time, the Amateur Radio Emergency Service®, (ARES®) sponsored by the American Radio Relay League has the longest history of public service of any Amateur Radio emergency communications provider organizations. It is also the largest program and is found in almost every sector of the country. Therefore, knowledge of the ARES program, organizational structure and the duties and responsibilities of key ARES positions is important. Those matters will be discussed in detail in the management level course.

ARRL AREC courses are specifically intended to provide more emergency communications tools to be used as may be appropriate for any given area. What works well fighting forest fires in Colorado may not work in conjunction with flooding in Pennsylvania. Use this information to benefit your community by adding whatever fits your particular area needs. Local protocol and training always takes precedence.

ARES is not an organization itself but a volunteer program of the ARRL and consists of licensed amateurs who have voluntarily registered their qualifications and equipment for communications duty in the public service when disaster strikes. Amateur Radio (and ARRL) exists largely due to its strong foundation of volunteers. Membership in ARRL, or any other local or national organization, is not required to participate in ARES-sponsored activities. ARRL membership is, however, required for the ARES leadership appointments described in this course. Through your commitment as an ARRL member, you support many national and local initiatives, such as ARES, and help supply local volunteers, like yourself, with the materials they need to provide excellent public service.

To learn more about ARRL and ARRL membership benefits visit www.ARRL.org.

Every year, thousands of ARES volunteers freely give their technical skills, time and use of equipment in service to their communities. Thank you for your participation.

The field of emergency response, including communications support, is rapidly changing. In the years following Hurricane Katrina, more and more communications systems are becoming "hardened" and there is more guidance and structure being given from the Department of Homeland Security (DHS) and the Federal Emergency Management Agency (FEMA). These

Introduction to Emergency Communication
Preface

changes are ongoing and whatever may be written today may well be outdated tomorrow.

This curriculum increases validity to our claims of significant training and positions us for the possibility of coming government certifications. It also provides an opportunity for other interested people to learn about Amateur Radio and our unique role in emergencies.

We're using "curriculum" because that's really what this is -- a program of study designed to train you in current practices and protocols. We have blended in FEMA independent study courses to cover many of the general topics which you need to know. These will change with time and experience, and this curriculum will change with it. Meanwhile, the materials presented here will focus on those unique activities specific to Amateur Radio.

This is not a course which you can complete in a weekend - it is not intended to be. Students who successfully complete the course activities and receive their certificates will indeed be ready for roles in situations where lives and property are at stake. Next time it just might be my town and family needing help but I will have confidence in those ARES volunteers who have completed this curriculum.

Finally, we understand that most who take this course are Amateur Radio operators that volunteer their time, skill, and equipment to provide an emergency communication resource to their community. For that we say "THANK YOU."

Mike Corey KI1U
ARRL Emergency Preparedness Manager

Introduction to Emergency Communication
Preface

How to Complete the Course

1. You will need to complete two DHS/FEMA trainings:

    - ICS-100 (IS-100.b) (Introduction to the Incident Command System)
    - IS -700 (National Incident Management System)

    These are free mini-courses you can take online at: http://training.fema.gov/IS/NIMS.asp

    Also recommended, but not required, are:

    - IS-250, Emergency Support Function 15 (ESF15), External Affairs
    - IS-288, The Role of Voluntary Agencies in Emergency Management

2. There are six sections of this course covering a total of 29 topics. Read each topic in this course and test yourself with the questions at the end of each unit.

3. Do the activities assigned with each course topic. If you are participating in a class, your instructor may assign alternative activities. Doing the activities is the best way to reinforce learning!

4. When you have completed the course and the two DHS/FEMA prerequisites, if you would like to earn a course completion certificate from ARRL, identify an opportunity to take the 35 question final exam. You can locate an EmComm Field Exam session or Field Examiner on the ARRL website at www.arrl.org/emergency-communications-training. A $15 exam fee will be required. A passing score is 80% or better.

Section 1: TOPIC 1

INTRODUCTION TO EMERGENCY COMMUNICATION

Objectives

Welcome to Topic 1:

This topic will introduce you to the general concepts of emergency communication. It will help prepare you to be the most helpful as a volunteer.

Student Preparation required:

You should have a sincere interest in improving your skills as an emergency communication volunteer.

As you begin this series of courses, let us first thank you for choosing to expand your knowledge of Amateur Radio emergency communication, or "emcomm" as it is often called. Our professionalism and the effectiveness of our public service efforts will be greatly improved if we all share a common base of knowledge, skills, and procedures.

In this course, you will learn new skills, and new ways of thinking about existing skills. Sometimes the way we have always done something is no longer useful or appropriate. We hope that this course will challenge you to become the best emergency communicator possible.

You may have ideas and material that could add to the base of knowledge presented here. Do not send these comments to your mentor as you take the course. Simply make a note of them and include them in the course evaluation form you will fill out at the end of the course. Since our methods and techniques must continually change to meet the needs of the communities and agencies we serve, so must this course. We will make changes after making careful periodic reviews of the course, and from all participants and mentor comments.

Section 1: The Framework: How You Fit In
Topic 1: Introduction to Emergency Communication

What is a Communication Emergency?

A communication emergency exists when a critical communication system failure puts the public at risk. A variety of circumstances can overload or damage critical day-to-day communication systems. It could be a storm that knocks down telephone lines or radio towers, a massive increase in the use of a communication system that causes it to become overloaded, or the failure of a key component in a system that has widespread consequences. Examples are easily found. Violent storms and earthquakes can knock down communication facilities. Critical facilities can also be damaged in "normal" circumstances: underground cables are dug up, fires occur in telephone equipment buildings, or a car crash knocks down a key telephone pole. Hospital or 911 telephone systems can fail. Even when no equipment fails, a large-scale emergency such as a chemical or nuclear accident can result in more message traffic than the system was designed to handle. Some emergency operations occur in areas without any existing communication systems, such as with backcountry searches or fires.

Most cellular phone systems are designed to handle only about 6-10% of their subscribers at any one time. This works well in normal situations and is economical for the company. But when a crisis happens, they quickly become overloaded as everyone (the other 90%) tries to talk at once.

What Makes A Good Emcomm Volunteer?

Emcomm volunteers come from a wide variety of backgrounds and with a range of skills and experience. The common attributes that all effective volunteers share are a desire to help others without personal gain of any kind, the ability to work as a member of a team, and to take direction from others. Emcomm volunteers need to be able to think and act quickly, under the stress and pressure of an emergency.

You cannot help others when you are worried about those you love. Your family should always be your first priority. Adequate personal and family preparation will enable you to get your own situation under control more quickly so that you are in a position to be of service to others.

Where Do You Fit In?

Amateur Radio operators (often called "Hams" or "Ham Radio Operators") have been a communication resource in emergency situations ever since there has been radio. To the agencies they serve, amateurs are their immediately available communication experts. Amateurs have the equipment, the skills, and the frequencies necessary to create expedient emergency communication networks under poor conditions. They are licensed and pre-authorized for national and international communication.

Hams have the ability to rapidly enlarge their communication capacity to meet growing needs in an emergency, something commercial and public safety systems cannot normally do. Many of the skills are the same ones that are used in everyday ham activities. However, just having

Section 1: The Framework: How You Fit In
Topic 1: Introduction to Emergency Communication

radios, frequencies, and basic radio skills is not enough. Certain emergency communication skills are very different from those you use in your daily ham radio life. Courses like this one help fill that need, as do local training programs and regular emergency exercises. Without specific emergency communication skills, you can easily become part of the problem rather than part of the solution.

As you might expect, technical and operating skills are critical. Just as important, though, is your ability to function as a team player within your own organization, and the organization you are serving. Those critical skills will also be covered in this course.

What You Are Not

As important as what you are, is what you are not. There are limits to your responsibilities as an emergency communicator, and it is important to know where to draw the line.

You are not a "first responder." Except in rare cases of chance, you will seldom be first on the scene. You do not need flashing lights and sirens, gold badges, or fancy uniforms. In most cases, beyond reporting the situation to the proper authorities, hams have little usefulness as communicators at the very beginnings of an emergency.

You have no authority. In most cases, you cannot make decisions for others, or make demands on the agency you serve or any other agency. The only decisions you can make are whether to participate or not, and those affecting your own health and safety.

You cannot do it all. When the agency you are helping runs short of doctors, cooks, or traffic cops, it is not your job to fill the void. In most cases, you are not trained for it. That does not mean you cannot lend a hand to fill an urgent need when you are qualified to do so, or perform other jobs for the served agency of which communication is an integral part, and for which you are trained and capable.

You are not in charge. You are there to temporarily fulfill the needs of an agency whose communication system is unable to do its job. They tell you what they need, and you do your best to comply.

"Day-to-Day" Versus "Emergency" Communication

In your daily ham radio life, there is no pressure to get any particular message through. You do things at your leisure, and no one's life depends upon you. In an emergency all that changes. Here are some differences you may see:

| Unlike general Amateur Radio activities, which involve primarily Amateur Radio operators, emergency communication involves both Amateurs and non-Amateurs. | Unlike regular activities, emergency operations happen in real time. Important activities cannot be delayed for convenience. |

Section 1: The Framework: How You Fit In
Topic 1: Introduction to Emergency Communication

Instead of one leisurely net a day, emergency communicators are often dealing with several continuous nets simultaneously to pass critical messages within a limited timeframe.	Unlike public service events that are scheduled and planned, emergency communicators are often asked to organize and coordinate field operations with little or no warning.
Unlike public service events where the communicators serve primarily under the direction of one lead organization, emergency communicators may need to interact with several key organizations simultaneously.	Unlike typical home installations, emergency stations must be portable and able to be set up and operate anywhere in a very short time.
Unlike contesting, which involves contacting any station for points; emergency communicators need to contact specific stations quickly to pass important messages. Teamwork is important, not competition between stations.	Unlike Field Day, where you can plan on a two-day operation, emergency operations have no schedule and are likely to continue for at least several days.
Unlike commercial communication solutions, where there is no reserve capacity for handling a sudden and massive increase in communication volume, Amateur Radio emergency communicators have the equipment, skills, and knowledge to create additional capacity in a very short time.	

The Missions

The job you are asked to do will vary with the specific agency you serve. If that agency is the American Red Cross, you will be providing the communications needed to maintain a system of shelters and other relief efforts. If it is a state or local emergency management agency, you could be handling interagency communications or serving as the eyes and ears of the emergency managers. When a hospital's telephone system fails, you might be handling the "mechanics" of communicating so that doctors and nurses can concentrate on patients. In a large forest-fire or search and rescue operation, you might be setting up personal phone patches for firefighters or rescuers to their families or assisting with logistical communications to insure that food, supplies, personnel and materials arrive when and where needed. For the National Weather Service you will be reporting storm locations and weather conditions so that they can better inform and warn the public. In any widespread disaster, hams could be assisting all the agencies listed above, and more, at the same time.

Section 1: The Framework: How You Fit In
Topic 1: Introduction to Emergency Communication

Communicating – Job #1

While you are proud of your skill as a radio operator, and the impressive equipment and systems you have in place, it is important to remember that your job is "communicating." If an agency asks us to deliver a long shelter supply list to headquarters, you should be prepared to use any means required – including the fax machine if it is still working. Our job is to get the message through, even if it means using smoke signals. Do not think about how to use ham radio to send the message – just think about the best and fastest way to send it. If that means using ham radio, so much the better. If all you have is CB or Family Radio, use it. If an agency asks you to use their radio system, do it. Your operating and technical skills are just as important as your ham radio resources.

Anatomy of a Communication Emergency

In the earliest stages of many disasters, there is no immediate need for emergency communication services. (An obvious exception would be a tornado or earthquake.) This phase might occur during a severe storm "watch" or "warning" period. You should use this time to monitor developments and prepare to deploy when and if a request for assistance comes. Some nets, such as the Hurricane Watch Net or SKYWARN, may be activated early in the storm watch or warning phases to provide the National Weather Service and other agencies with up-to- the-minute information.

Once a potential or actual need for more communication resources is identified, a served agency puts out the call for its volunteer communicators. Depending on the situation, operators and equipment might be needed at an Emergency Operations Center (EOC) or to set up in field locations, or both. In some areas, a "Rapid Response Team" (RRT) or similar small sub-group might deploy a minimal response in a very short time, to be backed up by a second, more robust response in an hour or two.

A "resource" or "logistics" net might be set up to handle incoming communication volunteers and direct resources where they are needed most. Any volunteer not presently assigned to a specific net or task should check into and monitor this net.

Once operations begin, all kinds of things can happen. The volume of messages can grow quickly, and confusion is common. In addition to handling messages, your team will need to think about relief or replacement operators, food and water, sleeping accommodations, batteries, fuel, and other logistical needs. Radios and antennas will fail and need to be replaced. Some operators will need to leave early for personal reasons.

Communication assignments might include staffing a shelter to handle calls for information, supplies, and personnel, "shadowing" an official to be their communication link, gathering weather information, or collecting and transmitting damage reports. Some nets might pass health and welfare inquiries to refugee/evacuee centers, or pass messages from refugees to family members outside the disaster area. Other nets might handle logistical needs for the served agency, such as those regarding supplies, equipment, and personnel.

Section 1: The Framework: How You Fit In
Topic 1: Introduction to Emergency Communication

Nets will be set up, rearranged, and dismantled as needs change. Volunteers will need to remain flexible in order to meet the changing needs of the served agency. Over time, the need for emergency communication networks will diminish as the message load decreases, and some nets will be closed or reduced in size. Operators will be demobilized (released to go home) one by one, in small groups, or all at once as the needs dictate.

Not long after the operation has ended, the emergency communication group should review the effectiveness of its response, either alone or with the served agency. This might be done on the air in a formal net, by email, or in a face-to-face meeting. However it is done, it should occur as soon as possible after operations have ended to be sure that events are fresh in everyone's mind. Critiques, done properly, can greatly improve your organization's – and your own – effectiveness

Reference links

ARRL Public Service Communications Manual:

http://www.arrl.org/public-service-communications-manual

Section 1: The Framework: How You Fit In
Topic 1: Introduction to Emergency Communication

Review

Communication emergencies can result from a variety of situations, including storms, earthquakes, fires, and equipment damage or failure. Normal communication systems are rapidly overloaded by the increase in usage caused by an emergency, and most have little or no reserve capacity. Amateur Radio operators are a national resource in a communication emergency, and your mission will vary with the agency you serve. Hams have the skills, equipment, and frequencies to rapidly expand the message carrying capacity of their networks. Specific emcomm skills are also required to meet the special needs of a communication emergency.

Activities

1. List three ways in which emergency communications are **similar** to day-to-day communications.

2. List six ways in which emergency communications **differ** from non-emergency communications.

3. In an emergency situation, a served agency asks you to forward an urgent message. Which one of the following methods would you NOT employ? Share your answers to each of these activities with your mentor.

    a. CB radio

    b. Family radio

    c. Informal, conversational grapevine

    d. The served agency's own radio system.

Section 1: The Framework: How You Fit In
Topic 1: Introduction to Emergency Communication

Welcome to Topic 1 Knowledge Review

In order to demonstrate mastery of the information presented in the topic, you will be asked a series of un-graded questions. There are approximately 5 questions on the following pages in multiple-choice or true/false format. Feedback will be offered to you based on the answer you provide.

Question 1:

When does a communication emergency exist?

a) Whenever the public is at risk.

b) When there is an earthquake in your area and the public is inconvenienced.

c) When a critical communication system fails and the public is inconvenienced.

d) When a critical communication system fails and the public is put at risk.

Question 2:

Which of the following actions is the most important for an emcomm group to do at the end of an emergency communication operation?

a) Review the effectiveness of its response.

b) Debate who was the most important person in the operation.

c) Tour the area to document the damages

d) Review the activities of the first responders.

Question 3:

Which of the following is NOT a responsibility of emergency communicators?

a) Making demands on the agency being served.

b) Having radios, frequencies and basic radio skills.

c) Being licensed and preauthorized for national and international communications.

d) Possessing emergency communication skills.

Section 1: The Framework: How You Fit In
Topic 1: Introduction to Emergency Communication

Question 4:

Which of the following describes the function of a Rapid Response Team (RRT)?

a) To handle large-scale emergencies over an extended period.

b) To deploy a quick response in a very short time.

c) To establish and operate a storm watch prior to any emergency.

d) To review of the effectiveness of an emergency communication group.

Question 5:

In an emergency situation — when a served agency asks you to forward an urgent message — which one of the following methods would you NOT employ?

a) CB radio

b) Family radio

c) Informal, conversational grapevine

d) The served agency's own radio

Section 1: The Framework: How You Fit In
Topic 2: Amateurs as Professionals

TOPIC 2:

Amateurs as Professionals —
The Served Agency Relationship

Objectives

Welcome to Topic 2.

This topic will help you appreciate the critical and delicate relationship between emergency communicators and the agencies they serve.

Student Preparation required:

None.

"What does my attitude have to do with emergency communications?"

In a word, everything! It is even more important than your radio skills. Historically speaking, the attitude of some Amateur Radio volunteers has been our weakest point.

In situations where a professional and helpful attitude is maintained, served agencies point with pride to ham's efforts and accomplishments. The opposite situation is clearly illustrated in the words of one emergency management official who said, "Working with ham radio operators is like herding cats—get them the heck out of here!" This man was clearly frustrated with the attitude of his volunteers.

Although our name says that we are "Amateurs," its real reference is to the fact that we are not paid for our efforts. It need not imply that our efforts or demeanor will be anything less than professional. "Professionalism" means getting the job done efficiently—with a minimum of fuss.

No matter which agency you serve — emergency management, the Red Cross or others, it is helpful to remember that emcomm volunteers are like unpaid employees. If you maintain the attitude that you are an employee of the agency you are serving, with all that employee status implies, there is little chance for you to go astray. You are there to help solve their communication problems. Do whatever you can, within reason, to accomplish that goal, and avoid becoming part of the problem.

Who Works For Whom?

The relationship between the volunteer communicator and served agency will vary somewhat

Section 1: The Framework: How You Fit In
Topic 2: Amateurs as Professionals

from situation to situation, but the fact is that you work for them. It doesn't matter whether you are part of a separate radio group like the Amateur Radio Emergency Service (ARES), or part of the agency's regular volunteer force. You still work for them.

Your job is to meet the communication needs of the served agency - period. It is not to show off your fancy equipment, nor to impress anyone with your knowledge of radio and electronics. A "know-it-all" or "I will show you how good I am, and how inadequate you are" attitude will end your—and our—relationship with the served agency in a hurry.

It is often said that volunteers don't have to take orders. This is true—we do not. However, when you volunteer your services to an organization, you implicitly agree to accept and comply with reasonable orders and requests from your "employer." If you do not feel comfortable doing this, do not volunteer.

There may be times that you find yourself unwilling or unable to comply with a served agency's demands. The reasons may be personal or related to safety or health, or it may be that you do not consider yourself qualified or capable of meeting a particular demand. On rare occasions, it may be that you are asked to do something not permitted by FCC rules. Regardless of the reason, respectfully explain the situation, and work with the served agency or your superiors in the communication group to come up with an alternative solution. If the discussion with the served agency becomes difficult or uncomfortable, you can always politely pass the discussion up to your immediate emcomm superiors so that they can handle it instead.

How Professional Emergency Responders Often View Volunteers

Unless a positive and long established relationship exists between professionals and volunteers, professionals who do not work regularly with competent volunteers are likely to look at them as "less than useful." There are several reasons for this. Fire departments have a long history of competitive relationships between professional and volunteer firefighters, and this attitude may carry over to volunteers in general. Police agencies are often distrustful of outsiders—often for legitimate information security concerns. Professionals in any field put a great deal of time and effort into their skills and training, and take considerable pride in their professional standing. As a result, they may view themselves as able to handle all possible situations without outside assistance.

Volunteers, on the other hand, are often viewed as "part timers" whose skill level and dedication to the job vary widely. Many agencies and organizations have learned that some volunteers cannot be depended on when they are needed most. Do not be offended if this attitude is obvious, and remember that you cannot change it overnight. It takes time for you to prove yourselves, and for a positive working relationship to develop and mature.

The middle of an on-going incident is not the time to try to change a "we do not need you" attitude. If your offer of assistance is refused, do not press the issue. The incident commander is busy with more pressing needs, and if he changes his mind about your offer, he will probably contact you.

Section 1: The Framework: How You Fit In
Topic 2: Amateurs as Professionals

> Remember: the served agency's authority should never be challenged—They are in charge, and you are not.

Performing Non-Communication Roles

It has been said many times that our job should be strictly limited to communication. But is this a hard and fast rule? When you work as a SKYWARN weather spotter, or collect and relay damage reports for the Red Cross, is this not going beyond your role as a communicator?

Well, yes and no. The old model of the emergency communicator was one where a written message would be generated by the served agency and handed to the radio operator. They would format and transmit the message to another station, whose operator would then write it out and deliver it to the addressee. In this role, hams were strictly communicators, and due to the radio technology of the times, it was appropriate. Except for rare occasions and situations, those days are gone forever. Some emcomm groups may still enforce a "communication only" policy, and in some agencies the old model may still be appropriate, but discuss this with your Emergency Coordinator or similar emcomm manager to be sure.

In today's fast paced emergency responses, there is often no time for this sort of system. Events are happening too quickly, and the agency's communications must move at the same speed. The job description will more likely be "any function that also *includes* communication," as defined by the served agency. For this reason, emergency communication groups should engage in pre-planning with the served agency to ensure that these jobs are clearly defined, and that any additional job-specific training required is obtained in advance.

In general, emcomm groups should be prepared to perform jobs for their served agency that include the need to communicate. Here are a few of the many possible job descriptions:

- Radio operator, using Amateur or served agency radio systems.
- Dispatcher, organizing the flow of personnel, vehicles and supplies.
- Resource coordinator, organizing the assignments of disaster relief volunteers.
- Field observer, watching and reporting weather or other conditions.
- Damage assessor, evaluating and reporting damage conditions.
- Van driver, moving people or supplies from location to location.
- Searcher, also providing communication for a search and rescue team.

Section 1: The Framework: How You Fit In
Topic 2: Amateurs as Professionals

To perform these jobs, you may need to complete task-specific training courses and take part in exercises and drills in addition to those required for emergency communication even beyond traditional Amateur Radio. In the ever- changing world of emergency response, this flexibility will become increasingly important if we are to continue our contribution to public safety as Amateur Radio operators.

Just as important as being prepared to embrace roles that involve an expanded understanding of "communication," is respecting the limits of your role to provide communication externally, specifically to the press. Avoid giving any information to the press until you understand both the served agency's and your own emcomm group's policies on speaking to the press. Most groups will want all information to come from a central official source, such as a "public information officer." The role of a public information officer (PIO) will be covered in more detail in a later topic.

Specific Agency Relationships

The relationship between the volunteer communicator and the served agency can be quite different from agency to agency, and even between different offices of the same agency. While the ARRL and other national communication groups have existing "Memoranda of Understanding" (MOU), sometimes called a "Statement of Understanding" (SOU) or "Statement of Affiliation" (SOA), in place with many served agencies that define our general relationships, the actual working relationship is more precisely defined at the local level. Different people have different ideas and management styles, agencies in one area can have different needs from others, and these can affect the working relationship between the agency and its emcomm volunteers. Emcomm groups often have their own written agreements with the agency's local office.

ARES and Local MOUs

While having an MOU is a good thing and can help clarify roles before problems actually happen, groups in the ARES program need to remember that they are making promises for the whole ARES organization. As such, these local MOUs and agreements must be reviewed before signing off on them. Talk to your DEC or SEC when considering making a local MOU. They can help you do it right.

Here are some examples of relationships:

Department of Homeland Security (DHS): In June 2003, ARRL and DHS signed a Statement of Affiliation, making ARES an affiliate member of DHS's Citizen's Corp community readiness program. The agreement provides for training and an accreditation of ARES members, raising public awareness of Amateur Radio's role in emergency communications, and coordination of shared activities.

Federal Emergency Management Agency (FEMA): In most cases Amateur Radio emcomm operators will have little direct contact with FEMA and other federal agencies, except within the Military Auxiliary Radio System (MARS) and at the national level with ARRL.

Section 1: The Framework: How You Fit In
Topic 2: Amateurs as Professionals

American Red Cross chapters may have their own communication teams that include Amateurs, or they may have a SOU with a local ARES group or radio club. Typical assignments include linking shelters and chapter houses, performing damage assessment, handling supply and personnel logistics and handling health and welfare messages.

The Salvation Army maintains its own internal Amateur Radio communication support group, known as the Salvation Army Team Emergency Radio Network (SATERN). In some areas, ARES or other groups provide local communication support. Assignments are similar to the Red Cross.

State and Local Emergency Management: Some state and local emergency management agencies include Radio Amateur Civil Emergency Service (RACES) teams as part of their own emergency communication plan. In a growing trend around the country, ARES members are also RACES and vice versa. Communication assignments may be similar to the Red Cross and Salvation Army, but may also include government command and control, and inter-agency communications.

SKYWARN is a self-contained program sponsored by the National Weather Service, and not all members are Amateur Radio operators. Many use other radio systems or telephone, fax or email to send in weather observations. SKYWARN volunteers collect on the spot weather observations that will allow forecasters to create forecasts that are more accurate, and issue timely warnings.

Volunteering Where You Are Not Known

In some cases, an emergency occurs in a neighboring area where you are not a member of the responding communication group. For whatever reason, you might feel obligated to offer your services. If at all feasible, it is best to make your offer through formal, leadership channels before making any significant preparations, or leaving home. Most ARES and other response groups will have protocols for bringing in volunteers from outside of their area if they are needed. Work with them. Trying to short-circuit their processes will just add to the confusion.

It is possible that your offer might be welcomed, but it is equally possible that it will be refused. There are good reasons for this, particularly where the served agency has specific requirements, such as specialized training, official IDs and time-consuming background checks.

Most emcomm managers prefer to work only with operators whose abilities and limitations they know. They may also have more volunteers than they need, or may feel that your skills or equipment are not suited to their mission. If you are turned away, please accept the situation gracefully.

On the other hand, if your offer of assistance is accepted, the situation you find may vary quite a bit. In a well-organized effort, there will be someone to help orient you to the response effort, provide any required information and answer your questions. Your assignment will be clear, a relief person will be sent along at the end of a pre-defined shift, and you will know of any arrangements for food, sanitation and sleep.

Section 1: The Framework: How You Fit In
Topic 2: Amateurs as Professionals

If the effort is not well organized, little, if any, of the above scenario could be true. You might be given an assignment, but with little additional information or support. In this case, you will need to improvise and fend for yourself, and you should be prepared to do so. This is one good reason for making your offer of assistance in advance. Learn as much as you can about the response before preparing to leave home.

In any event, the best time to offer your services to an emcomm group is well before any emergency occurs. This will allow you to obtain the proper training and credentials, and to become known to the group's managers. When the time comes to serve, you will be ready for your job, and a job will be ready for you.

Worker's Compensation Coverage and Legal Protections

In some states, Worker's Compensation insurance coverage can be extended to volunteers working on behalf of a government or non-profit agency. However, Worker's Compensation law is a rather complex matter regulated by individual state's laws. In many cases, it may not be possible for volunteers who are not also paid employees of a served agency to be covered by Worker's Compensation. Emcomm managers should investigate their state's laws on this subject rather than assume that the agency's Worker's Compensation coverage will automatically apply.

Volunteers providing services to government agencies or to private organizations exempt from income taxes under Section 501(c)(3) of the Internal Revenue Code are provided immunity from liability by Federal law through the Volunteer Protection Act of 1997, 42 U.S.C. Section 14501. This generally limits liability if the volunteer was acting at the time within the scope of official duties under a volunteer program. There are exceptions: the law does not cover volunteers who cause harm while operating motor vehicles, or if the volunteer is grossly negligent, or engages in criminal acts. The statute, however, provides broad liability protection for Amateurs in most contexts, and especially where Amateurs volunteer under ARES to provide emergency communications to served agencies.

Reference Links

American Red Cross: http://www.redcross.org

The Salvation Army: www.salvationarmy.org

SKYWARN: www.skywarn.org

Military Auxiliary Radio Service (Army): www.netcom.army.mil/mars/

Federal Emergency Management Agency: www.fema.gov

ARRL – Served Agencies and MOUs (SOUs): http://www.arrl.org/served-agencies-and-partners

Section 1: The Framework: How You Fit In
Topic 2: Amateurs as Professionals

Review

The relationship between Amateur Radio operators and a served agency is a critical one. Emcomm volunteers should maintain a professional attitude at all times and remember that their relationship to the served agency is much like that of an employee – without the paycheck. Agency relationships will vary with the agency, region, and the needs and style of local management.

Avoid giving any information to the press until you understand both the served agency's and your own emcomm group's policies on speaking to the press. Most groups will want all information to come from a central official source, such as a "public information officer."

When volunteering where you are not known, do not be surprised if your offer is refused. Response organizations often have requirements for training, localized protocols and skills that cannot be mastered during an actual emergency.

Activities

1. If you were asked to develop a Statement of Understanding (SOU) between your local emcomm group and a local served agency, what general topics would you include? Share your ideas with your mentor.

Section 1: The Framework: How You Fit In
Topic 2: Amateurs as Professionals

Welcome to Topic 2 Knowledge Review

In order to demonstrate mastery of the information presented in the topic, you will be asked a series of un-graded questions. There are approximately 5 questions on the following pages in multiple-choice or true/false format. Feedback will be offered to you based on the answer you provide.

Question 1:

Which of the following best describes your main job as an emergency communicator?

a) Dispatcher, organizing the flow of vehicles, personnel, and supplies.

b) Weather spotter.

c) Radio operator, using Amateur or served-agency radio systems.

d) Resource coordinator, organizing the assignments of disaster relief volunteers.

Question 2:

Which of following best describes the role of a modern emergency communicator?

a) You are strictly limited to communication tasks.

b) You may be asked to serve any function that includes communication.

c) You do anything a served agency asks.

d) You transmit and receive messages.

Section 1: The Framework: How You Fit In
Topic 2: Amateurs as Professionals

Question 3:

If you are asked by a served agency to perform a task that falls outside FCC rules, which of the following is a proper response?

a) Document the request, and then do what is asked.

b) Document the request, but refuse to do it.

c) Leave immediately.

d) Discuss the situation with the served agency, and develop an alternative solution.

Question 4:

An MOU is:

a) A legal contract between you and the served agency.

b) Volunteer information and make yourself helpful to them.

c) A document outlining what you can expect from each other.

d) Ignore them and hope they will go away.

Question 5:

Which of the following will most affect your relationship with a served agency?

a) Your radio and electronic equipment.

b) Your knowledge of FCC regulations.

c) Your attitude.

d) Your radio skills.

Section 1: The Framework: How You Fit In
Topic 3: Network Theory and the Design of Emergency Communication Systems

TOPIC 3:

Network Theory and the Design of Emergency Communication Systems

Objectives

Welcome to Topic 3.

Following completion of this topic, you will have a deeper understanding of the characteristics of messages and the modes for conveying those messages. This lesson, based on a comprehensive QST article by David Fordham, KD9LA, will help you choose which mode to use for sending different kinds of messages in an emergency communications situation.

Student Preparation required:

None required for this Learning Unit

Network Theory

The study of information transfer between multiple points is known as "network theory." During an emergency, messages vary greatly in terms of length, content, complexity and other characteristics. Similarly, the available communication pathways vary in how well they handle messages having different characteristics. Network theory can be thought of as the process of matching a particular message to the "best" communication pathway. The best pathway is that which can transfer the information with the most efficiency, tying up the communication resources the least amount of time, and getting the information transferred most accurately and dependably.

Hams are often invited to participate in emergency services planning, providing communications expertise. By incorporating some fundamental concepts about network theory into the planning of emergency communication systems, we can take advance steps to be sure that efficient and appropriate communication modes are available when the emergency strikes, thus providing a more valuable service to the public.

Let's start our discussion with the characteristics of messages.

Section 1: The Framework: How You Fit In
Topic 3: Network Theory and the Design of Emergency Communication Systems

Single Versus Multiple Destinations

There are major differences between broadcasting and one-to-one (exclusive) communication channels. Some messages are for one single addressee while others need to be received by multiple locations simultaneously. And some messages addressed to one destination can be useful and informative to "incidental" listeners, like the National Weather Service. A specific instruction to a particular shelter manager is a completely different kind of communication than an announcement to all shelters. Yet, it is common to hear these messages on the same communications channel.

High Precision versus Low Precision

Precision is not the same as accuracy. All messages must be received accurately. But sending a list of names or numbers requires **precision** at the "character" level, while a report that "the lost hiker has been found" does not. Both may be important messages and must be transferred accurately. But one involves a need for more **precision**.

Over low-precision communications channels (such as voice modes) even letters of the alphabet can be misinterpreted unless a phonetic system, feedback or error-correcting mechanism is used.

Conversely, typing out a low precision message that "the delivery van containing the coffee has arrived at this location" on a high-precision packet link can be more time consuming (and inefficient) than a simple voice report.

Complexity

A doctor at a hospital may use a radio to instruct an untrained field volunteer how to splint a fractured leg. A shelter manager may report that he is out of water. The level of complexity varies greatly between these two messages.

Some messages are so long and complicated that the recipient cannot remember or comprehend the entire message upon its arrival. Detailed maps, long lists, complicated directions and diagrams are best put in hard copy or electronic storage for later reference. This avoids the need to repeat and ask for "fills," activities that tie up the communication channel. Some modes, such as fax and packet radio, by their very nature generate such reference copy. Others (such as voice modes) do not, and require a time-consuming conversion step.

Section 1: The Framework: How You Fit In
Topic 3: Network Theory and the Design of Emergency Communication Systems

Timeliness

Some messages are extremely time-critical, while others can tolerate delays between origination and delivery without adverse effect. Relief workers and their communicators can be very busy people. Requiring a relief worker to handle a non-time-critical message may prevent him or her from handling a more pressing emergency. Also, a message might need to be passed at a time when the receiving station is tied up with other business, and by the time the receiving station is free the sending station is then occupied. In these cases, provision can be made for "time shifting"—the message can be left at a drop point for pickup when the receiving station becomes free. Conversely, highly time-critical messages must get through without delay.

Timeliness also relates to the *establishment* of a communications link. Some modes, such as telephones, require dialing and ringing to establish a connection. An operator of a base station radio may need to track down a key official at the site to deliver a message. What matters is the total elapsed time from the time the message originates to the time it is delivered to its final party.

Priority

The concept of priority as used by Network Theory is better known to hams as QSK, the ability to "break in" on a communication in progress. For example, a communication pathway is in use with a lengthy, but low-priority, message. A need suddenly arises for a high-priority message. Can the high-priority message take precedence and interrupt the low priority one to gain access to the channel? Some communications modes allow for this; others do not.

Characteristics of Communication Channels

Now that we have looked at the different message characteristics, let's consider the communication channels that might be used in an emergency. In addition to the concepts of destination, precision, complexity, timeliness, and priority, communication channels also can be evaluated in terms of their reliability and ease of use.

Telephones

The pathway most familiar to non-hams is the telephone. This voice-based mode is surprisingly reliable and can be operated without the need for specialized communication volunteers. It is often fully operational with plenty of unused capacity during localized and small-scale emergencies, but can quickly become overloaded during large-scale disasters.

The telephone system is very good for transferring simple information requiring low precision. Since this mode utilizes the human voice, transferring a large amount of high- precision data (such as spelling a long list of names or numbers) can become tedious and time consuming.

The telephone system is a one-to-one communication pathway, meaning it cannot be used for broadcasting. But, the one-to-one relationship between sender and receiver makes it ideal for messages containing sensitive or confidential information, such as casualty lists.

The exclusive nature of most telephone circuits makes it difficult or impossible to break-in on a conversation to deliver a higher-priority message. The need for break-in usually precludes leaving the channel open continuously between two points, resulting in the need to dial and answer each time a message needs to be sent.

The major drawback to telephones during emergencies is that the sending and receiving stations are not self-contained. The system requires wires and cables that can be damaged or destroyed during severe weather. When the central switching center goes down or becomes overloaded, all communications on this mode come to a halt, regardless of priority or criticality.

Cellular Phones

Cellular phones offer advantages that make them attractive: they are simple to operate and do not require a separate, licensed communication volunteer. They are lightweight and can be carried in a pocket, eliminating the need for tracking individuals as they move around.

Like landlines (and unlike devices used in Amateur Radio), cellular phones are ideally suited to one-to-one communications, avoiding distraction to stations not involved in the message exchange. They are unsuitable for multiple-recipient messages that are better handled on a broadcast-capable communications mode.

Like the landline telephone system, cellular phones are not self-contained communications units. They are reliant on a complex central switching and control system that is subject to failure or overloading. If the central base station goes down, or if its links with the other components of the phone system fail, cellular phone communication comes to a halt. There is no "go to simplex" contingency option with cellular phones.

Section 1: The Framework: How You Fit In
Topic 3: Network Theory and the Design of Emergency Communication Systems

Fax

Fax machines overcome the limitations of voice communications when it comes to dealing with high-precision, lengthy and complex information. A four-page list of first-aid supplies, for example, can be faxed much faster than it can be read over a voice channel and transcribed. Fax machines can transfer drawings, pictures, diagrams and maps—information that is practically impossible to transfer over voice channels.

Today, fax machines are widely available. Most organizations use them as a routine part of their business communications. It is becoming increasingly likely that a fax machine will be found at the school, church, hospital, government center, or other institution involved in emergency or disaster-relief efforts. Most of today's computers (even laptops!) are equipped with modems that can send and receive fax information.

Another advantage of fax machines is their production of a permanent record of the message as part of the transfer process. They also facilitate "time-shifting." But they rely on the phone system, and add one more piece of technology and opportunity for failure. Except for laptop modems, they generally require 120 V ac current, which is not always available during emergencies unless plans have been made for it.

Two-Way Voice Radios

Whether on the public service bands or ham frequencies, whether SSB or FM, via repeater or simplex, voice radio is simple and easy to operate. Most units can operate on multiple frequencies, making it a simple matter to increase the number of available communication circuits as the need arises. Most important, the units are generally self-contained, enhancing portability and increasing reliability of the system in adverse environmental conditions.

Radios are ideal for broadcasting. On the flip side, though, while a message is being transferred between two stations, the entire channel is occupied, preventing other stations from communicating. Using radio for one-to-one communication can be very distracting to stations not involved in the exchange. (The most common example of inefficient use of communication resources is a lengthy exchange between two stations on a channel being shared by a large number of users.) Also, radios suffer from the low precision inherent in voice modes of communication.

Section 1: The Framework: How You Fit In
Topic 3: Network Theory and the Design of Emergency Communication Systems

Trunked Radio Systems

These systems are becoming highly popular with public service agencies. They are similar to the standard voice radio systems described above with two exceptions. Unfortunately, both exceptions have a direct (and adverse) impact on the use of trunked systems in emergency and disaster situations.

The first has to do with the fundamental purpose behind trunking. Trunked systems came into being to allow increased message density on fewer circuits. In other words, more stations could share fewer frequencies, with each frequency being utilized at a higher rate. Under everyday circumstances, this results in more efficient spectrum use. But when an emergency strikes and communication needs skyrocket, the channels quickly become saturated. A priority queue results and messages are delayed. Medium- and low-priority messages, and even some high-priority messages, might not get through unless important stations are assigned a higher priority in the system's programming. Many times the trunked radio systems are shared between several departments within the local governments (i.e. Police, Fire, Highway, Courts, Justice Center, EMA, etc.)

The second difference deals with the way that frequencies are shared. Trunked systems rely on a complex central signaling system to dynamically handle the mobile frequency assignments. When the central control unit goes down for any reason, the entire system — base and mobile units — must revert to a pre-determined simplex or repeater-based arrangement. This fallback strategy is risky in emergencies because of the small number of frequencies available to the system.

Packet Radio

As already mentioned, voice modes are ideal for low-precision messages. Digital data modes, on the other hand, facilitate high-precision message transfer. Modes such as packet radio ensure near-perfect accuracy in transmission and reception. And like fax machines, packet has the ability to provide a relatively permanent record of the message for later reference.

The packet mode has another advantage when dealing with information that is in electronic form, there is no need for a conversion step before transmission. This is especially valuable when the information being sent is generated by machine (such as automated weather sensors, GPS receivers, or shelter management computers).

Packet stations are generally self-contained and if located within line-of-sight, do not need a central switching system. Unlike fax machines, packet radio systems are perfect for the distribution of high-precision information to a large number of destinations simultaneously. And the automated retry feature means that several connections can share a single frequency simultaneously, effectively increasing the capacity of the channel.

Among the disadvantages, real-time packet messages require the operator to use a keyboard. This makes the mode unacceptable for low- precision but lengthy messages, such as describing an injury or giving a status report, especially where the operator is not a fast typist. Due to its need for perfect transmission accuracy, packet may not be reliable along marginal RF paths.

Section 1: The Framework: How You Fit In
Topic 3: Network Theory and the Design of Emergency Communication Systems

And unlike fax machines, most of today's common packet protocols are inefficient when transferring precision graphics, drawings and all but the most rudimentary maps.

Store-and-Forward Systems

Sometimes considered a subset of packet radio, store-and-forward systems (bulletin boards, messaging gateways, electronic mailboxes, etc) can handle non-time-critical messages and reference material, enabling communication in situations where sender and receiver cannot be available simultaneously. These systems also increase the effective capacity of a communication channel by serving as a buffer. When a destination is overloaded with incoming messages, the store- and-forward unit can hold the messages until the receiver is free.

It is important to remember that store-and- forward systems are not limited to digital modes. Voice-answering machines and even an NTS-like arrangement of liaison stations can function as voice-based store-and-forward systems.

Winlink 2000 and D-Star

These two newer modes are gaining in popularity and are now "battle proven." Winlink http://www.winlink.org/ is a system that allows for email type messaging using both radio and the Internet. It can provide a digital bridge into and out of areas where the Internet is not available.
D-Star http://www.icomamerica.com/en/products/amateur/dstar/dstar/default.aspx
provides for both digital voice and data. We will discuss them in more depth later.

Other Modes

Slow-scan television, fast-scan television, satellite communications, human couriers, the Internet, email and other modes of communication all have their own characteristics. Space limitations prohibit more discussion, but by now you get the idea of how communications channels relate to different types of messages.

Section 1: The Framework: How You Fit In
Topic 3: Network Theory and the Design of Emergency Communication Systems

Planning and Preparation—The Keys to Success

Serious communication planners should give advance thought to the kinds of information that might need to be passed during each kind of emergency they wish to consider. Will maps need to be transferred? What about long lists of names, addresses, supplies or other detailed identification? Will the communications consist mostly of short status reports? Will the situation likely require transfer of detailed instructions, directions or descriptions? Will they originally be in oral, written or electronic form?

You may be able to assist a served agency to prepare for the handling of detailed or complex messages by recommending that preformatted (e.g., fill-in-the-blank) messages and named kit lists be developed and circulated in advance among all parties to a given type of communication, effectively creating a "shorthand" message that can be sent more quickly and is prone to fewer errors.

Planners should next consider the origins and destinations of the messages. Will one station be disseminating information to multiple remote sites? Will there be many one-to-one messages? Will one station be overloaded while others sit idle? Will a store-and-forward system, even via voice, be useful or necessary?

The content of the messages should also be considered. Will a lot of confidential or sensitive information be passed? Will there be a need for break-in or interruption for pressing traffic or can one station utilize (tie up) the communications link for a while with no adverse consequences?

Along with the message analysis described above, the frequency of occurrence (count of messages) of each type should also be estimated. Then, in the most important step, the characteristics of the high-volume messages should be matched to one or more appropriate communication pathways.

Once you have identified the ideal pathways for the most common messages, the next step is to take action to increase the likelihood that the needed modes will be available during the emergency. Hams take pride in their "jump kit" emergency packs containing their 2-meter radios, extra batteries and roll-up antennas. How about doing the same thing for some additional communication modes, too? Put a list of critical phone numbers (including fax numbers, pager numbers, and cellular numbers) in your kit. Make sure your local packet digipeater has battery backup. If you are likely to be assigned to a school, church, or office building, see if you can get a copy of the instructions for using the fax machine to keep in your kit.

Advance scouting may be needed. It is a good idea to see if fax machines are in place and

Section 1: The Framework: How You Fit In
Topic 3: Network Theory and the Design of Emergency Communication Systems

whether they will be accessible in an emergency. Is there a supply of paper available? Are the packet digipeaters within range of every likely communication post? Can computers be made available or will hams have to provide their own? How will backup power be provided to the computers? Can a frequency list be developed, along with guidelines of when and how to use each frequency?

Contingency planning is also of critical importance. How many times has a repeater gone down, and only then did the communicators wish they had agreed in advance on an alternate simplex frequency? What will you do if you need to send a map and the fax machine power fails? Suppose you are relying on cellular phones and the cellular network fails?

> ***Remember, if you plan for problems, they cease to be problems and become merely a part of the plan.***

Training

The final step is training. Your staffing roster, assignment lists, and contingency plans need to be tied in to the training and proficiency of your volunteers.

Questions you might want to ask are: Who knows how to best use all the capabilities of today's cellular phones? Who knows how to use fax software? Who knows how to upload or download a file from a packet BBS? Who knows how to touch-type? By matching your needs with your personnel, you can identify areas where training is needed.

Club meeting programs and field trips provide excellent opportunities for training as well as building enthusiasm and sharing knowledge of the plans. You will be surprised at how a little advance planning and effort can go a long way to turning a volunteer mobilization into a versatile, effective, professional-quality communication system.

Reference Links

For more information on this topic, see "Network Theory and the Design of Emergency Communication Systems—Part 1," October 1997 QST, Public Service column. Part 2 appears in November 1997 QST, Public Service.

See also a discussion of communications theory in http://www.arrl.org/public-service-communications-manual

For local information, or to learn more about ARES and NTS net operation in your area, contact your Section Manager (SM) http://www.arrl.org/sections

Section 1: The Framework: How You Fit In
Topic 3: Network Theory and the Design of Emergency Communication Systems

Review

In this Learning Topic, you have received a review of network theory and how it applies to emergency communication situations.

Activities

Make a list of the kinds of messages that might need to be handled during a communication emergency likely in your area. Match the kind of message (tactical messages, served agency manpower requests, welfare inquiries, medical information, casualty lists, requests for supplies, shelter resident lists, etc) with the appropriate communication mode(s) (packet or other digital modes, FM phone, CW, HF SSB, etc.). Share your ideas with your mentor.

Section 1: The Framework: How You Fit In
Topic 3: Network Theory and the Design of Emergency Communication Systems

Welcome to Topic 3 Knowledge Review

In order to demonstrate mastery of the information presented in the topic, you will be asked a series of un-graded questions. There are approximately 5 questions on the following pages in multiple-choice or true/false format. Feedback will be offered to you based on the answer you provide.

Question 1:

What mode should be used to send a list of casualties?

a) A VHF repeater system.

b) A secure mode.

c) Packet radio.

d) An HF net.

Question 2:

What types of messages are good to send by fax?

a) High precision, lengthy and complex messages.

b) Simple low-precision, and short messages.

c) Messages to many destinations simultaneously.

d) High detail color photographs.

Question 3:

What types of messages should be handled by a packet bulletin board system?

a) Time sensitive messages of immediate priority.

b) Low precision messages.

Section 1: The Framework: How You Fit In
Topic 3: Network Theory and the Design of Emergency Communication Systems

c) Non-time-critical messages and reference material, when the sender and receiver cannot be available simultaneously.

d) Messages to be "broadcast" to numerous stations.

Question 4:

What is the pitfall that is common to telephone, cellular phone and trunked radio systems?

a) They do not take advantage of the benefits of Amateur Radio.

b) They are all difficult to use.

c) They are seldom available at shelters and public safety agencies.

d) They all require the use of a complex central switching system that is subject to failure in a disaster situation.

Question 5:

Which of the following is an example of an efficient communication?

a) A ham communicating a lengthy list of needed medical supplies over a voice net.

b) A lengthy exchange between two stations on a primary voice net channel being shared by a large number of users.

c) Typing out a digital message that "the delivery van containing the coffee has arrived at this location" on a high-precision packet link.

d) Sending a shelter list on the office fax machine

Section 1: The Framework: How You Fit In
Topic 4: Emergency Communication Organizations & Systems

TOPIC 4:

Emergency Communication Organizations & Systems

Objectives

Welcome to Topic 4.

Emergency communication organizations are what make an emcomm response possible. After reading this material you will be able to identify the different organizations and systems that make it happen. This unit introduces several of the largest and best-known organizations, and a number of related emcomm and public warning systems.

Student Preparation required:

None.

Introduction

Imagine a random group of volunteers trying to tackle a full-scale disaster communication emergency, working together for the first time. They do not know each other well, have very different approaches to solving the same problem, and half of them want to be in charge. Get the picture?

It is not too farfetched. Just ask anyone who has been around emcomm for a while—they have seen it! This course is intended to help solve that problem.

Emcomm organizations provide training, and a forum to share ideas and develop workable solutions to problems in advance of a real disaster. This way, when the time comes to assist the served agency, you will be as prepared as you can be. The response will occur more smoothly, challenges will be dealt with productively and the served agency's needs met.

Some of the organizations discussed here do not directly involve Amateur Radio operators, but knowing about them and how they might assist in an emergency may be helpful. Your served agency may utilize or interact with one or more of these systems or organizations.

Section 1: The Framework: How You Fit In
Topic 4: Emergency Communication Organizations & Systems

Amateur Radio Emergency Service (ARES)

Among the largest and oldest emcomm groups is ARES, a program sponsored by the American Radio Relay League (ARRL) since 1935. ARES is part of the League's field organization, which is composed of "Sections". Most Sections are entire states, but some larger or more populous states have two or more Sections.

The elected Section Manager (SM) appoints the ARES leadership. The top ARES leader in each Section is the Section Emergency Coordinator (SEC).

Some larger Sections, like Wisconsin and Michigan, or heavily populated Sections like Connecticut, are further divided into two or more Districts. In this case, each District is guided by a District Emergency Coordinator (DEC), and Assistant DEC working directly under the SEC and/ or an assistant SEC.

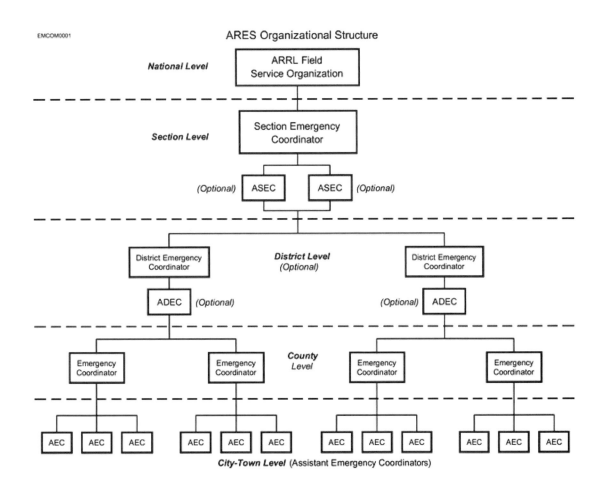

Section 1: The Framework: How You Fit In
Topic 4: Emergency Communication Organizations & Systems

The next subdivision within ARES is the "county" or similar region assigned to an Emergency Coordinator (EC). Most ECs will have one or more Assistant Emergency Coordinators (AEC), who may have responsibility for specific tasks or cities. A large city with complex needs may have its own EC, but most towns and smaller cities will have an AEC.

ARES has Memoranda of Understanding (MOUs) with a variety of agencies at the national level, including the Federal Emergency Management Agency (FEMA), American Red Cross, Salvation Army and the National Weather Service. These documents set out the general relationship between ARES and the agency at the national level, and provide guidance for local units of both organizations to draft more specific local MOUs.

In addition to local chapters of national groups, ARES groups often have MOUs or other written or oral agreements with state and city emergency management departments, hospitals, schools, police and fire departments, public works agencies, and others.

http://www.arrl.org/ares

Radio Amateur Civil Emergency Service (RACES)

The federal government created RACES after World War II. The RACES rules addressed the need for Amateur Radio operators to function as an integral part of a state, county or local Civil Defense (CD) agency in time of national emergency or war. The RACES authorization provided a means to continue to serve the public even if the President or the FCC suspended regular Amateur operations. In this situation, the RACES rules provided for use of all regular Amateur frequencies, but place strict limits on the types of communications made, and with whom. At one time, Civil Defense agencies could obtain a "RACES station license." These licenses are no longer issued.

Over the years, both "Civil Defense" (now known as "Emergency Management" in most states) and the way it utilizes Amateur Radio operators have changed dramatically. While there are no longer any RACES licenses, there are many Amateur Radio groups still serving their local governments and keeping "RACES" in the group's name. Some jurisdictions have renamed or revised such programs as "Auxiliary Communications Service" (ACS). Increasingly, RACES operators also belong to ARES, and can "switch hats" when the need arises. Emergency management officials like this arrangement since it provides more flexibility, and gives them more direct control over their ham radio volunteers.

Salvation Army Team Emergency Radio Network (SATERN)

SATERN members are also Salvation Army volunteers. Their HF networks are used for both logistical communication between various Salvation Army offices and for health and welfare messages. At the local level, ARES, REACT and other groups often help support the Salvation Army's operations.

The "Rapid Response Team" (RRT)

In the first minutes of an emergency, it is sometimes important to get the basic essentials of a network on the air quickly. The solution is the "RRT" concept, although its name may vary. In Hawaii, it is known as a "Quick Response Team" (QRT), and in New Hampshire, a "Rapid Emergency Deployment Team (RED Team). Rather than a stand-alone organization, a RRT is small team within a larger emcomm group. Their job is to put a few strategically placed stations on the air within the first half-hour to an hour. These stations will usually include the emergency operations center (EOC), a resource net and often a few field teams where needed most. This is commonly known as a "Level 1 RRT response."

A Level 2 RRT response follows within a few hours, bringing additional resources and operators. Level 1 teams have pre-assigned jobs, and short- term (12-24 hour) "jump kits," ready to go whenever the call comes. Level 2 teams have longer term (72 hour) jump kits, and a variety of other equipment, possibly including tents, portable repeaters, extended food and water supplies, sleeping gear, spare radios, and generators, depending on local needs.

ARES Mutual Assistance Team (ARESMAT)

When a communication emergency lasts longer than a day or two, or when the scale of the emergency is beyond the ability of a local ARES group to handle, help can be requested from neighboring areas. The ARESMAT concept was created to meet that need. These teams consist of hams who are willing and able to travel to another area for a period to assist ARES groups based in the disaster area. They may also bring additional resources in the form of radios, antennas and other critical equipment. If you travel to another area as part of an ARESMAT, remember that the local group is still in charge—you are there to do what they need done. In a sense, the host ARES group becomes a "served agency."

Section 1: The Framework: How You Fit In
Topic 4: Emergency Communication Organizations & Systems

Military Auxiliary Radio Service (MARS)

MARS is a United States Department of Defense sponsored program, separately managed and operated by the United States Army, Navy, and Air Force. The program is composed of civilians consisting primarily of licensed Amateur Radio operators who are interested in assisting the military with communications on a local, national, and international basis as an adjunct to normal communications. Hams operate disciplined and structured nets on assigned military radio frequencies adjacent to the Amateur bands. MARS has a strict set of rules regarding the type, content and format of messages. Special call signs are issued for MARS use.

In day-to-day service, MARS stations handle quasi-official and morale messages for the three services. During times of emergency, MARS provides backup communication networks to military, federal, state and local agencies. MARS' most publicly visible mission, providing phone patches to family members for US military personnel overseas, has diminished with the advent of new satellites that provide email and phone service almost anywhere. However, this was never MARS' largest or most important function. One advantage of the MARS system is that it is specifically authorized to communicate with other government radio services in time of emergency, including the federal SHARES HF networks.

National Traffic System (NTS)

Long before email and the Internet, there was ARRL's NTS. The concept on which NTS is based is as old as ARRL itself. The NTS consists of local, regional and national nets operating on a regular basis to pass messages (traffic) from place to place. In day-to-day usage, the NTS handles non-critical organizational messages for its own members and ARRL field organizations, radiograms for the public, and various personal messages.

Since email has become popular and long-distance calls have become inexpensive, the NTS has seen a significant decrease in the number of messages passed through the system, and a corresponding decrease in membership and overall effectiveness. However, NTS still has an important role in emergency communication, and discussions about modernizing the NTS are underway. A more in depth discussion of NTS will follow later.

Section 1: The Framework: How You Fit In
Topic 4: Emergency Communication Organizations & Systems

Local Radio Clubs

Not every area has a working ARES program or other nationally affiliated emcomm group. In many cases, the void is filled by local radio clubs who work with served agencies, either informally or with a formal MOU.

National Communications System (NCS)

A Federal agency, the NCS consists of 23 government organizations tasked with ensuring that the Federal Government has the necessary communication capabilities under all conditions from day-to-day use to national emergencies and international crises. These include the Forest Service, Federal Emergency Management Agency, Coast Guard, FBI, ATF and others who have a variety of communication assets. The Manager of the NCS is also the Director of the Defense Information Systems Agency (DISA), usually an Air Force general.

SHARES

Even those who have been involved with emcomm for years may not know of the US Government's "Shared Resources System," known as "SHARES." This system is part of the NCS. It pairs certain MARS operators with various federal agencies and state emergency operations centers to provide a high frequency (HF) communication backbone if normal communication systems should fail. In addition to government agencies, key communications companies such as AT&T, and agencies such as the Red Cross have SHARES radios. The SHARES system utilizes a number of nationwide and regional networks.

Section 1: The Framework: How You Fit In
Topic 4: Emergency Communication Organizations & Systems

Federal Emergency Management Agency — FEMA National Radio System (FNARS)

This is a FEMA high frequency (HF) radio network designed to provide a minimum essential emergency communication capability among federal agencies, state, local commonwealth, and territorial governments in times of national, natural and civil emergencies. FEMA monitors the FNARS HF frequencies on a daily basis. At the state level, FNARS radios are typically located at the state's emergency operations center (EOC).

Radio Emergency Associated Communications Teams (REACT)

REACT is another national emcomm group, whose members include Citizen's Band (CB) radio operators, hams and others. In addition to CB and Amateur Radio, they may use General Mobile Radio Service (GMRS), Family Radio and the Multiple Use Radio Service (MURS).

REACT has an organizational structure similar to ARRL/ARES, with local teams who directly serve many of the same agencies served by ARES and other ham radio emcomm groups. REACT has MOUs with many of these agencies, as well as with ARRL.

REACT's mission is somewhat broader than that of ARES. They offer crowd and traffic control, logistics, public education, and other services that usually (but not always) include a need for radio communication.

Emergency Warning Systems

Emergency Alert System—EAS—(Broadcast Radio & TV):

The current EAS system has evolved from the earlier Emergency Broadcast System (EBS) and the original "CONELRAD System" developed during World War II. The EAS relies on radio and TV broadcast stations to relay emergency alert messages from federal, state and local authorities. Messages may pertain to any immediate threat to public safety, including enemy attack, storm warnings, earthquake alerts and wildfires. Messages are relayed from station to station using automatic switching systems and digital signaling. You may have heard the required weekly EAS tests performed by radio and TV stations and their distinctive digital "squawk" sound.

NOAA Weather Alert and National Weather Radio (NWR):

The National Weather Service (NWS) division of the National Oceanic and Atmospheric Administration (NOAA) operates NWR. NWR uses seven frequencies in the 162MHz band to carry audio broadcasts to the public. In addition to routine weather reports, it carries forecast and warning information from the regional network of forecasting offices, and provides timely and quality alerts dealing with weather and other natural events.

Section 1: The Framework: How You Fit In
Topic 4: Emergency Communication Organizations & Systems

Newer "weather alert" radios are available from a variety of manufacturers with the digital Specific Area Message Encoding (SAME) alert mechanism. SAME equipped radios will remain silent until an alert is received for a specific geographic area. The user programs one or more five-digit FIPS codes for the areas they wish to monitor. When the NWS broadcasts the alert with the SAME code matching that programmed into the receiver, the receiver will activate and allow you to hear the audio message concerning the alert. Some receivers also provide a textual display of the alert information. The NWS tests the SAME network at least once weekly, and the radio will indicate that it has heard the test alert within the past week.

NAWAS (National Warning System):

The federal government maintains a "hardened" and secure national wire line phone network connecting the "warning points" in each state (usually the state police HQ or state EOC). The center of NAWAS operations is the National Warning Center at NORAD's Cheyenne Mountain command and control complex in Colorado. Its primary purpose is to provide notification in case of enemy attack, and to inform and coordinate alert and warning information among states in a given region. During peacetime, it carries alerts on a variety of wide- ranging emergencies. Roll call check-ins are taken periodically during the day to ensure that the phone circuits are functioning properly.

Statewide Warning Systems:

These systems are similar to NAWAS, but at a state level. For most states that have such a system, county warning points are part of a statewide alert and warning network. It is known by different names in each state. For example, in California, it is CALWAS. In Hawaii, HAWAS connects the warning points in each island county, the Pacific Tsunami Warning Center, the local National Weather Service Forecast Office and the Hawaii Air National Guard. It keeps these key entities informed on a real-time basis of bulletins crucial to these agencies. The warning systems in other states are similar.

Tsunami Warning System:

A national and international network of warning points are connected together to provide timely exchange of tsunami warning information. In the United States, it is known as the Tsunami Warning System (TWS). Information is relayed to a wide range of government, civil defense, military, and international tsunami research/warning points within each country or area.

Section 1: The Framework: How You Fit In
Topic 4: Emergency Communication Organizations & Systems

National Earthquake Information Center (NEIC):

The U.S. Geological Survey operates the National Earthquake Information Center, located in Golden, Colorado. The NEIC issues rapid reports for those earthquakes that register at least 4.5 on the Richter scale in the United States, or 6.5 on the Richter scale (or are known to have caused damage) anywhere else in the world. Public warning reports are disseminated in the affected areas via the NWR and EAS systems.

http://earthquake.usgs.gov/regional/neic/

Reference Links

National Communication System: www.ncs.gov

REACT International: www.reactintl.org

FEMA National Radio System www.fema.gov. Use site search box to find "FNARS"

Amateur Radio Emergency Service:

http://www.arrl.org/files/file/EMCOMM%20Broch%20for%20viewing.pdf

National Weather Radio: http://www.weather.gov/nwr/

Emergency Alert System (EAS): http://www.fcc.gov/pshs/services/eas/

Hawaii EAS: http://www.scd.hawaii.gov/documents/EAS_Plan.pdf

National Earthquake Information Center: http://earthquake.usgs.gov/regional/neic/

Army MARS: http://www.netcom.army.mil/mars/

Navy MARS: http://www.navymars.org/

Air Force MARS: http://www.afnic.af.mil/

SATERN: http://www.satern.org/

Section 1: The Framework: How You Fit In
Topic 4: Emergency Communication Organizations & Systems

Review

Organization is critical to any emergency response. Without an organization that plans and prepares in advance, an Amateur Radio emcomm response is likely to be disorganized and ineffective.

A variety of government and private emergency communication groups assist in time of disaster.

While Amateur Radio operators may not interact with many of these systems, it may help to know that they exist, since your served agency may utilize or interact with one or more.

Activities

Go to the ARRL website at http://www.arrl.org/ares-manual and familiarize yourself with the ARES information provided there. Discuss what you learned with your mentor.

Section 1: The Framework: How You Fit In
Topic 4: Emergency Communication Organizations & Systems

Welcome to Topic 4 Knowledge Review

In order to demonstrate mastery of the information presented in the topic, you will be asked a series of un-graded questions. There are approximately 5 questions on the following pages in multiple-choice or true/false format. Feedback will be offered to you based on the answer you provide.

Question 1:

Which of the following best describes the ARES organizational structure?

a) ARRL –District–Section–County

b) ARRL—Section–District—County

c) ARRL –County–Region–Section

d) ARRL –State – Region–Section

Question 2:

Which of the following best describes the ARES chain of command *within* a Section?

a) Section Manager–District Emergency Coordinator–Emergency Coordinator – Assistant Emergency Coordinator – Section Emergency Coordinator.

b) Section Emergency Coordinator– Section Manager—District Emergency Coordinator–Emergency Coordinator–Assistant Emergency Coordinator.

c) Section Manager–Section Emergency Coordinator–District Emergency Coordinator–Emergency Coordinator– Assistant Emergency Coordinator.

d) Section Manager–Section Emergency Coordinator–Emergency Coordinator – District Emergency Coordinator– Assistant Emergency Coordinator.

Section 1: The Framework: How You Fit In
Topic 4: Emergency Communication Organizations & Systems

Question 3:

Which of the following best describes a Level 2 RRT?

a) Is a first responder in any emergency.

b) Operates a few strategically placed stations within the first hour of an emergency.

c) Responds within a few hours and is prepared with longer term (72 hour) jump kits.

d) Is always affiliated with SATERN.

Question 4:

Which of the following best describes an ARES Mutual Assistance Team (ARESMAT)?

a) Is generally available for tasks lasting less than one day.

b) Is always from the local area.

c) An ARES team that is willing and able to travel to another area.

d) Is called out only when the President suspends regular Amateur operations.

Question 5:

Which of the following is true about REACT?

a) REACT is a part of ARRL.

b) REACT does not have an MOU with ARRL.

c) REACT's mission is more restricted than that of ARES.

d) REACT's resources include CB, Amateur Radio, GMRS, FRS, and MURS.

Section 1: The Framework: How You Fit In
Topic 5a: Served Agency Communication Systems

TOPIC 5a:

Served Agency Communication Systems

Objectives

Welcome to Topic 5a.

Emcomm volunteers may be asked to use the agency's own communication systems in addition to Amateur Radio. This unit attempts to familiarize you with some of the systems you are likely to encounter.

Student Preparation required:

Be familiar with the "Continuous Tone Coded Squelch System" (CTCSS), also known by various common trademarks, including Private Line (PL), and Channel Guard. (Private Line is a trademark of Motorola, Inc. and Channel Guard is a trademark of General Electric/Ericcson.)

Introduction

Most served agencies will have their own communication systems and equipment, ranging from modest to complex. In our ever-broadening role as emergency communicators, we may be asked to operate some of this equipment. If this occurs, you must become familiar with its operation. Your emcomm group should work with the served agency well in advance to determine whether the agency will need you to use its equipment, and under what conditions. Many of these radio systems are quite different from ham radio, and special training may be required. In addition to different equipment, on-air procedures will definitely be different. Training and drills may be necessary to make Amateur Radio emcomm operators proficient.

State and Local Government Radio Systems

These systems might include those licensed to police, fire, sheriffs, highway and other state, county, or city departments. If you are asked to use any of these systems, be sure to learn their standard operating procedures and "phonetic alphabet" system if one is used and adapt accordingly.

Some departments may use familiar ITU Phonetics, some will use APCO phonetics, and still others will make them up as they go along. In addition, a few departments still use a "10 code" or something similar, but most are moving away from special codes in favor of plain language. Be careful not to lapse into a ham radio operating style. Casual conversations are prohibited by

Section 1: The Framework: How You Fit In
Topic 5a: Served Agency Communication Systems

FCC rules and are usually not permitted by the agency. All transmissions must be directly related to the agency's mission.

Many police agencies are licensed for operation on 155.475 MHz, sometimes known as the "National Police Frequency." The FCC has set aside this channel to allow intercommunication between any police agency, regardless of state or jurisdiction. Unfortunately, many departments are not aware of its intended use and treat it as their own private "car to car" channel. Many will not know they have a common channel since they use "channel designators" rather than frequencies. In addition, CTCSS (the type of tone coded squelch abilities hams often have on our 2m repeaters and call "PL") was not supposed to be used on this channel to ensure interagency compatibility, but many departments use it anyway. This may become important if different police agencies must intercommunicate with each other in an emergency. If one or more use CTCSS, they will need to disable it by placing their radios in the "monitor" mode, if possible.

Medical Radio Systems

In order to standardize emergency medical radio systems across the country, the FCC assigned a number of dedicated frequencies. In theory, every ambulance in the country should be equipped to use all these frequencies. In practice, true compatibility is usually limited to a specific region.

The older system, often called "Med Star," used 10 simplex VHF frequencies with a dial-type pulsed-tone encoder to signal specific hospitals. This system is still in use in some rural areas, but is quickly being replaced by systems that are more modern. The newer Emergency Medical Radio Service uses 10 UHF duplex frequency pairs; one assigned to the hospital, the other to the ambulance and seven VHF simplex channels. The UHF channel sequence is designated "Med 1" to "Med 10."

Other systems such as HEAR and ReddiNet are found on the West Coast.

In some cases, the hospital's radio is located on a nearby mountain or tall tower in order to achieve the required coverage, and connected to the emergency department by a radio or telephone link.

You would do well to learn what your area hospital uses before any emergency.

American Red Cross

ARC has a nationally licensed frequency (47.42MHz) that can be used by all ARC chapters, and is intended primarily for disaster or emergency operations. This common channel ensures that ARC units responding from various chapters will be able to communicate with each other. Some chapters also use 47.50MHz. In addition, certain chapters may rent space on commercial systems or license their own VHF or UHF systems for day-to-day operations.

Section 1: The Framework: How You Fit In
Topic 5a: Served Agency Communication Systems

Types of Served-Agency Radio Systems

In larger jurisdictions, each agency will probably have its own radio system, completely independent of all other radio users in the same area. This is especially true of large city and state police and fire radio systems. Many agencies have more than one channel, each assigned to a different purpose. For instance, a fire department might have a "dispatch" channel, and one or more "fireground" channels. This allows local operations at a fire scene to be kept separate from on-going dispatch operations. A police department may have a separate channel for detectives, or one for each precinct. These systems may be on repeaters or use simplex frequencies.

The FCC allocates specific radio frequencies to different types of agencies, and some for multi-agency use. For instance, a frequency designated for use by police agencies may only be used for police business. The same is true of fire radio allocations. "Local Government" allocations may be used for any legitimate local government function.

In addition to "simple" systems where each user group has its own frequency, there are three different types of systems that allow multiple user groups to share resources. These are known as "community repeaters," "trunked repeater systems," and "shared simplex systems."

Community Repeater Systems

Unlike Amateur Radio repeater systems, a "community" or "shared" repeater uses a different CTCSS tone for each of several user groups. For instance, a city might have one repeater shared by the water, public works and sanitation departments, licensed as a single "local government" radio system. Since each department uses a different CTCSS tone, they will not normally hear one another's conversations, but only one department can use the system at any given moment. Some very small rural towns may even combine fire and police department operations on the same system, on either a repeater or simplex frequency.

When using any shared frequency—repeater or simplex—it is important to press the "monitor" button for a moment before transmitting. This disables the CTCSS decoder, temporarily allowing you to hear any transmissions being made on the frequency. Some mobile radios automatically switch to "monitor" mode when the mic is removed from its hang-up clip. In this way, you can be certain that no one else is using the channel before making your call.

In an emergency situation, these shared channel systems can quickly become overloaded. A common practice is to end all non-essential communications or perhaps move them to an Amateur system instead.

Section 1: The Framework: How You Fit In
Topic 5a: Served Agency Communication Systems

Trunked Systems

Trunked systems provide an efficient means for several "low volume" users to share a single radio system. They use several co-located repeaters tied together, using computer control to automatically switch a call to an available repeater. When one radio in a group is switched to a new frequency, all the others in the group automatically follow. This is accomplished by having a computer controller move the conversation from frequency to frequency in accordance with a pre-established algorithm. The number of available frequencies in the system depends on its design and the number of different user groups. Channel switching and assignment data is transmitted on a dedicated channel. Unlike a shared single-frequency repeater system using multiple CTCSS tones, a trunked system will provide almost instant on-demand clear channels in normal usage. Amateur Radio does not currently use this type of system.

In emergency situations, however, most trunked systems suffer from a lack of reserve capacity. To keep designs cost effective, there are always many more user groups than available channels. The number of available channels is designed to handle the normal day-to-day communications load. When an emergency occurs, these systems can be quickly overloaded with calls, and finding a clear channel can be difficult or impossible.

One "solution" to this problem is to assign certain users or user groups "priority" over others. If all the available channels are occupied, a higher priority user will bump the lowest priority user off the system and take over the channel. Priority status can either be full time or turned on in an emergency, depending on the system's design.

APCO Project 25 Radio Systems

In the 1990s, a new public safety radio system was developed to deal with problems of interoperability between agencies with different radios. The Association of Public Safety Communications Officers (APCO) created the Project 25 working group, which created what has become known as the Project 25 (P25) Standard.

P25 radios are extremely flexible, with both forward and backward compatibility. This means that they can be configured to operate in both analog and digital modes, and as part of trunked and conventional radio systems. P25 radio systems are becoming more common across the country as federal funds become available.

The advantages of P25 systems are obvious. Radios from several manufacturers can be programmed to communicate with each other seamlessly, as can radios from different agencies and jurisdictions. Digital modes can offer excellent audio quality under the right conditions, and optional encrypted modes offer message and data security. The disadvantages are less obvious. While P25 digital systems work well in urban environments, they are not as effective in rural or mountainous areas. Some agencies have resisted the use of digital modes because of higher signal-to-noise-ratio requirements. While analog signals can fade in and out, digital signals are either there or they're not, just like a digital cellular telephone signal. Further, the lengthy development time of P25 has led to the deployment of numerous proprietary solutions by commercial manufacturers, a result that works against true interoperability.

Section 1: The Framework: How You Fit In
Topic 5a: Served Agency Communication Systems

Telephone Systems

Telephone systems in use by public service agencies vary greatly. The served agency should be able to provide training in its use. Most telephone systems come with user manuals, and if possible, a copy of one should be included in your group's training materials.

Most business telephone systems allow the following basic functions, with which you should be familiar:

- Answering incoming calls
- Placing outside calls
- Placing and answering intercom calls
- Making "speed dial" calls
- Overhead paging
- Placing calls on hold, and then retrieving them
- Transferring calls to another extension
- Transferring calls to voice mail, if available
- Retrieving calls from a voice mailbox

There may be other more advanced functions available, but in most cases, you will not need to learn them for temporary operations. However, it is always a good idea to keep the user's manual nearby. You should also try to determine the extent to which the agency's telephone system is dependent on or susceptible to fluctuations in commercial power.

Satellite Telephones

Satellite phones and data terminals are becoming more common among served agencies as the cost of ownership and airtime decreases. Satellite telephone/data service is offered by a number of companies, including Inmarsat, Iridium, Thruway and Globalstar. Some of the services cover much of the earth's surface, others only certain regions.

Some phones or terminals require that an antenna be pointed directly at the satellite, others do not, but all require line-of-sight to the satellite. Some are handheld; others are contained in briefcases and must be set up before operating. In addition to voice communication, some companies offer paging, fax and data transmission, although at slower speeds than a typical land-based dial-up connection. A few phones also integrate a terrestrial cellular phone in the same unit.

Calls are typically expensive when compared to cellular telephone calls. All calls made through these systems are considered to be "international" calls, and each company has one or more "country codes." If you need to use one of these phones, keep conversations short and to the point. While most of the phones are fairly simple to use, due to the wide variety of phones and services it is essential that users be fully trained in their use.

Section 1: The Framework: How You Fit In
Topic 5a: Served Agency Communication Systems

In addition, there is some concern that the number of satellite telephones sold far outstrips the number of satellite channels available, so system overload remains a real possibility in a widespread incident.

Satellite Data Systems

Satellite systems in use by public service agencies also vary greatly. Some are used for two-way data and voice communication, others for one-way reception of voice, data or video. One popular system is the NOAA Emergency Management Weather Information System (EMWINS) system, which allows emergency management officials to obtain up-to-the-second weather maps and information. If you were trained on the system years ago, you will need to be retrained as it has changed and upgraded. As with many other served agency systems, the agency will need to provide prior training in their use if they want you to be able to operate this equipment in a crisis.

Other Agency-Owned Equipment

In addition to radio and telephone systems, you may need to use fax machines, copiers, computers, and similar devices. Since many of us use these items every day at work, learning their operation should not be a problem in most cases. However, some copiers and computer programs are quite complicated and may require instruction in their use. Computer software used in public safety applications is usually specially written for the purpose and may require extensive training in the rare situation where you will be required to use the system.

Reference Links

FCC – Public Safety & Homeland Security Radio Service www.fcc.gov/homeland/

FCC Rules – Ham Radio http://www.arrl.org/part-97-amateur-radio

APCO http://www.apco911.org/

International Municipal Signal Association (IMSA) http://www.imsasafety.org/

Dispatch Magazine http://www.911dispatch.com/

Project 25 http://www.project25.org/

Review

While some served agency systems may be familiar to Amateur Radio operators, others are not. Both equipment and procedures may vary greatly. If a served agency expects its emcomm volunteers to be able to operate any of its systems, specific training should be provided in advance.

Section 1: The Framework: How You Fit In
Topic 5a: Served Agency Communication Systems

Activities

Using the links provided, discuss with your mentor the answers to the following questions:

1. What do Sections 97.403 and 97.405 of the FCC Rules and Regulations (http://www.arrl.org/part-97-amateur-radio) Part 97 state about Amateur communications during emergencies?

2. Which courses offered by IMSA http://www.imsasafety.org/certify.htm) pertain to radio operations? To what extent do these courses pertain to emcomm operations?

Section 1: The Framework: How You Fit In
Topic 5a: Served Agency Communication Systems

Welcome to Topic 5a Knowledge Review

In order to demonstrate mastery of the information presented in the topic, you will be asked a series of un-graded questions. There are approximately 5 questions on the following pages in multiple-choice or true/false format. Feedback will be offered to you based on the answer you provide.

Question 1:

When emcomm team members are called upon to operate on Public Safety Radio Systems, which of the following may they NOT do?

a) Use special "10 codes."

b) Use the served agency's standard operating procedure.

c) Use the phonetic alphabet employed by the served agency.

d) Engage in casual conversations.

Question 2:

Which of the following modes/devices would not be appropriate for you to use to transmit a message for a served agency?

a) Email on a computer with Internet connections.

b) Fax machine.

c) Land line telephone.

d) ALL of these are appropriate and usable if needed.

Section 1: The Framework: How You Fit In
Topic 5a: Served Agency Communication Systems

Question 3:

Which of the following best describes the newer Emergency Medical Radio Services?

a) Ten UHF duplex frequencies and seven VHF simplex channels.

b) Ten simplex VHF frequencies with pulsed tone encoders for each hospital.

c) Seven UHF duplex frequencies and ten VHF simplex channels.

d) The Med Star system with channels Med 1 through Med 10.

Question 4:

Which one of the following statements is true about trunked systems?

a) Trunked systems are able to operate without the use of computer controllers.

b) The number of frequencies on a trunked system is always a multiple of 10.

c) Amateur radio does not currently use this type of system.

d) Most trunked systems have ample reserve capacity.

Section 1: The Framework: How You Fit In
Topic 5a: Served Agency Communication Systems

Question 5:

When emcomm teams work with a served agency, a number of assumptions are made. Which of the following assumptions are true?

a) Amateur Radio operators can operate any communication equipment they encounter.

b) There are NO significant differences between Amateur Radio operating procedures and the procedures used by the served agencies.

c) Served agencies must provide training if Amateur Radio operators are to be used effectively.

d) All phonetic alphabets are essentially the same and are thus interchangeable.

Section 1: The Framework: How You Fit In
Topic 5b: Working Directly with the Public

TOPIC 5b:
Working Directly With the Public

Objectives

Welcome to Topic 5b.

After reading this topic participants should identify ways to provide direct assistance to their local communities and integrate their skills with existing preparedness efforts.

Student Preparation required:

None.

Introduction

Many radio amateurs want to be of help when the need arises but are unable to commit the time or meet the schedule required for formal participation with an agency or Emcomm organization. These hams can still make valuable contributions to their communities by getting involved at the local level and making their skills available to their neighbors. Becoming a resource in your community can also enhance the public's understanding of and appreciation for Amateur Radio and help reduce the potential for conflicts when a ham wants to erect an antenna on his property. The more we are recognized as neighborhood assets, the more likely it is that our antennas, which are essential for effective station performance, will be accepted.

How Do I Get Started?

Neighbors may band together in a variety of ways to help one another. Some have formal associations with a defined leadership structure. Law enforcement agencies often sponsor a Neighborhood Watch programs, designed to deter local crime in residential areas. Many areas have implemented Community Emergency Response Team ("CERT") programs, which teach basic skills – such as fire suppression, triage, first aid and light search & rescue – needed to survive when a disaster swamps the resources of official first responders.

Find out what preparedness activities are going on in your area and join one or more local groups. Learn what plans are already in place and note the communication plan or absence thereof. Let the other participants know that you are a licensed Amateur Radio operator and want to help develop or improve the group's communication resources. Community groups are usually eager to learn from people with knowledge and experience in the areas of concern to them. It's also a good idea to take whatever local training is already offered in disaster

Section 1: The Framework: How You Fit In
Topic 5b: Working Directly with the Public

preparedness so that your understanding will be at least equal to that of your neighbors and so that you can present your suggestions regarding communications in context with that understanding. Participation in local preparedness courses will also let you meet like-minded individuals with whom you can share ideas. If there is no preparedness group or program in your area, consider starting one using resources available from FEMA and other public sources.

Using FRS and GMRS Radios

The most popular and ubiquitous communication tools not dependent on the telephone system or the Internet are Family Radio Service ("FRS") and General Mobile Radio Service ("GMRS") radios. These two services are described in detail in Learning Unit 24. You should be familiar with their use and limitations.

FRS radios may be operated without a license. Transmitting with GMRS radios requires a license. The fee covers a five-year term, and one license covers all the members of a family and as many separate radios as they may need. If you are going to use a GMRS radio, get the license!

A Project Medishare doctor communicating on a GMRS radio.

Channel numbering can be a source of confusion for FRS and GMRS users because different manufacturers may assign a different number to a given frequency. Sometimes channel numbering will vary even among different models from the same manufacturer. If you are advising a neighborhood group on the use of FRS or GMRS radios, you can suggest one of the following:

1. When equipping a group for the first time, have everyone buy one make and model of radio (or buy the same model in bulk for additional cost savings). This will assure consistent channel numbering.

2. If different makes and models are already employed by group members, prepare a chart to go with each radio showing the channel number that goes with each frequency.

Every radio owner should be able to power his or her transceiver from standard alkaline batteries. Rechargeable NiCd, NiMH or Li-Ion batteries are great for everyday use when AC power is available to recharge them, but recharging batteries when the power is out or when heavy use drains the batteries quickly can be a problem. Alkaline cells are inexpensive, can be replaced quickly, have a relatively long shelf life and are usually kept on hand already for use in flashlights and other devices. If an FRS or GMRS radio needs a separate shell to use these

Section 1: The Framework: How You Fit In
Topic 5b: Working Directly with the Public

disposable batteries, get one. If the alkaline batteries fit directly into the radio, keep some packed near (not in) the radio, and refresh the supply when necessary.

Radio Coverage

The limited range of FRS and GMRS radios is both good and bad news. The good news: the distance from which users may receive interference from other users is relatively small. The bad news: there may be parts of a desired coverage area that cannot be reached from a given location. You can suggest or organize a coverage-mapping exercise in which your neighbors test their radios from different locations, indoors and out, to identify any hot spots and dead spots. Find the places you can transmit with the most complete coverage and prepare to use relays for hard-to-reach areas if necessary. Knowing this before a disaster strikes will be most helpful, and it will get people used to using their radios.

Radio Protocol

During a disaster, time and radio resources may both be in short supply. People will be occupied with caring for their own families or performing their assigned team tasks. It benefits everyone to keep transmissions short and to minimize confusion over who is calling whom. Radio Amateurs are familiar with good radio protocol and can teach it to their neighbors to promote efficient use of whatever radios are in use. **Here are some basic practices to consider**.

- Fire, police and military radio operators make use of tactical callsigns, usually associated with a specific function or location, and civilian groups can do the same. First names may be fine for only a few users but can lead to confusion with many users on the same channel. Descriptive tactical callsigns such as "Utility One", "Farmington Command" or "Elm St, Fire" can reduce confusion in case another team is using the same channel nearby. Your group's communications plan should include any tactical callsigns you decide to use.

- It is good practice to start each transmission by stating the party you're trying to reach followed by your own call ("Supply, this is Triage"). Wait for an acknowledgement ("Triage, Supply, go ahead") before sending your message. Keep messages short ("Supply, Triage, we need six blankets at Elm & 1st right away") and sign off when the exchange is finished ("Triage clear" plus any required callsign) so the other party knows you're finished and can get back to other responsibilities. Any identification requirement is easily met using this method.
- It is also good practice to use the proword "Over" at the end of each transmission to another station. Since most FRS and GMRS is simplex, doubles could occur resulting in lost message content when it's unclear whose turn it is to transmit.

- Speak – don't yell – somewhat more slowly and distinctly than you would in face-to-face conversation. Yelling into an FM transceiver usually produces distortion rather than making one louder, the very opposite of what the user is trying to achieve. Speaking

Section 1: The Framework: How You Fit In
Topic 5b: Working Directly with the Public

across rather than into the microphone will help reduce the popping of "P"s and the hissing of "S"s, producing clearer speech on the receiving end. Have your group practice with their radios and encourage honest "signal reports" so each user can make the most effective use of his or her radio.

- Avoid noisy locations when possible. Background noise makes it harder for you to hear and harder for you to be heard.

When people not accustomed to using radios practice these techniques, they are more likely to find their radios to be useful communication tools rather than distractions from their other duties.

Linking To the Outside

In addition to helping with neighborhood communications plans, Radio Amateurs may be called upon or expected to provide a link to adjacent areas or to first responders. You should be aware of the other Amateurs in your area who are active in the local Emcomm organizations and know the frequencies on which you can reach them. They will probably be your best access to first responders and aid organizations if there is any access to be had.

You should set realistic expectations as to what you can accomplish. Surrounding areas may be experiencing the same problems you have locally. Fire department and law-enforcement agency communications will be very busy and will give priority to those groups with which they are familiar. You can learn more by getting to know the formal Emcomm organizations in your area. Even if you don't have time to participate with the local Emcomm group regularly, you need to find out where they are likely to be stationed and how you can contact them. For example, if you know which hospitals will have Ham coverage and the best way to reach them, you may be able to determine whether a given facility is functioning in a disaster so that a seriously injured person can be transported there.

Section 1: The Framework: How You Fit In
Topic 5b: Working Directly with the Public

Community Emergency Response Teams (CERT)

The Community Emergency Response Team (CERT) Program educates people about disaster preparedness for hazards that may impact their area and trains them in basic disaster response skills, such as fire safety, light search and rescue, team organization, and disaster medical operations. Using training learned in the classroom and during exercises, CERT members can assist others in their neighborhood or workplace following an event when professional responders are not immediately available to help. CERT members also are encouraged to support emergency response agencies by taking a more active role in emergency preparedness projects in their community.

The basic CERT trainings include:

* IS-317: Introduction to CERTs and the CERT Basic Training Course

"Introduction to Community Emergency Response Teams", IS-317, is an independent study course that serves as an introduction to CERT for those wanting to complete training or as a refresher for current team members. It has topics that include an Introduction to CERT, Fire Safety, Hazardous Material and Terrorist Incidents, Disaster Medical Operations, and Search and Rescue. It takes between six and eight hours to complete the course. Those who successfully finish it will receive a certificate of completion. IS-317 can be taken by anyone interested in CERT. However, to become a CERT volunteer, one **must complete the classroom training** offered by a local government agency such as the emergency management agency, fire or police department. If your home area has the program, you can contact your local emergency manager to learn about the local education and training opportunities available to you. Let this person know about your interest in taking CERT training."

Reference Links

CERT http://www.citizencorps.gov/cert/training_mat.shtm#basictraining

REACT http://www.reactintl.org/

North Hills Community Association as an example

http://www.northhillscommunity.org/index.php?page=frs-radios

Section 1: The Framework: How You Fit In
Topic 5b: Working Directly with the Public

Review

The Community Emergency Response Team (CERT) Program is a volunteer program of trained people operating in teams under ICS protocols. In the role of gathering initial information, radio communication capabilities can be a major asset to CERT and other community teams. Many local community organizations are using FRS, GMRS or CB radios within neighborhoods and then Amateur Radio to relay information in to formal operations centers.

Activities

Inquire as to the existence of a CERT or similar team in your area. Contact members and interview them about their role. Who would be the person in your area to contact to learn about local education and training opportunities available with their program? Share what you find with your mentor.

Section 1: The Framework: How You Fit In
Topic 5b: Working Directly with the Public

Welcome to Topic 5b Knowledge Review

In order to demonstrate mastery of the information presented in the topic, you will be asked a series of un-graded questions. There are approximately 5 questions on the following pages in multiple-choice or true/false format. Feedback will be offered to you based on the answer you provide.

Question 1:

Which of the following is not a good practice when using FRS / GMRS radios?

a) Using tactical call signs.

b) Operating away from sources of loud noise.

c) Waiting for a frequency to be cleared by other users before transmitting.

d) Speaking very loudly directly into the microphone.

Question 2:

Which group might an Amateur contact about community-preparedness efforts?

a) Neighborhood Watch.

b) Homeowners association.

c) CERT team.

d) All the above.

Section 1: The Framework: How You Fit In
Topic 5b: Working Directly with the Public

Question 3:

CERT is:

a) A national certification program for ICS

b) A volunteer program of trained people operating in teams under ICS protocols.

c) A program mandated by FEMA for all parts of the country.

d) An auxiliary of local Fire Department

Section 2: The Networks for Messages
Topic 6: Basic Communication Skills

TOPIC 6:

Basic Communication Skills

Objectives

Welcome to Topic 6.

This lesson introduces communication skills that are specific to emcomm operations, and will help you appreciate differences from normal Amateur Radio operations.

Student Preparation required:

None.

Introduction

An emergency communicator must do his or her part to get every message to its intended recipient, quickly, accurately, and with a minimum of fuss. A number of factors can affect your ability to do this, including your own operating skills, the communication method used, a variety of noise problems, the skills of the receiving party, the cooperation of others, and adequate resources. In this unit, we will discuss basic personal operating skills. Many of the other factors will be covered in later units.

Life–and–death communications are not part of our daily experience. Most of what we say and do each day does not have the potential to severely impact the lives and property of hundreds or thousands of people. In an emergency, any given message can have huge and often unintended consequences. An unclear message, or one that is modified, delayed, mis-delivered or never delivered at all can have disastrous results.

Listening

Listening is at least 50% of communication. Discipline yourself to focus on your job and "tune out" distractions. If your attention drifts at the wrong time, you could miss a critical message. Listening also means avoiding unnecessary transmissions. A wise person once said, "A man has two ears and one mouth. Therefore he should listen twice as much as he talks." While you are asking, "When will the cots arrive?" for the fourth time that hour, someone else with a life and death emergency might be prevented from calling for help.

Sometimes the job of listening is complicated by noise. You might be operating from a noisy location, the signal might be weak or other stations may be causing interference. In each of these cases, it helps to have headphones to minimize local noise and help you concentrate on the radio signal. Any veteran of a major emergency situation will tell you, headphones are one of the "must have" items in emcomm operations. Digital Signal Processing (DSP), filters and

Section 2: The Networks for Messages
Topic 6: Basic Communication Skills

other technologies may also help to reduce radio noise and interference.

Microphone Techniques

Even something as simple as using your microphone correctly can make a big difference in intelligibility. For optimum performance, hold the mic close to your cheek, and just off to the side of your mouth. Talk across, rather than into, the microphone. This will reduce breath noises and "popping" sounds that can mask your speech.

Speak in a normal, clear, calm voice. Raising your voice or shouting can result in over-modulation and distortion, and will not increase volume at the receiving end. Speak at a normal pace—rushing your words can result in slurred and unintelligible speech. Pronounce words carefully, making sure to enunciate each syllable and sound. Radios should be adjusted so that a normal voice within 2 inches of the mic element will produce full modulation. If your microphone gain is set so high that you can achieve full modulation with the mic in your lap, it will also pick up extraneous background noise that can mask or garble your voice.

A noise-canceling microphone is a good choice since it blocks out nearly all unwanted background noise, and is available in handheld and headset boom configurations.

Headset boom microphones are becoming less expensive and more popular, but care should be taken to choose one with a cardioid or other noise-canceling type element. Many low-cost headset boom mics have omni-directional elements, and will pick up extraneous noise.

"Voice operated transmission" (VOX) is *not* recommended for emergency communication. It is too easy for background noise and off-air operator comments to be accidentally transmitted, resulting in embarrassment or a disrupted net. Use a hand or foot switch instead.

When using a repeater, be sure to leave a little extra time between pressing the push-to-talk switch and speaking. A variety of delays can occur within a system, including CTCSS decode time, and transmitter rise time. Some repeaters also have a short "kerchunk" timer to prevent brief key-ups and noise from keying the transmitter. It also gives time for some handhelds to come out of the "power-saver" mode. Leaving extra time is also necessary on any system of linked repeaters, to allow time for all the links to begin transmitting. Momentary delay in speaking after keying up will ensure that your entire message is transmitted, avoiding time-wasting repeats for lost first words.

Lastly, pause a little longer than usual between transmissions any time there is a possibility that other stations may have emergency traffic to pass. A count of "one, one thousand" is usually sufficient.

Brevity & Clarity

Each communication should consist of only the information necessary to get the message across clearly and accurately. Extraneous information can distract the recipient and lead to misinterpretation and confusion. If you are the message's author and can leave a word out without changing the meaning of a message, leave it out. If the description of an item will not add to the understanding of the subject of the message, leave it out. Avoid using contractions

Section 2: The Networks for Messages
Topic 6: Basic Communication Skills

within your messages. Words like "don't" and "isn't" are easily confused. If someone else has drafted the message, work with the author to make it more concise.

Make your transmissions sound crisp and professional, like the police and fire radio dispatchers and the air traffic controllers. Do not editorialize, or engage in chitchat. An emergency net is no place for "Hi Larry, long time no hear", "Hey, you know that rig you were telling me about last month…." or any other non-essential conversation.

Be sure to say exactly what you mean. Use specific words to ensure that your precise meaning is conveyed. Do not say, "That place we were talking about," when "Richards School" is what you mean. Using non-specific language can lead to misunderstandings and confusion.

Communicate one complete subject at a time. Mixing different subjects into one message can cause misunderstandings and confusion. If you are sending a list of additional food supplies needed, keep it separate from a message asking for more sand bags. Chances are that the two requests will have to be forwarded to different locations. If combined, one request will be lost.

Plain Language

As hams, we use a great deal of "jargon" (technical slang) and specialized terminology in our daily conversations. Most of us understand each other when we do, and if we do not on occasion it usually makes little difference. In an emergency, however, the results can be much different. A misunderstood message could cost someone's life.

Not everyone involved in an emergency communication situation will understand our slang and technical jargon. Even terms used by hams vary from one region to another, and non- hams or new hams will have no knowledge of most of our terminology. Hams assisting from another region might understand certain jargon very differently from local hams.

For these reasons, all messages and communications during an emergency should be in plain language. "Q" signals (except in CW communication), 10 codes and similar jargon should be avoided. The one exception to this is the list of standard "pro-words" (often called "pro-signs") used in Amateur traffic nets, such as "clear", "say again all after" and so on.

Avoid words or phrases that carry strong emotions. Most emergency situations are emotionally charged already, and you do not need to add to the problem. For instance, instead of saying, "horrific damage and people torn to bits," you might say "significant physical damage and serious personal injuries."

And please watch your speed of speech. It should be at a normal rate. Many times emergency operators get too excited and talk very fast, making it hard for receiving stations to understand.

Phonetics

Certain words in a message may not be immediately understood. This might be the case with an unusual place name, such as "Franconia" or an unusual last name, like "Smythe." The best way to be sure it is understood correctly is to spell it. The trouble is, if you just spell the word

Section 2: The Networks for Messages
Topic 6: Basic Communication Skills

using letters, it might still be misunderstood, since many letters sound alike at the other end of a radio circuit. "Z" and "C" are two good examples. For that reason, radio communicators often use "phonetics." These are specific words that begin with the letter being sent. For instance, "ARRL" might be spoken as "alpha romeo romeo lima".

To reduce requests to repeat words, use phonetics anytime a word has an unusual or difficult spelling, or may be easily misunderstood. Do not spell common words unless the receiving station asks you to. In some cases, they may ask for the phonetic spelling of a common word to clear up confusion over what has been received. Standard practice is to first say the word, say "I spell," and then spell the word phonetically. This lets the receiving station know you are about to spell the word he just heard.

Several different phonetic alphabets are in common use, but most hams and public safety agencies use the ITU Phonetic Alphabet, shown below, and others use military alphabets. Many hams like to make up their own phonetics, especially as a memory aid for call signs, and often with humorous results. **This practice has no place in emergency communication**. In poor conditions, unusual phonetic words might also be misunderstood. We need to be sure that what we say is always interpreted exactly as intended— this is why most professional communicators use standardized phonetics.

ITU Phonetic Alphabet:

A—alfa (AL-fa)
B—bravo (BRAH-voh)
C—charlie (CHAR-lee)
D—delta (DELL-tah)
E—echo (ECK-oh)
F—foxtrot (FOKS-trot)
G—golf (GOLF)
H—hotel (HOH-tell)
I—india (IN-dee-ah)
J—juliet (JU-lee-ett)
K—kilo (KEY-loh)
L—lima (LEE-mah)
M—mike (MIKE)
N—november (no-VEM-ber)
O—oscar (OSS-cah)
P—papa (PAH-PAH)
Q—quebec (kay-BECK)
R—romeo (ROW-me-oh)
S—sierra (SEE-air-rah)
T—tango (TANG-go)
U—uniform (YOU-ni-form)
V—victor (VIK-tor)
W—whiskey (WISS-key)
X—x-ray (ECKS-ray)
Y—yankee (YANG-key)
Z—zulu (ZOO-loo)

Numbers are somewhat easier to understand. Most can be made clearer by simply "over-enunciating" them.

Phonetics:

One: "Wun"
Two: "TOOO"
Three: "THUH-ree"
Four: "FOH-wer"
Five: "FY-ive"
Six: "Sicks"
Seven: "SEV-vin"
Eight: "Ate"
Nine: "NINE-er"
Zero: "ZEE-row"

Numbers are always pronounced individually. The number "60" is spoken as "six zero", not "sixty". The number "509" is spoken as "five zero nine", and not as "five hundred nine" or "five oh nine".

Section 2: The Networks for Messages
Topic 6: Basic Communication Skills

Pro-words

Pro-words, called "pro-signs" when sent in Morse code or digital modes, are procedural terms with specific meanings. ("Pro" is short for "procedural.") They are used to save time and ensure that everyone understands precisely what is being said.

Some pro-words are used in general communication, others while sending and receiving formal messages. The usage and meaning of some pro-words in other services, such as police, fire or military, may differ from amateur radio usage.

Here are some pro-words and pro-signs in common usage in amateur radio communications:

Voice	Morse	Meaning and Digital function
Clear	SK*	End of contact; end of communication. In CW, SK is sent before final identification.
Over	KN*	Used to let a specific station know to respond.
Go ahead	K	Used to indicate that any station may respond
Out	CL*	End of contact; end of communication, no reply expected.
Stand by	AS*	A temporary interruption of the contact.
Roger	R	Indicates that a transmission has been received correctly and in full

* Two letters are sent as one character in CW.

Tactical Call Signs

Tactical call signs can identify the station's location or its purpose during an event, regardless of who is operating the station. This is an important concept. The tactical call sign allows you to contact a station without knowing the FCC call sign of the operator. It virtually eliminates confusion at shift changes or at stations with multiple operators.

Tactical call signs should be used for all emergency nets and public service events if there are more than just a few participants. If one does not already exist, the Net Control Station (NCS) may assign the tactical call sign as each location is "opened." Tactical call signs will usually provide some information about the location or its purpose. It is often helpful if the tactical call signs have a meaning that matches the way in which the served agency identifies the location or function.

Some examples are:

"**Net**"— for net control station
"**Springfield EOC**"— for the city's Emergency Operations Center
"**Firebase 1**"— for the first fire base established, or a primary fire base
"**Checkpoint 1**"— for the first check point in a public service event
"**Canyon Shelter**"— for the Red Cross shelter at Canyon School
"**Repair 1**"— for the roving repair vehicle at a bike-a-thon
"**Mercy**"— for Mercy Hospital

Section 2: The Networks for Messages
Topic 6: Basic Communication Skills

To be effective, a tactical call sign, once assigned, should be used consistently (i.e., don't use EOC" one time and "Command" the next). A list of tactical callsigns and the locations or functions to which they are assigned should be made known to all who might make calls to or receive calls from each such location or function.

Calling with Tactical Call Signs

If you are at "Aid 3" during a directed net and want to contact the net control station, you would say "Net, Aid 3" or, in crisper nets (and where the NCS is paying close attention), simply "Aid 3". If you had emergency traffic, you would say "Aid 3, emergency traffic," or for priority traffic "Aid 3, priority traffic." Notice how you have quickly conveyed all the information necessary, and have not used any extra words.

If you have traffic for a specific location, such as Firebase 5, you would say "Aid 3, priority traffic for Firebase 5." This tells the NCS everything needed to correctly direct the message. If there is no other traffic holding, the NCS will then call Firebase 5 with, "Firebase 5, call Aid 3 for priority traffic." Note that no FCC call signs have been used - so far...

Station Identification

In addition to satisfying the FCC's rules, proper station identification is essential to promoting the efficient operation of a net. The FCC requires that you identify at ten-minute intervals during a conversation **and** at the end of your last transmission. During periods of heavy activity in tactical nets it is easy to forget when you last identified, but if you identify at the end of each transmission, you will waste valuable time. What to do?

The easiest way to be sure you fulfill FCC station identification requirements during a net is to give your FCC call sign as you complete each exchange. Most exchanges will be far shorter than ten minutes. This serves two important functions:

1. It tells the NCS that you consider the exchange complete (and saves time and extra words)
2. It fulfills all FCC identification requirements.

Completing a Call

After the message has been sent, you would complete the call from Aid 3 by saying "Aid 3, *<your call sign>*". This fulfills your station identification requirements and tells the NCS that you believe the exchange to be complete.

If the Net Control Station believes the exchange is complete, and Aid 3 had forgotten to identify, then the NCS should say, "Aid 3, do you have further traffic?" At that point, Aid 3 should either continue with the traffic, or "clear" by identifying as above

For this method to work properly, the NCS must allow each station the opportunity to

Section 2: The Networks for Messages
Topic 6: Basic Communication Skills

identify at the close of an exchange.

A Review of Habits to Avoid

- Thinking aloud on the air: "Ahhh, let me see. Hmm. Well, you know, if…"
- On-air arguments, criticism, or rambling commentaries
- Shouting into your microphone
- "Cute" phonetics
- Identifying every time you key or un-key the mic
- Using "10" codes, Q-signals on phone, or anything other than "plain language"
- Speaking without planning your message in advance
- Talking just to pass the time.

Reference Links

The Public Service Communications Manual:

http://www.arrl.org/public-service-communications-manual

ARRL ARES Field Resources Manual:

http://www.arrl.org/ares-field-resources-manual

Section 2: The Networks for Messages
Topic 6: Basic Communication Skills

Review

Clear, concise communications save time and reduce misunderstandings. Avoid any non-essential transmissions. Use tactical call signs to call other stations, and give your FCC call sign only at the end of the complete exchange, or every ten minutes during longer exchanges. Plain language is more easily understood by a wider range of people than most codes and jargon.

Activities

1. Looking at the following exchanges, tell your mentor how you might revise the language to make them more clear and concise.

    a. "KA1XYZ at Ramapo Base, this is Bob, K2ABC at Weston EOC calling."
    b. "K2ABC, this is KA1XYZ. Hi, Bob. This is Ramapo Base, Harry at the mic. Go ahead. K2ABC from KA1XYZ."
    c. "KA1XYZ, this is K2ABC returning. Hi, Harry. I have a message for you. By the way, remember to call me later about the get-together the club is having next month. Are you ready to copy the message? KA1XYZ, this is K2ABC, over to you Harry."

2. Based upon what you have read in this lesson, list five common errors to avoid when communicating during an emergency.

Share the results of both activities with your mentor.

Section 2: The Networks for Messages
Topic 6: Basic Communication Skills

Welcome to Topic 6 Knowledge Review

In order to demonstrate mastery of the information presented in the topic, you will be asked a series of un-graded questions. There are approximately 5 questions on the following pages in multiple-choice or true/false format. Feedback will be offered to you based on the answer you provide.

Question 1:

In emergency communication, which one of the following is NOT true?

a) Listening is only about 10% of communication.

b) Message errors can have huge and unintended consequences.

c) A message that is never delivered can yield disastrous results.

d) Listening also means avoiding unnecessary communications.

Question 2:

Which of the following procedures is best for using a microphone?

a) Hold the microphone just off the tip of your nose.

b) Talk across, rather than into, your microphone.

c) Shout into the microphone to insure that you are heard at the receiving end.

d) Whenever possible, use voice operated transmission (VOX).

Question 3:

In emergency communications, which of the following is true?

a) Never use "10 codes" on Amateur Radio.

b) Use "Q signals" on served-agency radio systems.

c) Under NO circumstances use "Q" signals on a CW net.

d) Use technical jargon when you feel that it is appropriate.

Section 2: The Networks for Messages
Topic 6: Basic Communication Skills

Question 4:

Which of the following is always true of a tactical net?

a) Personal call signs are never used.

b) Personal call signs are always preferred over tactical call signs (such as "Aid 3").

c) Personal call signs are required at ten- minute intervals during a conversation or at the end of your last transmission.

d) Personal call signs are required at ten- minute intervals during a conversation and at the end of your last transmission.

Question 5:

Which of the following is the most efficient way to end an exchange on a tactical net?

a) Say "Over".

b) Say "Roger".

c) Give your FCC call sign.

d) Ask Net Control if there are any further messages for you.

Section 2: The Networks for Messages
Topic 7a: Basic Net Operations

TOPIC 7a:

Basic Net Operations

Topic 7a: Basic Net Operations

Objectives

Welcome to Topic 7a.

This topic will provide a brief review of basic net operations as a foundation for other material to follow in this section of the curriculum.

Student Preparation required:

If you are unfamiliar with network (net) operations, monitor several sessions of an Amateur Radio scheduled or emergency net.

Why We Have Nets

Any list of the major strengths of Amateur Radio in an emergency setting includes our abilities to share information in a "group setting" in real time across multiple locations and even multiple served agencies. Unlike many other types of communications, our radio messages can be heard by everyone in the group at once - and they can respond. This gives flexibility to emergency response managers that is very useful. But, it can cause a problem if not organized.

During an emergency communication situation, a high volume of disorganized messages can quickly turn an overloaded communication system into a disaster of its own. To prevent this from happening, Amateur Radio operators use regular protocols called a "network" or "net" to organize the flow of messages. The mission of the net is to effectively move as much traffic accurately and quickly as possible. Nets can be either formal or informal as needs dictate. Nets can be in voice, Morse code, or digital modes depending on the situation.

Anatomy of Net Operations

The Net Manager is the person in charge of a net, but is most often not the person who actually conducts the net on the air. Managers ensure that there is a Net Control Station (NCS) with enough operators for each shift, and monitors net and band conditions to see if changes in frequency are needed. If more than one net is operating, a Net Manager may be responsible for a group of nets. The Net Manager coordinates the various nets and their NCSs to ensure a smooth flow of traffic within and between nets. Managers may assign various human and equipment resources to meet the needs of each net.

Section 2: The Networks for Messages
Topic 7a: Basic Net Operations

Net Managers may be responsible for a regularly scheduled net, or may be temporarily appointed to manage one or more ad hoc nets created for a particular emergency incident.

An NCS directs the minute-by-minute operation of the net on the air. The NCS controls the flow of messages according to priority, and keeps track of where messages come from and where they go, and any that have yet to be sent. They also keep a current list of which stations are where, their assignments, and their capabilities. In a busy situation, the NCS may have one or more assistants to help with record keeping.

Liaison Stations handle messages that need to be passed from one net to another. The NCS or Net Manager may assign one or more stations to act as liaisons between two specific nets. These stations can monitor one or both nets, depending on resources. It is easier to monitor only one net at a time. This can be accomplished by having one station in each net assigned as the liaison to the other, or by having a single liaison station check into both nets on a regular schedule. In the event that an "emergency" precedence message needs to be passed to another net when the liaison is not monitoring that net, any net member can be assigned to jump to the other net and pass the message.

Learning proper NCS technique and handling such duties is one of the most important functions in Emergency Communications. During an emergency or disaster, the first operator to arrive on frequency is the NCS operator– at least until a Net Manager or a leadership official arrives on frequency to take control and perhaps to assign someone else to be the NCS.

Net Types

Open (Informal) Nets

During an open emergency net, there is minimal central control by a Net Control Station, if indeed there is an NCS at all. Stations call one another directly to pass messages. Unnecessary chatter is usually kept to a minimum. Open nets are often used during the period leading up to a potential emergency situation and as an operation winds down, or in smaller nets with only a few stations participating.

Net Types

| Refer to audio file 1 |

Directed (Formal) Nets

A directed emergency net is created whenever large numbers of stations are participating, or where the volume of traffic cannot be dealt with on a first-come first-served basis. In a communication emergency of any size, it is usually best to operate a directed net. In such situations the NCS can prioritize traffic by nature and content.

| Refer to audio file 2 |

In a directed net, the NCS controls all net operations. Check-ins may not "break into" (interrupt) the net or transmit unless specifically instructed to do so by the NCS, or unless they have an emergency message. The NCS will determine who uses the frequency and which traffic will be passed first. Casual conversation is strongly discouraged and tactical call signs will probably be

Section 2: The Networks for Messages
Topic 7a: Basic Net Operations

used. Tactical call signs can be assigned to stations at various sites, locations and different purposes. For example mobile operators can often be assigned the sign "rover 1", "rover 2" and so on.

At his/her discretion, the NCS operator may often elect to create a "sub net" depending on the volume of traffic and its content and nature. In this case a "sub net" NCS may be appointed to take over the newly created net.

Net Missions

Each net has a specific mission, or set of missions. In a smaller emergency, all the communication needs may be met by one net. In a larger emergency, multiple nets may be created to handle different needs. Here are some examples:

Traffic Net:– Handles formatted written messages between served agency locations or between other nets. In emergency operations, these nets may handle the majority of message originations and deliveries. Messages to or from outside the immediate area may be handled by a Section-level net, and depending on the distances involved and the degree to which the public telephone network and Internet are impaired, by Region Nets and Area Nets. Even if you expect to handle traffic primarily on VHF/UHF repeaters, understanding how these layers of nets operate will help you to optimize your use of the system. HF traffic nets can provide you additional practice and expose you to traffic handling that you might not encounter on VHF/UHF. During an emergency ARES and the National Traffic System (NTS) work together closely, so it's a good idea to understand emergency traffic from the NTS operator's perspective.

Resource Net: When incoming operators arrive on scene this is the net that they would check into to receive assignments, or to be reassigned as needs change. A resource net may also be used to locate needed equipment, or operators with specific skills. Several different resource nets may be used in large-scale events. One might be used for collecting new volunteers over a wide area, and other local nets could be used for initial assignments. If required due to geography or high net activity, a third net could handle on-going logistical support needs.

Tactical Net: In general, the tactical net(s) handle the primary on-site emergency communication. Their mission may be handling communications for a served agency, weather monitoring and reporting, river gauging, or a variety of other tasks that do not require a formal written message. Often a tactical net may be set up as a "sub net" to handle specific types of traffic during high volume emergency situations. In such cases an additional NCS may be assigned for the sub net.

Information Net: An information net might be used to make regular announcements, disseminate official bulletins or answer general questions that might otherwise tie up other nets that are busy handling incident-related communications.

Health and Welfare (H&W) Nets: These nets usually handle messages between concerned friends, families and persons in the disaster area. Most H&W nets will be on HF bands, but local VHF or UHF "feeder" nets may be needed within a disaster area. Band conditions, operator license constraints and specific use needs will most always determine which mode may be the best choice for determining the mode of certain net operations.

Section 2: The Networks for Messages
Topic 7a: Basic Net Operations

[Refer to video file 3]

Reference Links

For more information on any of the elements presented, please consult the following links:

Public Service Communication Manual http://www.arrl.org/public-service-communications-manual

Section 2: The Networks for Messages
Topic 7a: Basic Net Operations

Review

Amateur Radio allows for multiple participants to hear and pass messages in a group setting. This capability is a major strength of Amateur Radio and is put to best use by using nets. Nets are used to control the flow of message traffic on a specific frequency. The net's mission and overall operation is handled by a Net Manager, while the Net Control Station (NCS) is like a traffic cop directing the flow of traffic on the air. Liaison Stations pass messages between two different nets. Nets can be directed (formal) or open (informal) depending on the number of participants and volume of messages. Nets can serve many needs, including welfare message handling, resource management, and tactical message handling.

Activities

Outline a net plan for a possible disaster in your own area. Describe the types of nets you would include and the links between them. Discuss this plan with your mentor.

Monitor three HF or VHF/UHF traffic nets. Identify each net by category. If you do not have a receiver capable of monitoring such nets, contact your local ARES group or Amateur Radio club – a member may be able to let you listen to a few nets at their station. Share the results of this activity with your mentor.

Section 2: The Networks for Messages
Topic 7a: Basic Net Operations

Welcome to Topic 7a Knowledge Review

In order to demonstrate mastery of the information presented in the topic, you will be asked a series of un-graded questions. There are approximately 5 questions on the following pages in multiple-choice or true/false format. Feedback will be offered to you based on the answer you provide.

Question 1:

Which of the following requires no NCS to control net operations?

a) An Open Net.

b) A Directed Net.

c) An NTS Net.

d) A Health and Welfare Net.

Question 2:

Which of the following is true of Directed Nets?

a) There is minimal direction from a Net Control Station.

b) There is no clearly assigned mission.

c) They serve only as Liaison Nets between several simultaneous nets during large operations.

d) They are used when the volume of traffic is too great to be handled on a first-come, first-served basis.

Question 3:

Who is responsible for ensuring a smooth flow of traffic within and between nets?

a) The Official Observer.

b) The Net Manager.

c) The Liaison Station.

d) The NTS Emergency Coordinator.

Section 2: The Networks for Messages
Topic 7a: Basic Net Operations

Question 4:

Which type of net would handle non-formal communications for a served agency?

a) Health and Welfare Net.

b) Tactical Net.

c) Resource Net.

d) Traffic Net.

Question 5:

Which of the following statements concerning nets is true?

a) Resource Nets are used to assign operators as they become available.

b) Health and Welfare Nets operate only on HF bands.

c) NTS Traffic Nets handle both formal and informal long distance messages.

d) Tactical Nets handle only formatted, written messages.

Section 2: The Networks for Messages
Topic 7b: Introduction to Emergency Nets

TOPIC 7b:

Introduction to Emergency Nets

Objectives

Welcome to Topic 7b.

This topic will provide an overview of operations in a radio network, or "net" environment. It sets the stage for the following topic lessons, which present various aspects of net operation and message handling in greater detail. After reading the topic content you will identify information that is appropriate for net operations in a variety of settings, and is representative of nets around the country. Local procedures may vary slightly.

Student Preparation required:

Learn the following definitions:

Net: A group of stations who gather on one frequency, with a common purpose. The net provides a structure and organization to allow an orderly flow of messages.

Net Control Station (NCS): The station in charge of the net, and directing the flow of messages and general communications.

Formal Messages: Written messages that are sent in a standardized format.

Informal or "Tactical" Messages: brief oral or informal written messages, intended for direct and immediate delivery.

Traffic: A term referring to messages sent over Amateur Radio, usually formal, written messages. More generally, any messages or activity on a particular frequency.

Pass: to send messages from one station to another.

Third-Party Traffic: Messages transmitted on behalf of a person or organization other than a licensed Amateur Radio operator. This term also applies when a person other than a licensed operator is allowed to use the microphone.

Liaison Station: A station responsible for passing messages between different nets.

Section 2: The Networks for Messages
Topic 7b: Introduction to Emergency Nets

What is an Emergency Net?

The purpose of any net is to provide a means for orderly communication within a group of stations. An "emergency" net is a group of stations who provide communication to one or more served agencies, or to the general public, in a communications emergency. An emergency net may be formal or informal, depending on the number of participants and volume of messages.

Net Formats

Directed (formal) Nets:

In a directed net, a "net control station" (NCS) organizes and controls all activity. One station wishing to call or send a message to another in the net must first receive permission from the NCS. This is done so that messages with a higher priority will be handled first, and that all messages will be handled in an orderly fashion. Directed nets are the best format when there are a large number of member stations. (Be careful not to confuse "formal nets" with "formal messages." There is no definite link between the two. A formal net may handle informal messages, and vice versa.)

Open (informal) Nets:

In an open net, the NCS is optional. Stations may call each other directly. When a NCS is used at all, he usually exerts minimal control over the net. The NCS may step in when the message volume increases for short periods, or to solve problems and keep the net operating smoothly. Open nets are most often used when there are only a few stations and little traffic

Types of Emergency Nets

Emergency nets may have different purposes, and a given emergency may require one or more of each type of net. During a small operation, all functions may be combined into one net.

A **traffic net** handles formal written messages in a specified (i.e. ARRL) format. The nets operated by the National Traffic System (NTS) are an excellent example of traffic nets. ARES or RACES traffic nets may be directed or open depending on their size

Tactical Net – In general, the tactical net(s) handle the primary on-site emergency communication. Their mission may be handling communications for a served agency, weather monitoring and reporting, river gauging, or a variety of other tasks that do not require a formal written message. Often a tactical net may be set up as a "sub net" to handle specific types of traffic during high volume emergency situations. In such cases an additional NCS may be assigned for the sub net.

A **"resource" or "logistics"** net may be needed to acquire resources and volunteers, and handle assignments. It is usually a directed net. Resource nets accept check-ins from arriving volunteers, who are then directed to contact an appropriate station or to proceed to a specific location. It might also be used to locate needed resources, such as equipment, food, water and other supplies for emcomm volunteers.

Section 2: The Networks for Messages
Topic 7b: Introduction to Emergency Nets

An **information net** is usually an open net used to collect or share information on a developing situation, without overly restricting the use of the frequency by others. Net members send updated local information as needed, and official bulletins from the served agency may be sent by the NCS (if the net has one), an agency liaison station or an Official Bulletin Station (OBS). The NCS and many of the participants monitor the frequency, but a "roll call" is seldom taken and stations may not be expected to check in and out of the net. The operation of an information net also serves as notice to all stations that a more formal net may be activated at any moment if conditions warrant. A good example is a SKYWARN weather net activated during a severe storm watch.

Checking Into an Emergency Net

There are two situations where you will need to "check in" to a net.

1. When you first join the net.

2. When you have messages, questions or information to send.

If you are part of the organization operating the net, simply follow the instructions for checking into directed and open nets as discussed below.

To become part of a **directed net**, listen for the NCS to ask for "check-ins" and listen to any specific instructions, such as "check-ins with emergency traffic only." At the appropriate time, give only your call sign. If you have a message to pass, you can add, "with traffic." If it is an emergency message, say "with emergency traffic." The same is true for stations with priority traffic. Wait for a response before offering more information. Checking into a directed net when the NCS has not asked for check-ins is usually considered a bad practice. However, if a long period passes with no request, you might wait for a pause in the net's activity and briefly call the NCS like this: "Net control, W1FN, with traffic."

To check in to an **open net** for the first time, briefly call the net control station as above. If there appears to be no NCS, call anyone on the net to find out if anyone is "in charge" and make contact with them. If you are already part of the net and have a message to send, simply wait for the frequency to be clear before calling another station.

If you are *not* **part of the organization** operating the net, do not just check in and offer to assist. Listen for a while. Be sure you have something specific to offer before checking in, (such as the ability to deliver a message close to your location when none of the regular net members can). If they really do seem to need help that you feel you can provide, you might check in briefly to ask if they have a "resource" net in operation, then switch to that frequency. If not, make a brief offer of assistance to the NCS.

Do not be too surprised if you receive a cool reception to your offer of help. It is usually nothing personal. Emergency nets are serious business. Most emcomm managers prefer to deal with people with known training and capabilities, and with whom they have worked before. You may not have the experience, skills or official credentials they require—and they have no way of knowing what your true capabilities are. Some emcomm managers will assign you as an

Section 2: The Networks for Messages
Topic 7b: Introduction to Emergency Nets

apprentice, logger, or as a "runner." If you are given such an opportunity, take it! It is all good experience and a great way to introduce yourself to the group. Better yet, become involved with your local emcomm group now—do not wait for the next disaster.

Passing Messages

If you told the NCS you have traffic to send when you checked in, he will probably ask you to "list your traffic" with its destination and priority. After you send your list, the NCS will direct you to pass each message to the appropriate station in the net, either on the net frequency, or another frequency to avoid tying up the net. When moving to another frequency to pass the message, always check to see if the frequency is in use before beginning.

When you are asked by the NCS to send your message, the standard procedure is for the NCS to tell the receiving station to call the sending station.

The entire exchange might sound like this:

NCS: "W1AW, list your traffic."
    You: "W1AW, two priority for Springfield EOC, one welfare for the Section net."
        NCS: "Springfield EOC, call W1AW for your traffic."
        Springfield EOC: "W1AW, Springfield EOC, go ahead."
            You: "Number 25, Priority…"

(After you have sent your messages to the Springfield EOC, the NCS will next direct the section net liaison station to call you for their message.)

When you have finished, simply sign with any tactical call sign and your FCC call.
(You will learn more about messages and message handling and "emergency," "priority," and other precedences later.)

"Breaking" the Net

If the net is in progress, and you have emergency traffic to send, you may need to "break" into the net. Procedures for doing this vary from net to net, but the most common method is to wait for a pause between transmissions and simply say, "Break, WA1ZCN." The NCS will say, "Go ahead WA1ZCN," and you respond, "WA1ZCN with emergency traffic."

Section 2: The Networks for Messages
Topic 7b: Introduction to Emergency Nets

Checking Out of an Emergency Net

Always let the NCS know when you are leaving the net, even if it is only for a few minutes. If the NCS believes you are still in the net, they may become concerned about your unexplained absence. This could result in someone being unnecessarily dispatched to check on your well-being.

There are three reasons for checking out of (leaving) a net.

1. The location of your station is closing.

   If the NCS has given you directions to close the location, simply acknowledge the request, and sign with your tactical call sign, if you are using one, and your FCC call sign. If the order to close has come from a local official, state that your location has been closed, along with the name and title of the official who ordered it, and sign off as above. Long "goodbyes" only tie up the net needlessly, and do not sound very professional.

2. You need a break and there is no relief operator.

   Tell the NCS that you will be away from the radio for a certain length of time, the reason and sign with your tactical call sign, if you are using one, and your FCC call sign.

3. You have turned the location over to another operator.

   Tell the NCS that you have turned the station over to (give the new operator's name and FCC call sign), and that you are leaving. Sign with your tactical call sign, if you are using one, and your FCC call sign.

There are two special situations to be aware of: If someone in authority asks you, such as a law enforcement officer, to move your station, then move immediately and without argument. Notify the NCS of the situation at the first appropriate opportunity. If you are requested by someone in authority to turn off your radio, or to refrain from transmitting, do so immediately and without question. Do not notify Net Control until you have permission to transmit again, and can do so safely. There is usually a good reason for such a request. It may be an issue of security, or it may be a potential hazard, such as an explosive device that could be triggered by RF energy.

Levels of Nets

Network systems are often "layered" for greater operating efficiency. Some networks are designed to handle messages within specific areas, and others to handle messages between areas. Think of this much like you would the Interstate Highway System. Local messages (cars) travel between destinations directly on local nets (local roads). When a message has to go to a distant city, it is passed to a regional net (state highway), and if it is really distant, to a long distance net (interstate highway). At the other end, it is returned to regional, then local nets for delivery. What has been just described is the extensive National Traffic System (NTS), discussed further below.

Section 2: The Networks for Messages
Topic 7b: Introduction to Emergency Nets

ARES or RACES can use a similar structure on a smaller scale. For instance, each city might have a local FM net. A county net would handle messages going from city to city. A section HF net would handle messages from county to county. Any net in such a system could have "liaison" stations to pass into the NTS any messages that need to travel out of the section.

Non-Voice Nets

Emergency nets may also use other modes of communication besides voice (phone). Traffic nets have used CW since the beginning of Amateur Radio, and it is still a viable option for long distance formal traffic. High-speed CW nets can actually handle more messages per hour than most voice nets. Packet communication on VHF and UHF is often used for local communication where accuracy and a record of the message are required. HF digital modes such as AMTOR and PACTOR are used on long distance circuits. Many groups are now experimenting with emergency communication applications for newer modes such as PSK31 on HF and VHF/UHF bands.

Most CW nets are directed nets. Packet nets are not generally directed by a human, due the automatic "store and forward" nature of the mode, and are usually operated as open nets with no NCS.

There are two systems which have gotten significant attention by many emcomm groups and offer digital message handling capabilities:

"WinLink 2000," an automatic system that blends radio and Internet transmission paths to permit rapid and seamless email message transfer to stations anywhere on Earth. For most emergencies, it will be possible for stations in the affected area to link to a WinLink 2000 PACTOR node outside the affected area, allowing contact with the outside world.

More recently, the D-Star digital voice and data protocol specification, developed as the result of research by the Japan Amateur Radio League (JARL), is an on-air and packet-based standard that is now widely deployed and sold by a major radio manufacturer. D-Star compatible radios are available on VHF, UHF, and microwave amateur radio bands. In addition to the over-the-air protocol, D-Star also has network connectivity, enabling D-Star radios to be connected to the Internet or other networks. It also has provisions for routing data streams of voice or packet data directly to specific callsigns.

More on these later, but one new point needs to be made...

Practice and train using Digital as you would on any other mode.

How do you hold a training net on D-Star or Winlink? Digital modes are often not keyboard-to-keyboard in real time, and messages might take a while to get to their intended destination. Therefore, any attempt at a "conventional" net must be truly in slow motion. But without taking this time, net members will not know who else is up and operating, that equipment is working properly, and there are no "bugs" in the system. An emergency is not the time to see if your digital planning works – try it out in a drill or net before you really need it.

Section 2: The Networks for Messages
Topic 7b: Introduction to Emergency Nets

Reference Links

To learn about NTS in your area, contact your Section Manager (SM), or Section Traffic Manager (STM). To locate your Section Manager (SM), see the ARRL Section Manager List at: http://www.arrl.org/sections

For a list of ARES and NTS nets in your area, see:
http://www.arrl.org/arrl-net-directory.

D – Star: http://en.wikipedia.org/wiki/D-STAR

Winlink 2000: http://en.wikipedia.org/wiki/Winlink

Section 2: The Networks for Messages
Topic 7b: Introduction to Emergency Nets

Review

Large nets are usually directed (formal) nets with a NCS in charge. Smaller nets may be "open" (informal), and a NCS is optional. Nets can serve many purposes, including passing formal messages, handling logistics, or passing informal tactical messages. Large emergencies may require more than one of each type of net – small emergencies may have one combined net. Medium and long distance messages are often handled by the National Traffic System (NTS).

Activities

1. Discuss with your mentor the various types of emergency nets and how they are used.

2. Find a local emergency net in your area and listen in. Describe this experience to your mentor

Section 2: The Networks for Messages
Topic 7b: Introduction to Emergency Nets

Welcome to Topic 7b Knowledge Review

In order to demonstrate mastery of the information presented in the topic, you will be asked a series of un-graded questions. There are approximately 5 questions on the following pages in multiple-choice or true/false format. Feedback will be offered to you based on the answer you provide.

Question 1:

Which of the following best describes a net?

a) A group of stations who purposely frequent the airwaves.

b) A group of stations who gather on one frequency with a purpose.

c) A group of stations who occasionally meet on various frequencies.

d) A group of stations who propose to meet at a particular time.

Question 2:

What is a major difference between an "open net" and a "directed net"?

a) The presence or absence of full control by a Net Control Station.

b) The presence or absence of formal traffic.

c) The type of radio traffic on the net.

d) The approval or sanction of net operations by the FCC.

Question 3:

Which of the following is true of a "tactical net"?

a) The net is used to acquire volunteers and to handle assignments.

b) The net is used for the coordination of activities associated with future emergencies.

c) The net may be directed or open, but will usually have a Net Control Station.

d) The net handles only formal traffic.

Section 2: The Networks for Messages
Topic 7b: Introduction to Emergency Nets

Question 4:

When should you check in to an emergency net?

a) When you want to comment on something that someone else has said.

b) When you are tired of listening.

c) When you first join the net and when you have messages, questions or relevant information.

d) When you first join the net and when you would like to send greetings to one of the participating stations.

Question 5:

What should you do if someone in authority asks you to move your station?

a) Do so immediately without argument and report to the NCS as soon as possible.

b) Call the NCS for advice before moving.

c) Tell the person in authority how difficult it is for you to comply.

d) Demand a written order before complying.

Section 2: The Networks for Messages
Topic 7c: Net Operating Guidelines

TOPIC 7c:
Net Operating Guidelines

Objectives

Welcome to Topic 7c.

This unit will help net members understand how to operate efficiently and effectively in a net environment under emergency conditions.

Student Preparation required:

None.

Introduction

Every organization needs an executive-level manager to oversee the entire operation and ensure that everything runs smoothly. Depending on the type of net, the Net Manager will be responsible for recruiting and training NCS operators, liaison stations and other net members.

The Net Manager sets up the net's schedule and makes sure that one or more qualified NCS operators will be available for each session of the net. In a long-term emergency net, the Net Manager may also arrange for relief operators and support services. Some net managers may be responsible for more than one net.

The NCS

Think of the NCS as a "ringmaster" or "traffic cop." The NCS decides what happens in the net, and when. If the EOC has a Priority message for Red Cross Shelter 1, and Medical Station 4 has an Emergency message for Mercy Hospital, it is the NCS's job to make sure that the Emergency message is sent first. He decides when stations will check in, with or without traffic, and whether messages will be passed on the net's frequency or a different one. The NCS needs to be aware of everything going on around him and handle the needs of the net, its members and served agency as quickly and efficiently as possible. It can be a daunting task in a busy and challenging net.

The NCS can be located anywhere but should be in a position to hear most, if not all, stations in the net. This helps avoid time-consuming "relays." Some groups place their NCS at the EOC or command post; others like to keep them away from the noise and confusion.

The NCS is in charge of one specific net but should not be responsible for the entire emcomm operation. That is the job of the EC or similar emcomm manager. It is not possible to be in command of all aspects of an emergency response, and still run a net effectively, since both jobs require 100% of your attention.

Section 2: The Networks for Messages
Topic 7c: Net Operating Guidelines

Net Scripts

Many groups open and close their nets with a standard script. The text of the script lets listeners know the purpose and format of the net. Using a standard script also ensures that the net will be run in a similar format each time it operates regardless of who is acting as the NCS. A typical net script might look like this:

Opening: *This is [call sign], net control station for the New Hampshire ARES/RACES Emergency Net. This is a directed emergency net for liaison stations from all New Hampshire ARES/RACES regions. Please transmit only when requested to, unless you have emergency traffic,*

Any station with emergency traffic, please call now. (Stations call in and emergency traffic is passed.)
Any station with priority traffic, please call now. (Stations call in and priority traffic is passed.)

All other stations with or without traffic, please call now. (Stations call in and any traffic is passed.)

Closing: *I would like to thank all stations that checked in. This is [call sign] securing the New Hampshire ARES/RACES Emergency Net at [date and time] returning the [repeater or frequency] to regular use.*

A backup NCS needs to be readily available should there be an equipment failure at the primary NCS location, or if the primary NCS operator needs to take a break. There are two types of backup NCS. Either the Net Manager or the primary NCS, depending on the situation, appoints both. All members of the net should be made aware of the backup NCS assignment early in the net's operation.

The first type is at the same location as the primary NCS operator. The second is a station at a different location that maintains a duplicate log of everything happening during the net. Whenever possible, an offsite backup NCS should be maintained, even if an on-site backup is present. This is especially important during an emergency where antennas can be damaged or power lost. Equipment can fail even during less demanding operations.

Section 2: The Networks for Messages
Topic 7c: Net Operating Guidelines

Acting as a "fill-in" NCS

Even before you have had a chance to be trained by your group to act as a NCS operator, an opportunity might arise for you to handle the job temporarily. During an emergency, anyone and everyone can be asked to take on new and unfamiliar tasks in order to deal with a rapidly changing situation. Fortunately, basic NCS skills are not difficult to teach or learn. Here are some basic dos and don'ts:

- Remember that although you are in control of the net, you are not "God." Treat members with respect and accept suggestions from other experienced members.

- If you are taking over an existing net, try to run it much as the previous NCS did.

- Always follow a script if one is provided.

- Write your own if necessary, but keep it short and to the point.

- Handle messages in order of precedence: Emergency—Priority—Welfare—Routine.

- Speak clearly and in a normal tone of voice. Use good mic technique.

- Make all instructions clear and concise, using as few words as possible.

- Keep notes as you go along. Do not let your log fall behind.

- Write down which operators are at which locations. When one leaves or is replaced, update your notes.

- Ask stations to pass messages off the main net frequency whenever possible.

- All the reading and study in the world will not replace actual experience. You should look for opportunities to practice being the NCS operator well before an emergency occurs.

Net Members

Operators at various sites are responsible for messages going to and from their location. They must listen to everything that happens on the net, and maintain contact with the served agency's people at the site. They assist the served agency with the creation of messages, put them into the appropriate format and contact the NCS when they are ready to be sent.

Whenever possible, two operators should be at each site. When the station is busy, one can handle logging, message origination, and work with the served agency's staff while the other monitors the net, sends messages, and copies incoming traffic. During slower periods, one member can be "off-duty" for rest, meals or personal needs.

Bulletin Stations

Section 2: The Networks for Messages
Topic 7c: Net Operating Guidelines

In some nets, the NCS does not send out bulletins and other incident related information. That is the role of the "bulletin station." This station relays ARRL bulletins or those authorized by the served agency to all stations in the net. They may also be transmitted on a preset schedule, such as at the top and bottom of each hour. The bulletin station must be located at the served agency or have a reliable communication link to them.

Liaison Stations

Liaison stations pass messages between two different nets. The NCS or Net Manager, depending on the type of organization, usually assigns these stations. Messages may be passed as needed, or on a pre-set schedule. In some cases, a liaison station will monitor one net full time. When a message must be passed to another net, they leave the net temporarily to pass it, and then return. The other net has a liaison station who does exactly the same thing, but in reverse.

In other situations, a single liaison station may need to handle messages going both ways between two nets. There are two ways to do this. You can use two radios to monitor both nets at the same time, a difficult task if either or both nets are busy. The radios antennas must be separated sufficiently to prevent interference between radios when one is used to transmit. In the second method, one radio is used, and the liaison station switches between the two nets on a regular schedule.

Relay Stations

While not a regular net position, a relay station is one that passes messages between two stations in the net that cannot hear each other. Relay stations are generally designated by the NCS on an "as needed" basis. If you can hear a station or stations that the NCS cannot, it is OK to volunteer to act as a relay station.

Workload and Shift Changes

Although it happens frequently, no operator should try to work excessively long hours. When you become tired, your efficiency and effectiveness decline, and your served agency is not getting the best possible service. Net managers and NCS operators should work with the EC or other emcomm manager to ensure that all net members get some rest on a regular basis. It is a good practice for any replacement NCS, liaison, or net member to monitor the net for at least fifteen minutes and review the logs with the present operator before taking over. This assures continuity in the net's operation.

Non-voice Modes

Packet modes include FM packet, HF packet and PACTOR. Because packet modes can provide an automatic connection between two stations, it is not really proper to speak of a "packet net." Although messages can be transmitted between two stations "keyboard to keyboard" as with RTTY or PSK31, it is usually better to transmit them as "traffic," using the

Section 2: The Networks for Messages
Topic 7c: Net Operating Guidelines

bulletin board or mailbox facility of the terminal node controller (TNC). Packet messages are automatically routed and stored without any action by the receiving station's operator or a NCS.

Non-packet digital modes are not automatic, and may require a NCS operator to manage the net in much the same way as a phone or CW net. These include RTTY, PSK31, AMTOR and GTOR.

CW Procedures: Clean and accurate code sent at 10 words per minute is better than sloppy code sent at 30 words per minute. Sending speed is not a true measure of effectiveness, but accuracy is.

When propagation or interference makes communication difficult, or when the receiving operator cannot keep up, it is time to reduce the sending speed. Always send at a speed that the receiving station can copy comfortably.

There are variations used when passing traffic via CW, especially when both stations are operating "full break-in" mode (both stations are capable of receiving signals between each Morse character sent). The receiving station can "break" (stop) the sending station at any point for needed fills, instead of waiting for the entire message to be sent. There are additional special pro-signs used, and interested Amateurs should be familiar with ARRL Publication FSD-218 (http://www.arrl.org/public-service-field-services-forms). This publication is sometimes referred to as the "pink card" and contains CW net procedures as well as a description of the Amateur Message Form, message precedences and Handling Instruction abbreviations.

When formatting an ARRL Radiogram message, use abbreviations and prosigns consistently and appropriately. For instance, do not send "R," meaning you have received everything correctly, and then ask for repeats like "AA" (all after) or
"AB" (all before).

Interference Problems

If your net experiences interference, the NCS has several options. If the interference is coming from adjacent or co-channel stations that may be unaware of the emergency net, the NCS should politely inform them of the net and ask for their cooperation. Alternatively, the NCS might ask an HF net to move over a few kHz. If the problem cannot be resolved in this manner, each net should have one or more alternative frequencies that it can move to as required. If possible, the frequencies themselves should not be published or mentioned on the air.

Never discuss, acknowledge or try to speak with an intentionally interfering station. Many years of experience has proven that this only encourages the offender. If the interference is making communication difficult, simply announce to the net that everyone should move to the alternate frequency and sign off. Better yet, put a plan in place so that when interference occurs, all net members know to move to the alternate frequency without being told to do so on the air. If intentional interference persists, the Net Manager or NCS can contact an elected League official or an Official Observer Station, and ask that the FCC be notified of the interference. In some cases, they may be able to track down and contact the responsible station.

Section 2: The Networks for Messages
Topic 7c: Net Operating Guidelines

Reference Links

For information about ARRL Public Service Communications, please see The ARRL Public Service Communications Manual:

www.arrl.org/public-service-communications-manual

ARRL Publication FSD-218:

http://www.arrl.org/public-service-field-services-forms

Section 2: The Networks for Messages
Topic 7c: Net Operating Guidelines

Review

As the net's "ringmaster," the NCS operator is responsible for keeping the net operating smoothly and assuring that messages are sent in order of priority. An off-site backup or alternate NCS operator is essential for long- running nets in the event of equipment failure or operator fatigue. Net member stations should monitor the net continuously whenever possible, as well as maintaining contact with the served agency's staff at that location. Liaison stations pass traffic between two different nets, sometimes only in one direction, and sometimes in both directions. Bulletin stations transmit bulletin messages from the served agency to the net. CW nets can move messages very quickly and accurately, but slightly different procedures are used than with phone. Packet radio doesn't use a conventional net format due to its automatic nature, and is well suited to handling large volumes of traffic, or highly detailed and lengthy messages.

Activities

1. What are the major topics found in ARRL's FSD-218? Share what you learned with your mentor.

2. Many nets open and close their sessions with a standard script. Listen in on your local net and discuss with your mentor the language of the opening and closing script used.

Section 2: The Networks for Messages
Topic 7c: Net Operating Guidelines

Welcome to Topic 7c Knowledge Review

In order to demonstrate mastery of the information presented in the topic, you will be asked a series of un-graded questions. There are approximately 5 questions on the following pages in multiple-choice or true/false format. Feedback will be offered to you based on the answer you provide.

Question 1:

Which of the following best describes the responsibilities of the NCS in an emcomm operation?

a) The NCS is responsible for all aspects of the emcomm operation.

b) The NCS is responsible for station check in.

c) The NCS is responsible for all aspects of the net's operation.

d) The NCS is responsible for writing the net script.

Question 2:

As acting "fill in" NCS, which of the following practices would you *avoid*?

a) Try to run an existing net much as the previous NCS did.

b) Handle messages in order of precedence: Emergency-Priority-Welfare.

c) Keep notes as you go along: do not let your log fall behind.

d) Ask stations to pass messages on the main net frequency whenever possible.

Question 3:

Which of the following is true of a liaison station?

a) The liaison station mainly relays bulletins authorized by the served agency to all stations on the net.

b) A liaison station passes messages only on a pre-set schedule.

c) A liaison station handles only one-way traffic.

d) A liaison station passes messages between two nets.

Section 2: The Networks for Messages
Topic 7c: Net Operating Guidelines

Question 4:

Packet modes include which of the following groups?

a) FM packet, HF packet and PACTOR.

b) HF packet, PACTOR and PSK31.

c) PACTOR, PSK31 and RTTY.

d) PSK31, RTTY and PACTOR.

Question 5:

You are the NCS of a net involved in an emcomm operation and you notice that some other station is intentionally interfering with your net. Which of the following represents your best course of action?

a) Shut down the net and go home.

b) Address the interfering station directly and inform them of the error of their ways.

c) Move the net to an alternate frequency.

d) Contact the EOC and continue to operate.

Section 2: The Networks for Messages
Topic 7d: The FCC Ruling on Drills and Employees

TOPIC 7d:

The FCC Ruling on Drills and Employees

Objectives

Welcome to Topic 7d.

After reading this topic the participant will learn about the prohibition on using Amateur Radio for the benefit of an employer except as now being allowed in drills but under very limited circumstances.

Student Preparation required:

None.

Introduction

On July 14, 2010 the FCC issued a Report and Order amending the rules to permit amateur radio operators to transmit messages, *under certain limited circumstances*, during either government-sponsored or non-government sponsored emergency and disaster preparedness drills, regardless of whether the operators are employees of entities participating in the drill.

Tests or drills that are not government-sponsored are limited to a total time of one hour per week; except that no more than twice in any calendar year, they may be conducted for a period not to exceed 72 hours.

Federal Communications Commission FCC 10-124

Although public safety land mobile radio systems are the primary means of radio-based communications for emergency responders, experience has shown that amateur radio has played an important role in preparation for, during, and in the aftermath of, natural and man-made emergencies and disasters. We emphasize, however, that the amendment does not permit communications unrelated to the drill or exercise being conducted.

Section 2: The Networks for Messages
Topic 7d: The FCC Ruling on Drills and Employees

Final Rules

Part 97 of Chapter 1 of Title 47 of the Code of Federal Regulations is amended as follows:

§ 97.113 Prohibited transmissions.

(a) * * *

(3) Communications in which the station licensee or control operator has a pecuniary interest, including communications on behalf of an employer, with the following exceptions:

(i) A station licensee or control station operator may participate on behalf of an employer in an emergency preparedness or disaster readiness test or drill, limited to the duration and scope of such test or drill, and operational testing immediately prior to such test or drill. Tests or drills that are not government-sponsored are limited to a total time of one hour per week; except that no more than twice in any calendar year, they may be conducted for a period not to exceed 72 hours.

(ii) An amateur operator may notify other amateur operators of the availability for sale or trade of apparatus normally used in an amateur station, provided that such activity is not conducted on a regular basis.

(iii) A control operator may accept compensation as an incident of a teaching position during periods of time when an amateur station is used by that teacher as a part of classroom instruction at an educational institution.

(iv) The control operator of a club station may accept compensation for the periods of time when the station is transmitting telegraphy practice or information bulletins, provided that the station transmits such telegraphy practice and bulletins for at least 40 hours per week; schedules operations on at least six amateur service MF and HF bands using reasonable measures to maximize coverage; where the schedule of normal operating times and frequencies is published at least 30 days in advance of the actual transmissions; and where the control operator does not accept any direct or indirect compensation for any other service as a control operator.

Note that not every Amateur transmission from a work location is necessarily on behalf of an employer. For example, an ARES member using an employer-provided station to check into a local ARES net as an individual is not necessarily transmitting on behalf of the employer. This is a new ruling for us all and specific examples will be debated and discussed for a long time to come. Use your very best judgment. We all want to be helpful, but keep Amateur Radio as "amateur."

Section 2: The Networks for Messages
Topic 7d: The FCC Ruling on Drills and Employees

Reference Links
See the FCC document (PDF)

> Find FCC 10-124 in the Appendix to this course transcript.

Activities

Understand the FCC's ruling on drills and employees. Discuss with your mentor how this ruling may apply to you.

Section 2: The Networks for Messages
Topic 7d: The FCC Ruling on Drills and Employees

Welcome to Topic 7d Knowledge Review

In order to demonstrate mastery of the information presented in the topic, you will be asked a series of un-graded questions. There are approximately 5 questions on the following pages in multiple-choice or true/false format. Feedback will be offered to you based on the answer you provide.

Question 1:

What is a maximum amount of time a radio amateur can participate in a government sponsored drill on behalf of their employer?

a) One hour.

b) 72 hours twice a year.

c) There is no limit.

d) Never.

Question 2:

What is the maximum amount of time a radio amateur can participate in a non-government sponsored drill on behalf of their employer?

a) One hour a week.

b) Never.

c) There is no limit.

d) No limit if it is for a hospital.

Question 3:

Your employer wants you to design and operate an Amateur Radio system between office buildings so his business can still function even if the phones and intranet are down. He says that, for him, "No phones is an emergency." Should you do it?

a) Yes

b) No

Section 2: The Networks for Messages
Topic 8: The Net Control Station

TOPIC 8:

THE NET CONTROL STATION (NCS)

Objectives

Welcome to Topic 8.

Following completion of this Learning Topic, you will acquire knowledge on how the Net Control Station (NCS) runs a net, and many of the skills required.

Student Preparation required:

None required for this Learning Topic.

Introduction

The NCS

Formal (directed) nets will always have one station "in control." This station is known as the *"Net Control Station" (NCS)*, and its operator as the *"NCS operator."* Think of the NCS operator as sort of a "traffic cop," directing the orderly flow of messages. His or her skills are critical to the success of any emergency communication net. For this reason many emergency communication groups elect to have training and even classes designed to teach and train operators in NCS skills. Practice sessions are often helpful for this purpose, and many ARES groups schedule regular weekly practice sessions.

When Do You Need An NCS?

All formal (directed) nets require an NCS. Formal nets are used to maintain order when a large number of stations are in the net, or when a large volume of messages are being sent. The NCS operator decides who speaks when, in which order messages are passed, and keeps a log of which messages went where and when, and a list of messages that have yet to be passed.

Some informal nets will have a "standby" NCS, although by definition informal nets are not controlled. This person is there to keep things organized when necessary, to answer questions, keep the frequency clear, and to step in and "upgrade" the net to "formal" status if it becomes necessary. This often happens with initially light-duty nets that have the potential to grow as the situation evolves. SKYWARN® tornado watch nets are a good example. During the "watch" phase, not much is happening other than informal sharing of information between observers. If a tornado appears, the traffic on channel will increase, and if damage occurs on the ground, the net could quickly evolve into a high-volume disaster relief net. Having an NCS operator on standby helps make this a smooth transition.

Section 2: The Networks for Messages
Topic 8: The Net Control Station

How Important Is A Well-Trained NCS Operator?

Have you ever listened to or participated in a poorly run net? One where routine messages are passed on-channel, while emergency or priority messages wait in line? Or where the NCS operator "loses his cool" and alienates half the net's members? Or nets where messages are not kept organized, are lost, changed, or misdirected?

The value of the NCS operator's skill is unquestionable. A well run net meets the needs of the served agency – a poorly run net can end Amateur Radio's relationship with the agency altogether.

The NCS operator must be a good organizer, and know how to defuse tension and stress with an appropriate sense of humor. The NCS operator also must have the ability to absorb new terminology quickly, as there is no more fertile environment for the growth of jargon than in the emergency management community!

The Right Stuff

Do you have what it takes to become a good NCS operator? Here is a short list of basic pre-requisites:

- A clear speaking voice – someone who talks as though they have a mouthful of marbles won't do.

- Fluency in the language – if you have a thick accent or cannot use the language precisely, it may make it difficult for others to understand you accurately.

- The ability to handle mental and physical stress for long periods. Information and demands will be coming at you from all directions all at once, sometimes for hours on end. Can you handle it without losing your composure, or your voice? Can you think and act quickly when seconds count using prudence and are you able to make decisions under pressure?

- The ability to listen and comprehend in an often noisy and chaotic environment. Can you tune out all the distractions and focus only on the job at hand?

- Good hearing - If you have a hearing loss that makes it tough to understand human voices, NCS of a voice net is not the job for you. Hams with limited hearing problems may elect to act as NCS for a digital mode net, according to one's abilities.

- The ability to write legibly what you hear, as you receive it, and to make good notes as you go, not rely on memory.

- Above-average general knowledge and operating skills in the modes used (phone, digital, or CW).

Section 2: The Networks for Messages
Topic 8: The Net Control Station

"Transferable" Skills

Some of the skills you use in everyday amateur radio activities will be useful in your position as NCS operator.

- A well-designed and maintained station is critical to success. You must be able to choose the correct antenna, know how to get the best sound from your microphone, be radio agile, knowing how to operate, program and maintain the radio on short notice and have all controls and supplies within easy reach.

- You need to understand propagation so that you can choose the appropriate frequency as band conditions change. DXers learn how to pick weak signals out of the noise, and deal with crowded band conditions. Many of the skills used in contesting are applicable to controlling a net. Both activities involve dealing with many stations on the same frequency at the same time. The contester running a pile-up will try to contact as many stations as possible in the least amount of time. The mission of the NCS operator is to move as much traffic as possible in the least amount of time, accurately and effectively.

"Learned" Skills

A good NCS operator is trained, not born. Here are some skills you may need to learn to perform at your best.

- Working as a team player to achieve the goals of the net

- Effective leadership skills – keeping the team on track and motivated by developing a confident, self-assured management style

- Decisiveness – the ability to make quick and appropriate decisions

- Record keeping – log sheets (writing, thinking and talking all at once)

- Planning ahead – net scripts, assignments, materials on-hand

- HF propagation and antenna choices – knowing when to move to a different band

- Dealing with stress – a "burned-out" operator is a danger to the net

- Delegation – knowing when and how to "hand off" some jobs and responsibilities

- A working knowledge of the Incident Command System (ICS) and how we fit in

Section 2: The Networks for Messages
Topic 8: The Net Control Station

Learning and Practicing Your Skills

Book learning alone will not make you a competent NCS operator. It takes practice to learn these skills in a way that they will be ingrained and useful in a real emergency. Continued practice is necessary to maintain these skills once learned. Local nets on a weekly basis with rotation of NCS operators are a good way to gain practice, which is often done by many ARES groups.

Net control skills can be learned and honed through classroom sessions, tabletop exercises, and regularly scheduled training nets. Actual emergency conditions can be simulated with periodic drills and simulations such as the annual Simulated Emergency Tests (SET), and public service events such as road races, marathons and bike rides. Some ARES units have simulated emergency nets weekly. For example, some have simulated emergency weather nets during the severe weather season.

To begin your own NCS training, find out if your local group offers any formal training. Some will begin with tabletop exercises, in which a group sitting around a table will simulate a net operation, taking turns as NCS and net member stations. Tabletop exercises allow quick feedback and greater interaction among participants.

Other groups will simply let you take over as NCS for several scheduled training nets. Before you do this, try to listen to other, more experienced, operators on your own net, and as many other formal nets as you can. Pay close attention to how they run the net, what scripts (if any) they use, and any mistakes they make.

If your group or local club provides communication support for events such as marathons, large parades, or races, these provide additional opportunities to get some "real world" NCS operator experience.

A real emergency is not the time to learn or practice new skills, unless there is no other option. A poorly trained or inexperienced NCS operator can do as much harm as good. Participation in regularly scheduled nets is important so that anyone who is or may become an NCS during a disaster or emergency can be effective and vital to the overall success of the mission.

What the NCS Operator is Not

The duties of the NCS operator should be limited to running the net. This is a full-time job all by itself. The NCS operator should not be in charge of the overall communication effort, or of any portion of the response beyond his or her own net and shift. The Net Manager generally handles the assignment of NCS operators, frequencies, and schedules, and may also recruit members for the net. Also, it is best for the Net Control Station to work away from any location that is also a significant originator or destination of message traffic.

Section 2: The Networks for Messages
Topic 8: The Net Control Station

Reference Links

For more information on any of the elements presented, please consult the following links:

Public Service Communications Manual: http://www.arrl.org/public-service-communications-manual

To learn more about local ARES and NTS net operations, contact your Section Manager (SM), your Section Emergency Coordinator (SEC) or District Emergency Coordinator (DEC). For other localized information, see http://www.arrl.org/sections

See the **ARRL Net Directory** for a list of ARES and NTS nets operating in your area. The directory can also be searched on the ARRL Web site at http://www.arrl.org/arrl-net-directory

Section 2: The Networks for Messages
Topic 8: The Net Control Station

Review

The NCS operator is in charge of controlling the flow of information on a net. In addition to training and practice, a good NCS operator has several attributes including a clear speaking voice and patience. The Net Manager assigns an NCS for each net session or operating shift. The duties of the NCS operator should be limited to running the net.

Activities

1. Participate in a formal net as a member. Review the performance of the net control stations. List five positive features and any negative features of net operation that you encountered. If you do not have the capability to check into a net yourself, listen to nets on VHF/UHF or HF and review their operations and the effectiveness of the NCS operators. Share these notes with your mentor.

    While net frequencies or times change, see the ARRL Net Directory book or go to the ARRL Web site at http://www.arrl.org/arrl-net-directory find the latest known information about major nets.

    - US Coast Guard Amateur Radio Net 14.300 or 14.313 MHz
    - International Assistance and Traffic Net: 14.303 MHz
    - East Coast Amateur Radio Service Net: 7.255 MHz. South CARS 7.251 MHz; mid CARS 7.258 MHz.
    - Mobile Emergency & County Hunter's Net: 14.336, 14.0565 MHz (continuous)

If you do not have a receiver capable of monitoring such nets, contact your local ARES group or Amateur Radio club – a member may be able to let you listen to a few nets at their station.

Section 2: The Networks for Messages
Topic 8: The Net Control Station

Welcome to Topic 8 Knowledge Review

In order to demonstrate mastery of the information presented in the topic, you will be asked a series of un-graded questions. There are approximately 5 questions on the following pages in multiple-choice or true/false format. Feedback will be offered to you based on the answer you provide.

Question 1:

Which is the primary purpose of a "standby" NCS in an informal net?

a) To make certain that the informal sharing of information flows smoothly.

b) To encourage others to join in the informal conversations.

c) To upgrade the net to formal status if it becomes necessary.

d) To acquire monthly service points.

Question 2:

The NCS operator is responsible for which of the following?

a) Being in charge of the overall communication effort.

b) Being in charge of the net during his shift.

c) Being in charge of net operations beyond his net and shift.

d) Being in charge of frequencies, schedules and recruiting.

Question 3:

Which is *least* desirable time to train new operators?

a) During an emergency.

b) During a tabletop exercise.

c) During a public service event.

d) During a regularly scheduled training event.

Section 2: The Networks for Messages
Topic 8: The Net Control Station

Question 4:

Which best describes the *primary* mission of the NCS operator?

a) To train net operators.

b) To understand the Incident Command System (ICS).

c) To help the net move as much traffic as possible in the least amount of time, accurately and effectively.

d) To tune out all distractions and to focus on the job at hand in an often noisy and chaotic environment.

Question 5:

Which of the following does *not* represent "the right stuff" to become a good NCS operator?

a) The ability to handle mental and physical stress for long periods.

b) The ability to write legibly.

c) The desire to be seen as important in a response despite lack of training.

d) Above average operating skills.

Section 2: The Networks for Messages
Topic 9: Net Control Station Operator Practices

TOPIC 9:

Net Control Station (NCS) Operator Practices

Objectives

Welcome to Topic 9.

Following completion of this Learning Topic, the participant will have gained knowledge of the basic steps to serve as the Net Control operator for a net.

Student Preparation required:

On-going observation of local, regional, or national traffic and emergency nets.

The following is a list of questions the NCS operator should answer before opening the net.

- **Can the NCS hear all the stations in the net from his location?**

    The NCS should be in a position to hear all the stations in the net whenever possible. Relays may be used, but they slow the operation of the net significantly. For best results, some area testing via simplex to see which stations can communicate with which others should be conducted well in advance so that during an emergency relay stations can properly be put in place to insure good communications.

- **Is the NCS location sufficiently separated from the served agency's operations?**

    It is good practice to assign net control duty to a station in a low-traffic location. The noise and commotion in an Emergency Operations Center (EOC) can greatly degrade the ability to run a net well. Establishing net control at another location permits the EOC station to concentrate on passing traffic and working with the served agency. Of course, the NCS and the EOC station need to work together as a team. It is common for the overall incident to be managed from the EOC, while the off-site NCS assumes responsibility for managing check- ins and net traffic. In practice, it's not hard to work out a productive division of labor.

- **Do you have the best performing antenna for the conditions?**

    A "rubber duck" (short, flexible, helically-wound antenna) is not adequate unless you can see the repeater antenna, and if the repeater fails, you are out of business. A higher gain flexible or telescopic antenna would extend the range of the handhelds over that of the rubber duck antenna. On HF, an NVIS antenna (Near Vertical Incidence Skywave

Section 2: The Networks for Messages
Topic 9: Net Control Station Operator Practices

antenna) is essential for skip-zone communication. For long-range nets, conventional vertical, beam or dipole antennas, or a combination of these will work best.

- **If you are running your radio with battery power, do you have at least one hour of battery capacity available?**

  Ideally you will have a fully charged battery and access to backup batteries. If you are the only choice for NCS, make sure that you can run the net long enough to have someone else get ready to assume the duty so you can recharge your batteries when needed.

- **Are you using a headset with a noise-canceling microphone?**

  Even from home, background noise can affect how well you can hear and be heard.

  Refer to video file 4.

- **Do you have sufficient pencils/pens and paper to run the net for your shift?**

  You will not be able to remember enough about the traffic or participants to be effective unless you write it down. A sheet to track net participants and their requests and a good supply of NTS Traffic forms and ICS forms which may be required should also be kept on hand.

- **For VHF/UHF repeater operation, are you familiar with the characteristics and control commands of the repeater system hosting your net?**

  Your effectiveness as NCS may be adversely affected if you do not, particularly with linked systems.

- **Do you have a runner, liaison, or logging person to support you?**

  For large emergency events, all three are required. It is nearly impossible to handle the net, keep accurate and complete logs, and handle messages at the same time.

- **Do you have a designated back-up net control station?**

  In case you go off the air, another station should be ready to take control of the net.

- **Do you have a designated relief operator?**

  Everyone gets tired and the NCS must be the most alert operator on the net.

Opening and Closing the Net

Nets may be opened or closed on a specific schedule, or when the situation dictates. For instance, training and regular traffic nets may open at specific times, and may run for a specified period of time or as long as it takes to complete the net's business. Emergency nets are often

Section 2: The Networks for Messages
Topic 9: Net Control Station Operator Practices

opened and closed as needs dictate. NTS nets operate on a "cycle" that can be increased or decreased as the traffic load dictates.

Each net session should begin with the reading of a standard script that describes the purpose of the net and its basic procedures and protocols. Here is a sample script:

> "***This is W1HQ calling the Elmer Fudd County Emergency Net. This is a directed net, and all stations must call Net Control only. This net is handling only Emergency and Priority Traffic at this time. Only ARES stations assigned to this net should participate. Once checked in, please check out with Net Control before leaving the frequency. Stations with emergency traffic may check in now, or break the net at any time.***"

At the end of each net session, you can read a similar script, also briefly thanking members for participating, and reminding them of any future nets or other obligations. All scripts should be kept short and to the point.

The Importance of Message Precedence

In a communication emergency, one of the NCS operator's primary concerns is "information overload." When this happens, a message requesting "more bedpans for a shelter" may be sent before one requesting "a trauma team for a train wreck." This condition is usually caused by messages that are fed into the "system" in an unregulated manner. Failure to organize this information flow could result in critical messages being delayed or lost. **There are four message precedences**:

1. **Emergency** (relating to the immediate protection of life or property)

2. **Priority** (served agency and ARES messages directly related to the emergency, but not as time sensitive as an Emergency precedence message.)

3. **Health & Welfare** (Inquiries or information about the whereabouts or condition of persons in the affected area.)

4. **Routine** (Messages unrelated to any emergency: birthday greetings, net activity reports, etc.)

Section 2: The Networks for Messages
Topic 9: Net Control Station Operator Practices

Highest Precedence

The primary job of the NCS operator is to ensure that messages with the highest precedence are sent first – *emergency*, **then** *priority*, **then** *health and welfare*, **then** *routine*.

Most emergency nets refuse to handle any *routine* messages at all, since they usually have little or no bearing on the emergency itself or the served agency's needs. Other nets may handle only *emergency and priority* messages, or primarily *health and welfare* messages.

Asking for Check-Ins

Ask for check-ins immediately after reading the opening script, and then periodically during the net's operation. If the net is handling only *emergency and priority* messages, but not *welfare* or *routine* messages, it is important to state this in the opening script and when asking for "check-ins with messages." If *emergency* precedence messages are likely, it is a good idea to ask for them first, then move on to *priority*, and finally *welfare*. Try to ask for "check-ins with traffic only" as often as possible, and ask for "check-ins with or without traffic" at least every fifteen minutes, so that new stations may join the net. In a busy net, it can be difficult to balance the need to handle the current message backlog and still take check-ins on a regular basis. It is important to ask for check-ins with traffic frequently to ensure that priority or emergency messages get through expeditiously. When taking check-ins, NCS should read back the calls they received, and then ask if they missed anyone. This method can cut the time required for check-ins.

Studies show that "This is" and unkeying before sending callsign just *wastes* time. Better for the NCS to just read back the calls they received.

Time Tested Techniques

Listen! When asking for reports or soliciting traffic, ***listen carefully***! This might seem obvious, but it is easy to miss critical information when operating under the stress of an emergency. Wear headphones and reduce any distractions around you.

Check-ins - After asking for check-ins, note on your net worksheet as many calls as you can before you acknowledge anyone. Acknowledge all stations heard by call, ask for fills on any partial calls heard and then ask if you've missed anyone.

Section 2: The Networks for Messages
Topic 9: Net Control Station Operator Practices

Pair up stations to pass traffic on a different frequency whenever possible. This practice results in net "multi-tasking" and a higher rate of traffic handling. This is especially true when longer formal messages are being passed, or when a protracted discussion or exchange of information is required.

Every net has a particular style of operating, suited to the needs of the net. Most participants will catch on to the methods used, but if they do not, take time to explain. Things get done much more quickly if everyone uses the same techniques.

Be as concise as possible. Use the fewest words that will completely say what you mean. This will minimize the need for repeating instructions and messages.

Take frequent breaks. While you may not recognize the stress that being a NCS produces, it is constant, and will become evident in your voice. If you find yourself asking when your last break was, you know it is time to take one. Turn over the net to your backup at least every two hours and rest. Do not listen to the net – rest. Once rested, listen to the net for a few minutes before resuming as NCS.

Control the tone of your voice. Be as calm as possible. Tension tends to cause voices to increase in pitch, and net members will detect this change. When you use a calm tone, other members of the net will tend to remain calm as well. Remember to speak with confidence and authority. A weak or indecisive demeanor undermines your effectiveness as NCS, and consequently the productivity of the net.

Legally Identify Yourself. In the heat of things, especially using tactical callsigns, it is easy to forget the requirement to identify. But a good NCS will ID at least every 10 minutes as required by FCC rules and regulations.

> **When conducting a net using a repeater with a PL tone, don't forget to announce the PL tone! Valuable time can be lost trying to find it, and emergency messages could be waiting.**

Net Disciplines

You can reasonably expect trained net members to:

- Report to the NCS promptly as they become available.
- Ask the NCS operator for permission to call another station.
- Answer promptly when called by the NCS operator.
- Use tactical call signs.
- Identify legally at the end of each exchange
- Follow established net protocol.

Expectations aside, you must keep in mind that you are working with volunteers. You cannot *order* compliance -- you can only *ask* for cooperation.

Section 2: The Networks for Messages
Topic 9: Net Control Station Operator Practices

Probably the best way to enlist the cooperation of the net is to explain what you are doing in a calm and straightforward manner. This may involve supplying a small amount of real-time training. The one thing you must **never** do is criticize someone on the air. It is better to lead by example – it produces better results. If a problem persists, try to resolve it on the telephone or in person afterward.

Microphone Technique

Know how to use your microphone. The worst NCS operator is one that cannot be understood due to poor microphone technique.

Articulate, don't slur. If your natural speech is rapid-fire, you may want to train yourself to slow down a bit on the air.

Different microphones perform differently. Experiment to find the best microphone placement. Have another station listen while you make adjustments. There are no general rules that apply to all situations. If your mic came with a manual, following its guidance is a good starting point, but you'll still want to experiment to find what works best for you.

Three major categories of microphones are commonly used in amateur stations

1. noise-canceling,
2. unidirectional,
3. omnidirectional

If you are using a *noise-canceling* microphone, you have to get quite close to it for best effect.

If you are using a *unidirectional* microphone, you'll probably want to speak directly into it (on axis) for best performance. However, these mics tend to get bassy as you get closer; this is called "proximity effect." You can sometimes compensate for too much bass by backing off or speaking slightly off-axis. Consistent technique is critical with these microphones because small changes in angle and distance can have a pronounced effect on volume and frequency response - making it hard for others to understand you.

The common electret mics that are supplied with most rigs are *omnidirectional* - equally sensitive in all directions. These mics tend not to suffer from proximity effect, but they often do a great job of picking up unwanted background noise in addition to your voice. If you are using an omni in a noisy environment, get up close to the mic and reduce the mic gain on the rig to make the mic less sensitive to the background noise.

Some microphones are prone to sibilance (a hissing sound when "s," "f," or "ch" sounds are spoken) or "popping" (during "p" or "b" sounds). Much of this extraneous noise is caused by turbulence produced when air flowing from your mouth strikes some part of the microphone. The trick is to aim the mic so that it responds to the pressure wave produced by your voice while avoiding the high-velocity air flow. For example, you can sometimes improve things by changing the angle of the mic slightly (i.e., speaking "across" the mic instead of directly into it) or pointing the mic at the corner of your mouth. In the most severe cases, try placing a foam windscreen over the microphone. You can use a rubber band to hold it in place. The best microphones are relatively impervious to wind noise, and speaking directly into the mic may yield the best sound.

Section 2: The Networks for Messages
Topic 9: Net Control Station Operator Practices

On HF, it is critical to adjust the mic gain and compression to achieve a good signal. Overmodulation and distortion should be avoided at all costs. The goal is maximum intelligibility. Even on VHF and UHF FM rigs, it is a mistake to assume that mic gain and deviation controls are adjusted to optimum levels for your voice and operating style. All band radios have speech compression that can be turned on and off. It is meant to be used with SSB, and should never be used with FM. It can cause over-deviation, or at least distorted transmit audio. Sometimes a small adjustment makes a big difference in the quality of your audio.

Road noise can be a huge problem when operating mobile. It is human nature to speak louder as the vehicle's speed increases - simply because we have trouble hearing ourselves over the noise. The problem is, the louder we holler, the more strained and distorted we sound. The solution is to get close to the mic, turn down the mic gain, and force yourself to speak at a constant volume regardless of background noise. With a little practice, you can train yourself to keep your volume and tone uniform regardless of speed and background noise.

Here's a good hint:

For good microphone technique, use the "Monitor" function that is available on most modern transceivers to monitor your audio quality through your headphones. Then you yourself can hear what you sound like and make corrections.

Last but not least, when you find a technique that works, **use it consistently**.

More Hints for Successful Operation:

Keep transmissions as short as possible without losing message clarity.

For voice nets, use only plain English and standard "prowords" (procedure words). "Q" signals are only for CW, and 10-codes are passé even for CB - most served agencies have abandoned codes in favor of plain English. Keep the net formal and professional, but friendly. *An informal or casual style during an emergency net promotes sloppiness, and does little to impress served agencies.*

If the net is a scheduled net, start on time! *Tardiness indicates poor management and doesn't inspire confidence in the NCS.*

Use a script to promote clear and concise communication. Scripts can be used to open and close the net, and for periodic "housekeeping" announcements. If you don't have a pre-printed script, take a moment to write one.

Frequently identify the name and purpose of the net. Advise listeners of the sub-audible squelch tone (CTCSS or DCS) required, if applicable. This can be part of your periodic "housekeeping" script.

If the net is an emergency operation, use your scripts to tell listeners where to find other nets, such as resource or specialized nets. In some cases, this may help prevent un-needed but well-meaning stations from checking-in just to offer their services, which distracts the net from its mission.

Section 2: The Networks for Messages
Topic 9: Net Control Station Operator Practices

Be friendly, yet in control. Speak slowly and clearly with a calm, even, tone – not a monotone. Speak with confidence, even if you are inwardly nervous.

Acknowledge requests promptly and specifically so that net participants are not left wondering if they were heard or which one of several callers was recognized.

Ask specific questions – give specific instructions. This reduces the need for "repeats" and prevents confusion.

Have pencil and paper ready – write down ALL calls and tactical call signs. Practice writing down everyone's calls when you are not the NCS.

Read your radio's owner's manual and know your radio before an emergency occurs. Random fumbling with the knobs wastes valuable time and is very unprofessional.

Know how to use your microphone. Have another station advise you on the best distance and angle from your mouth to the microphone, and the proper mic gain setting. You may have to adjust your mic technique to compensate for increased background noise – talking louder will likely cause overmodulation or distortion. Articulate, don't slur.

When there is a "double" (i.e., when two or more stations transmit on the same frequency at the same time), listen to see if you can identify either station by call sign or by text. Then, ask all stations to stand by while you solicit clarification or repeats from each station involved, as needed.

During check-ins, recognize participants by their tactical call sign whenever possible—it helps to let everyone else know which stations are on the air and become familiar with what the tactical call signs are.

Don't be afraid to ask for assistance if you need it. The net manager should be able to assist you or locate additional help. That is part of their job.

You will make mistakes. Acknowledging them will earn the respect and support of net members, but don't dwell on them.

NEVER think out loud. If you need a moment to consider what to do next, say something like "stand by" or "please wait" and un-key your microphone while you think.

Transmit only facts. If there is a real need to make an educated guess or to speculate, make it clear to others that it is only speculation and not fact.

Avoid becoming the source for general information about the event. If it is an emergency, refer event status questions to the proper public information net or Public Information Officer (PIO). Avoid casual discussions about the served agency's response efforts on the air, since the press or the general public might be listening and take information out of context.

When necessary, use standard ITU phonetics. There is no such thing as "common spelling." Send all numbers as individual numbers, e.g., 334 is "three three four" not "three hundred thirty four."

Section 2: The Networks for Messages
Topic 9: Net Control Station Operator Practices

Reference Links

For more information on any of the elements presented, please consult the following links:

Public Service Communications Manual:
http://www.arrl.org/public-service-communications-manual

For more information on the NCS operator's function, please see the ARRL *Operating Manual*: http://www.arrl.org/shop/The-ARRL-Operating-Manual chapter on emergency communications. See also the ARRL *ARES Field Resources Manual* http://www.arrl.org/ARES-Field-Resources-Manual.

For a list of nets in the nation and in your area, see the ARRL *Net Directory* on the Web at http://www.arrl.org/arrl-net-directory.

To learn more about local and section-wide ARES and NTS net operation, contact your Section Manager (SM), your Section Emergency Coordinator (SEC) or District Emergency Coordinator (DEC). To locate your Section Manager, see http://www.arrl.org/sections.

For more information on NVIS see http://www.arrl.org/nvis

Section 2: The Networks for Messages
Topic 9: Net Control Station Operator Practices

Review

The NCS operator has many skills, some of which are transferable, and some specific to the NCS' job. He or she must not only control the flow of messages, but also keep the net moving quickly and professionally. The NCS operator must effectively handle any problems with net members, interference, special situations, and urgent messages.

Activities

1. Develop your own set of guidelines for operating the ideal net. These guidelines should show what you imagine to be the best way to operate. Monitor two or more nets if you can and compare each net's performance with your guidelines. Alternatively, describe efficient and effective communications techniques that you observe being used in a well-operated DX operation or a contest. Share these guidelines with your mentor.

2. Formal nets have both opening and closing scripts. Develop outlines for both an opening and closing script.

3. Develop a method that works for you so that you can have immediate access to critical phone numbers, email addresses and other contact information for local served agencies, police, fire, section officials and others who you might need to contact in a hurry while still working a net.

Section 2: The Networks for Messages
Topic 9: Net Control Station Operator Practices

Welcome to Topic 9 Knowledge Review

In order to demonstrate mastery of the information presented in the topic, you will be asked a series of un-graded questions. There are approximately 5 questions on the following pages in multiple-choice or true/false format. Feedback will be offered to you based on the answer you provide.

Question 1:

Which of the following statements is *true*?

a) The NCS should ask for check-ins immediately before reading the opening script.

b) The NCS should ask for check-ins just before reading the closing script.

c) The NCS should ask for check-ins immediately after reading the opening script and periodically thereafter.

d) The NCS should ask for check-ins every ten minutes during the operation of the net.

Question 2:

In which order should messages be handled during an emergency?

a) Priority, Emergency, Health & Welfare, Routine.

b) Emergency, Priority, Health & Welfare, Routine.

c) Emergency, Health & Welfare, Priority, Routine.

d) Health & Welfare, Emergency, Routine, Priority.

Question 3:

Which of the following should the NCS operator *not* expect of trained net members?

a) To ask the NCS operator for permission to call another station.

b) To answer promptly when called by the NCS operator.

c) To follow established net protocols.

d) To rely exclusively on FCC call signs during net operations.

Section 2: The Networks for Messages
Topic 9: Net Control Station Operator Practices

Question 4:

Which of the following are appropriate to use in an emergency phone net?

a) Plain English and 10-Codes.

b) Plain English and prowords.

c) Q-signals and prowords.

d) Q-Signals and 10-Codes.

Question 5:

Which is the best way to enlist the cooperation of the net?

a) Immediately criticize net operators who make a mistake so that other operators will learn from the error.

b) Issue an order demanding the cooperation of all net operators.

c) Explain what you are doing in a calm and straightforward manner.

d) Immediately expel operators from the net who do not follow net protocol.

Section 2: The Networks for Messages
Topic 10: The Net Manager

TOPIC 10:

The Net Manager

Objectives

Welcome to Topic 10.

After reading this Learning Topic you will be able to comprehend the importance and functions of the position of Net Manager, as used in both the National Traffic System (NTS) and Amateur Radio Emergency Service (ARES). This topic is based on the official job description published by ARRL.

Student Preparation required:

You should have a basic knowledge of the National Traffic System, Amateur Radio Emergency Service, and the ARRL Field Organization, obtainable by reviewing the ARRL's Public Service Communications Manual.

Introduction

The Net Manager (NM) has overall responsibility for the planning and operation of one or more nets. Net Managers are used in both the National Traffic System (NTS) and in ARES organizations. This person works with ARES or NTS leadership to define the net's purpose, sets standards of operation, and communicates that information to net members. In NTS, he or she also handles human resource and training issues, but this may not be true in ARES organizations.

Whether you have one net or a dozen, you need a Net Manager. You might ask, "Could the NCS (Net Control Station) operator do this job as well?" During an emergency, NCS operators might change every few hours. In addition, both jobs must be done simultaneously.

The NTS Net Manager is a full ARRL member appointed by the Section Manager, usually on the recommendation of the Section Traffic Manager. In ARES, the appointment is recommended to the SM by either the SEC, DEC, or EC, depending on the level of the net. The NM may choose one or more assistants to take over when he or she needs a break, or to handle certain aspects of the net's operation, such as training. It is also the NM's responsibility to make sure that the NCS operators on the roster have received the proper training in the way nets should be conducted before appointing them as NCS.

During an emergency, "ad hoc" nets may be created to meet specific needs. These may either be assigned to the permanent NM, or to a temporary NM for the duration of the event. Those in such a position should be prepared in advance should this need arise and be trained in protocol of different types of nets, their purposes and how they should be conducted.

Section 2: The Networks for Messages
Topic 10: The Net Manager

Organization

Net Managers may be assigned to handle only one net, or many. The number of NMs appointed might depend on a Section's physical size, the number of nets, how often the nets meet, or factors having to do with the way the Section is organized. In small sections, there may be only one NTS or ARES NM in charge of all section nets. In larger sections there may be several NMs, each having responsibility for a different region, mode, or type of net. Separate NMs should be appointed for ARES and NTS, since the needs and functions of the nets of the two organizations can be quite different.

All ARRL NMs, both NTS and ARES, should work under the Section Traffic Manager (STM) and/or Section Emergency Coordinator (SEC) guided by a coordinated section traffic and ARES Communications Plan.

Some NTS nets cover more than one section but operate within the NTS at the section level. In this case, the NM is selected by agreement among the STMs concerned and their resident SM confirms the appointment. Some NMs are system operators of, or sysop-recommended operators active on, participating NTS or ARES packet bulletin boards or other digital nets.

Duties

The Net Manager's duties include resource management and quality control. He/she makes certain that a NCS operator and alternate are assigned to each session, and that replacements are available for each shift. This person may also recruit net members for certain types of nets to ensure that delivery of messages is possible everywhere. The NM is also responsible for assigning regular liaison stations to move messages to and from other nets, although the NM may delegate this task to the NCS to handle on an ad hoc basis.

The nature of this job, like other leadership positions, demands excellent people and management skills. At times, the NM will need to work with a group of volunteers performing under stressful conditions. The NM's own operating and message handling skills should be superior so that the NM can help teach others and ensure that they are all properly trained before giving them an assignment.

The Net Frequency

In most cases, the **Net Manager (NM)** will choose the net's frequency(s). Scheduled and pre-planned nets usually operate on designated frequencies, but temporary nets often choose a frequency based on which bands and frequencies are available. HF nets that operate on a regular schedule will usually have less difficulty getting a clear frequency than those who only operate when needed. Net frequencies on HF should always be listed as "plus or minus 5 kHz" to allow for interference. In some emergencies, it may be necessary for an emergency management official to request an FCC emergency communications declaration (ECD) to clear a particular VHF/UHF frequency. But in the MF/HF Amateur Service bands, an ECD will, at best, only authorize use of 1 or 2 channels in the 60 Meter Amateur Service band. The FCC is not providing ECD's for MF or HF frequencies as was done in the past. This policy became effective August 2, 2004.

Section 2: The Networks for Messages
Topic 10: The Net Manager

> Section 97.401(b) provides that when a disaster disrupts normal communication systems in a particular area, the FCC may declare a temporary state of communication emergency. The declaration will set forth any special conditions and special rules to be observed by stations during the communication emergency. However, the FCC has not done this in several years and there are no expectations they will resume this option.

One or more alternate frequencies should be chosen in advance, and should be known by all net members. In the case of VHF/UHF nets, alternate frequencies should be chosen for both repeaters as well as simplex frequencies since in an emergency, many repeaters may be off the air. In the event that interference or band conditions render the primary frequency unusable, net members should automatically switch to the alternate.

FM simplex nets should use a frequency that is seldom used by local hams for day-to-day conversations, and never on a national calling frequency such as 146.52 or 446.000 MHz. Nets that use repeaters should make prior arrangements with the repeater's owner. If a net uses a repeater as its primary meeting place, a backup simplex frequency should be chosen and publicized in the event the repeater fails. One way to do this is to give instructions that in the event of repeater failure, the first place to meet is the OUTPUT of the repeater. All NCS operators and responders must know and fully understand how to operate their individual radios so that they can adjust the offset for simplex duty.

Another ploy used by some ARES units to provide a backup for their own repeater is to have an agreement with a local radio club to use their repeater in the event that the ARES repeater fails during an emergency. This goes over very well if the ARES unit also invites the radio club to use the ARES repeater, if the radio club's repeater goes down (during non-emergency periods). This win-win arrangement provides both organizations with a back up machine and fosters good relations.

Some Points for Net Managers to Remember:

- You are responsible for managing the net, but do so with tact and diplomacy. Teach net discipline by setting a good example, and take the net yourself from time to time to do so. .
- Ensure that traffic on the net is handled in a timely manner. Do not let the net become too informal and waste time.

- Know your operators' capabilities, and their locations, especially when you may need to go simplex and what their coverage range is, taking terrain and other factors into account. One way to gather such information is to organize periodic practice nets using simplex, in place of using the repeater. It is often surprising how many net members can be heard and can hear on simplex. Do not assume; you will never know unless you try it. A good practice exercise to keep operators sharp is to take the repeater out of service with no advance warning (just like it might during a true disaster) and find out how good your simplex coverage is.

- Know how and where your net fits into the overall net structure at all times, since the situation may change periodically. Working with SEC's, DEC's and EC's will help produce good results.

Section 2: The Networks for Messages
Topic 10: The Net Manager

• Assign or identify liaison stations to move traffic from one net to the other(s).

• Assign an alternate NCS to stand by in case the primary NCS goes off the air.

• Get all the information you can (type of situation, needed station locations, potential shift lengths, frequencies, agency or agencies involved, etc.) before you put a net into service, but do not delay too long waiting for any single piece of information.

• Provide direction in the routing and handling of various types of messages. Determine the physical location of each served agency site early on to ensure proper routing.

• Monitor the net(s) to be sure proper procedures and message formats are being used.

• Training is crucial to success "when the big one hits." A varied and interesting training schedule will help keep net members ready to go. The practice net on simplex mentioned previously is an interesting training session.

Section 2: The Networks for Messages
Topic 10: The Net Manager

Reference Links

For more information on any of the elements presented, please consult the following links:

ARRL Public Service Communications Manual
http://www.arrl.org/public-service-communications-manual

For more information on the Net Manager function, please see the ARRL Operating Manual, chapters on emergency communications and traffic handling. See also the ARRL ARES Field Resources Manual. To learn more about ARES and NTS net operation, contact your Section Manager (SM), your Section Emergency Coordinator (SEC) or District Emergency Coordinator (DEC).
http://www.arrl.org/sections

Section 2: The Networks for Messages
Topic 10: The Net Manager

Review

The Net Manager has overall responsibility for the operation of a net, including recruiting and training NCS operators, net members, frequency choices, and scheduling. A Net Manager may be appointed permanently for one or more regularly scheduled nets, or temporarily to manage ad hoc nets created for a particular event or disaster.

Activities

1. Describe to your mentor the importance and functions of the net manager.

2. Imagine that you have just been appointed the NM for a section-wide ARES tactical net. Your mission is to provide an HF link between local FM nets and the State EOC. Create a simple plan to accomplish this and list the tasks you would need to complete in order to be successful. Share with your mentor the different considerations you would face if this was to be a recurring net.

Section 2: The Networks for Messages
Topic 10: The Net Manager

Welcome to Topic 10 Knowledge Review

In order to demonstrate mastery of the information presented in the topic, you will be asked a series of un-graded questions. There are approximately 5 questions on the following pages in multiple-choice or true/false format. Feedback will be offered to you based on the answer you provide.

Question 1:

What are the requirements and qualifications of the ARRL Net Manager position?

- a) There are no specific requirements or qualifications for the position.
- b) Amateur Radio license; full ARRL membership; and any appropriate local or Section qualifications.
- c) An Amateur Extra Class license; and the approval of ARRL Headquarters.
- d) The approval of the emergency management agency holding jurisdiction in the area.

Question 2:

Which statement best describes the Section Net Manager's job?

- a) Coordinate public information in the Section.
- b) Provide technical information to members of ARES and/or NTS.
- c) Appoint the local Emergency Coordinators.
- d) Coordinate and supervise traffic handling and net activities in the Section.

Question 3:

Which factor does NOT affect the number of Net Managers appointed in each Section?

- a) The Section's geographical size.
- b) The number of nets operating in the Section.
- c) Other factors having to do with the way the Section is organized.
- d) The ARRL Emergency Preparedness Manager.

Section 2: The Networks for Messages
Topic 10: The Net Manager

Question 4:

Who appoints the NTS Net Manager?

a) Section Manager.

b) Division Director.

c) ARRL Headquarters staff.

d) Local EC.

Question 5:

To whom does the Section Net Manager report?

a) Division Director is responsible for supervising all Field Organization activity.

b) ARRL HQ staff is responsible for supervising all Field Organization activity.

c) Section NMs work under the STM and/or SEC, guided by a coordinated Section traffic or ARES communications plan.

d) Emergency Management personnel.

Section 2: The Networks for Messages
Topic 11: Introduction to The National Traffic System

TOPIC 11:

Introduction to
The National Traffic System (NTS)

Objectives

Welcome to Topic 11.

This Learning Topic is designed to offer a basic understanding of NTS and its function during an emergency. After you have completed the topic, you will understand how messages are passed from one location to another, and which nets are involved. You will also know how the NTS is designed to facilitate the timely and orderly flow of messages.

Student Preparation required:

None.

What is the NTS?

The National Traffic System (NTS) is a unique arrangement for handling messages that was designed over 50 years ago. Organized traffic handling was a central purpose of ARRL at its founding in 1914! Its goal is to enable a message to be passed across the continent within 24 hours. NTS does this with a group of specialized nets operating in a "cycle" that allows messages to move smoothly from a local net, to a regional net, to various transcontinental nets, and then back down to regional and local nets at the destination. Ultimately, someone in a local net near the addressee should be able to deliver the message by phone, in person, by mail, or email and even amateur radio. Many NTS messages reach their address by radio, and it should be included as a viable delivery resource.

One of the most important features of the NTS is the "system concept." No NTS net is an independent entity; it interfaces with other NTS nets. Each net performs a specific function in the overall organization. To the extent a net fails to perform any of its functions, it can affect the performance of the overall system. (A net whose exclusive purpose is to pass messages between its own stations would not be considered part of NTS.)

In the days before inexpensive long-distance telephone, and well before the Internet and email, the NTS was used heavily for routine daily communication between Amateur Radio operators,

Section 2: The Networks for Messages
Topic 11: Introduction to The National Traffic System

family, and friends. This daily traffic kept NTS members in practice for handling large volumes of traffic during emergencies and disasters, the ultimate reason for the NTS's existence. Today, routine daily traffic on the NTS is light, and large-scale emergency operations are generally during major disasters with widespread infrastructure damage. However, this does not lessen the importance of the NTS in assisting our served agencies. One of the most important duties of NTS and its benefits to served agencies is "health and welfare" traffic as we will discuss. However use of NTS is dependant to a large degree upon the served agency and their traffic requirements. It is wise to note that not all served agencies will elect to use the NTS system, opting instead to use their own forms, such as during an incident where an ICS-213 form may be required. We must remember the principal that we serve at their pleasure and must employ the format which they direct us to use.

The NTS is not part of ARES, but is a separate and distinct ARRL program. The NTS and ARES work together. Think of the NTS as a "long distance carrier," and of ARES as the "local exchange carrier." This analogy is not perfect, but it is close.

The NTS is not intended as competition for the many independently organized traffic networks. When necessitated by overload or lack of outlet for traffic, the facilities of independent networks can function as alternate traffic routings where this is indicated in the best interest of efficient message relay and/or delivery.

Nets may sometimes find it necessary and expedient to adopt temporary measures to ensure the movement of traffic. This is considered improper operation only when no attempt is made to return to the normal schedule. Nevertheless, improper operation of any NTS net is the concern of all NTS nets, and every effort should be made to assist in returning any non-functioning or improperly functioning net to its normal operation.

> The NTS is not part of ARES, but is a separate and distinct ARRL program. The NTS and ARES work together. Think of the NTS as a "long distance carrier," and of ARES as the "local exchange carrier."

How the NTS Works

The National Traffic System consists of four different levels of nets. These operate in an orderly time sequence to move messages in a definite pattern from origin to destination. A message flows through the NTS in a manner similar to a business-person who travels between two small rural towns at opposite ends of the country. This person has to change carriers many times in the process, starting with a drive to the local airport, then a feeder airline to a major airport, to a transcontinental airline, to another feeder airline, and finally by ground again to the destination. In a very similar manner, the transcontinental message starts with the originating station in a local net, is carried up to the "Section" net, then up to the "Region" net, then up to the "Area" net, across to another "Area" net, and then back down the line to the point of delivery.

Of course, the message, like the passenger, can "get on" or "get off" at any point if that is the origin or destination. Thus, a message from San Francisco to Los Angeles would not go beyond Region level, and one from Syracuse to Buffalo would remain in the Section net(s). At the local

Section 2: The Networks for Messages
Topic 11: Introduction to The National Traffic System

level, messages may be passed into or out of local ARES or other nets for delivery to served agencies, or may be delivered to private citizens directly.

NTS nets may use FM, SSB, CW, and IRLP and VoIP (Voice over Internet Protocol). Messages may also be passed through NTS-affiliated local and Section traffic nodes that employ digital modes such as AMTOR, packet, D-Star, Winlink, PSK-31 and other such new technology modes with store-and-forward capabilities and bulletin-board operations. Long hauls can be made by the NTS digital stations on HF that interface with Section traffic nodes and the traditional nets of the system.

Local Nets

"Local" NTS nets are those that cover small areas such as a town, city, county or metropolitan area, but not a complete ARRL Section. They usually operate on two-meter or 70cm bands at times and on days most convenient to their members. Other nets are designated as "emergency" (ARES) nets that do not specialize in routine traffic handling. These nets generally become active only for training and during emergencies.

Local nets are intended mainly for local delivery of traffic, with a goal of delivery by non-toll telephone calls. They provide outlets for locally originated traffic, and route the incoming traffic as close as possible to its actual destination before delivery.

A local net, or "node", may also be conducted on a local packet system, where messages may be stored, forwarded, and picked up by local operators for subsequent delivery. A Net (Node) Manager is appointed by the Section Traffic Manager to manage these functions, and assure that traffic is moved expeditiously.

Section Nets

The purpose of the "Section" net is to handle messages within the Section, and to handle messages moving to and from the "Region" nets.

Either liaison stations from local NTS nets and nodes, individual stations, or both, handle messages passing within the Region. In most areas, all stations in the Section are invited to take part. However, in a highly populated Section with several metropolitan areas covered by local nets, representation may be by liaison stations, plus individual stations in cities or towns not covered by local nets.

The Section may have more than one net (e.g. a CW net, a VHF net, an SSB net, or a Section packet BBS). In an area with low population density or NTS activity, two or more Sections may combine to form a single net operating at Section level. Section nets are administered through the office of the Section Manager, with authority for this function often delegated to an appointed Section Traffic Manager and/or designated Net Managers. In the case of combined-Section nets, officials of the Sections concerned should collaborate on the designation of a qualified Amateur to manage the net.

Section 2: The Networks for Messages
Topic 11: Introduction to The National Traffic System

Region Nets

"Region" nets cover a wider area, such as a call area. At this level, the object is representation of each ARRL Section within the Region. Participants normally include:

- A Net Control Station, designated by the Region net manager.

- Representatives from each of the various Sections in the Region, designated by their Section Net Managers.

- One or more stations designated by the Region net manager to handle traffic going to points outside the Region.

- One or more stations bringing traffic down from higher-level NTS nets.

- Any other station with traffic.

There may be more than one representative from each Section in the Region net, but more than two are usually superfluous and will only clutter the net. However, all Section representatives are required to represent the entire Section, not just their own net.

The purpose of the Region net is to exchange traffic between the Sections in the Region, put out-of-Region traffic in the hands of liaison stations, and distribute traffic coming into the Region among the Section net representatives. Regional nets are administered by managers elected by the NTS volunteers and supported through the Membership and Volunteer Programs Department (MVP) at ARRL Headquarters.

Area Nets

At the top level of NTS nets is the "Area" net. Participation at the area level includes:

- A Net Control Station, designated by the Area Net Manager.

- One or more representatives from each Region net in the Area, designated by the Region Net Managers.

- Transcontinental Corps (TCC) stations designated to handle traffic going to other Area nets.

- TCC stations designated to bring traffic from other Area nets.

- Any station with traffic.

There are three Areas, designated "Eastern," "Central" and "Pacific," the names roughly indicating their coverage of the US and Canada except that the Pacific Area includes the Mountain as well as the Pacific time zones. Area nets are administered by managers elected by the NTS volunteers and supported through the Membership and Volunteer Programs Department (MVP) at ARRL Headquarters.

Section 2: The Networks for Messages
Topic 11: Introduction to The National Traffic System

For a map of NTS areas and regions, see below:

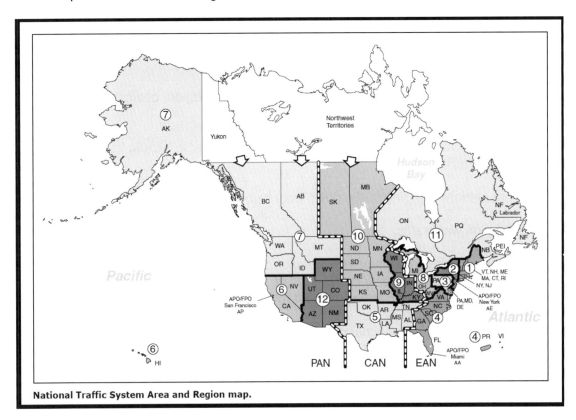

National Traffic System Area and Region map.

Map key: **National Traffic System Routing Guide**

State/Province	Abbrev.	Region	Area
Alaska	AK	7	PAN
Alabama	AL	5	CAN
Alberta	AB	7	PAN
Arizona	AZ	12	PAN
Arkansas	AR	5	CAN
British Columbia	BC	7	PAN
California	CA	6	PAN
Colorado	CO	12	PAN
Connecticut	CT	1	EAN
Delaware	DE	3	EAN
Dist. of Columbia	DC	3	EAN
Florida	FL	4	EAN
Georgia	GA	4	EAN
Guam	GU	6	PAN
Hawaii	HI	6	PAN
Idaho	ID	7	PAN
Illinois	IL	9	CAN
Indiana	IN	9	CAN
Iowa	IA	10	CAN

Section 2: The Networks for Messages
Topic 11: Introduction to The National Traffic System

Kansas	KS	10	CAN
Kentucky	KY	9	CAN
Labrador	LB	11	EAN
Louisiana	LA	5	CAN
Maine	ME	1	EAN
Manitoba	MB	10	CAN
Maryland	MD	3	EAN
Massachusetts	MA	1	EAN
Michigan	MI	8	EAN
Minnesota	MN	10	CAN
Mississippi	MS	5	CAN
Missouri	MO	10	CAN
Montana	MT	7	PAN
Nebraska	NE	10	CAN
Nevada	NV	6	PAN
New Brunswick	NB	11	EAN
New Hampshire	NH	1	EAN
New Jersey	NJ	2	EAN
New Mexico	NM	12	PAN
New York	NY	2	EAN
Newfoundland	NF	11	EAN
North Carolina	NC	4	EAN
North Dakota	ND	10	CAN
Nova Scotia	NS	11	EAN
Ohio	OH	8	EAN
Oklahoma	OK	5	CAN
Ontario	ON	11	EAN
Oregon	OR	7	PAN
Pennsylvania	PA	3	EAN
Prince Edward Is.	PEI	11	EAN
Puerto Rico	PR	4	EAN
Quebec	PQ	11	EAN
Rhode Island	RI	1	EAN
Saskatchewan	SK	10	CAN
South Carolina	SC	4	EAN
South Dakota	SD	10	CAN
Tennessee	TN	5	CAN
Texas	TX	5	CAN
Utah	UT	12	PAN
Vermont	VT	1	EAN
Virginia	VA	4	EAN
Virgin Islands	VI	4	EAN
Washington	WA	7	PAN
West Virginia	WV	8	EAN
Wisconsin	WI	9	CAN
Wyoming	WY	12	PAN
APO New York APO	NY	2	EAN
APO San Francisco APO	SF	6	PAN

Section 2: The Networks for Messages
Topic 11: Introduction to The National Traffic System

Transcontinental Corps

The handling of higher priority messages between "Area Nets" is accomplished through the facilities of the Transcontinental Corps (TCC). TCC members handle "routine" messages only in times of extreme overload. This is not a net, but a group of designated liaison stations that have the responsibility for seeing that inter-Area traffic reaches its destination Area. TCC is administered by TCC directors, or as delegated to the Area Digital Coordinator, in each Area who assign stations to report into Area nets for the purpose of "clearing" inter-Area traffic, and to keep out-of-net schedules with each other for the purpose of transferring traffic from one Area to another.

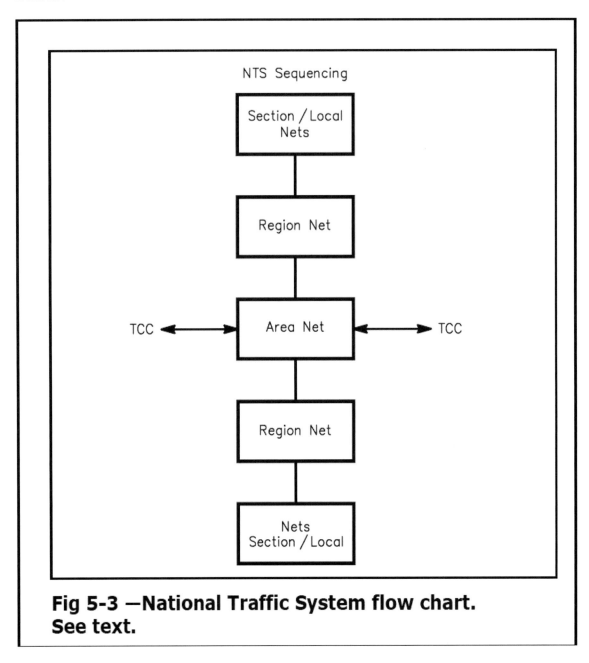

Fig 5-3 — National Traffic System flow chart. See text.

Section 2: The Networks for Messages
Topic 11: Introduction to The National Traffic System

Review an example of an NTS message routing in the NTS manual at:
http://www.arrl.org/chapter-nine-nts-traffic-routing.

"Hotline" Circuits

In certain situations, a large volume of traffic may be moving between two locations, such as from a large refugee center to an American Red Cross office. Rather than attempting to move these messages through the normal system, a "hotline" circuit is established between two or more stations at or near these locations. This avoids overloading normal nets, and speeds delivery of critical messages.

Increased Operations During Disasters

In day-to-day operation, the National Traffic System passes routine messages around the country. In its emergency role, the NTS is dedicated to disaster communication on behalf of ARES. The NTS is capable of expanding its cyclic operation partially or fully depending on the level of need. The normal cycles can be expanded to handle an increasing volume of messages with greater speed. In extreme cases, the cycles can operate continuously. This requires all nets to be on the air full time, with stations designated for liaison operation replacing each other as stations are dispatched to the higher or lower nets with which they make liaison.

Activation for Disasters

Emergency Coordinators in disaster areas consult with served agencies to determine which communication resources will need to be activated.

The Section Emergency Coordinator, working along with and in direct communications with the appropriate Section Manager(s), consults with affected DECs and ECs, and makes an activation recommendation to the Section Traffic Manager, and Section or Regional NTS managers as appropriate. The decision to alert the NTS Region management may be made by any combination of these officials, depending upon the urgency of the situation.

The scope of the activation will depend on the scope of the disaster. If messages need to be passed only within the Section, then only those nets will be activated. However, if the disaster is widespread and communications are disrupted over a large area, Region or Area nets may be needed. In such cases the Traffic Managers and SEC's, working with their Section Managers will need to coordinate the effort between sections or regions. The TCC then needs to become involved. Handling outbound Health and Welfare (H&W) traffic has a higher priority than inbound H&W – each outbound H&W message delivered may head-off several more H&W inquiries about the same person, since the person receiving the outbound H&W message may share the news with other friends and relatives.

Managers of NTS nets at local, Section, Region, and Area levels are directly responsible for activation of their nets at the request of ARES or NTS officials. Each EC is directly responsible for activating their local ARES nets.

Section 2: The Networks for Messages
Topic 11: Introduction to The National Traffic System

NTS Alerting Plan

Section Traffic Manager (STM) and Section Net Manager Roles:
During a disaster, the STM and certain Section net managers may be contacted by the Section Emergency Coordinator or the Section Manager to activate needed Section NTS and ARES nets, either to provide Section-wide contact or, in the case of NTS nets, to provide liaison with the nets outside the Section.

The STM and Section Net Managers make contact with NTS Region Net Managers in the event that messages connected with the disaster need to cross Section boundaries, and may recommend extraordinary activation of the Region net.

Specific Section net stations are designated to conduct liaison with the NTS Region net, either through another Section net or directly. This is the responsibility of Section officials, not the Region net manager.

Region Net Manager Functions:
Should a disaster situation's needs extend beyond the Section level, any one of the Section officials in a Region or a neighboring NTS Region may contact the Region Net Manager. The Region Net Manager should be able to predict such contact based on the circumstances, and should be available to receive their recommendation.

The Region Net Manager makes contact with the NTS Area Net Manager in the event that communications connected with the disaster transcend Region boundaries, recommending extraordinary activation of the Area NTS net.

Area Net Manager Functions:
There are only two Area Net Manager appointees for each of the three Areas in the US, but their function during and after disasters is of paramount importance. Area Net Managers maintain a high sensitivity to disasters that extend to or beyond Region boundaries. When one does, Area Net Managers take the initiative to alert the Region Net Manager involved to determine if extraordinary NTS operation is indicated.

In the event that high-precedence inter-Area traffic is involved, the Area Net Managers contact the two Transcontinental Corps directors in the Area to assist by arranging to pass the traffic directly to other Areas.

The Area Net Managers in the affected Area also contact the other NTS Area Net Managers to discuss the possibility of opening extra net sessions if required to handle the traffic reaching them through NTS inter-Area handling. Under some circumstances, direct representation or "hotlines" may be indicated.

The Area Net Managers maintain close contact with all Region Net Managers in the Area and make decisions regarding overall NTS operation in consultation with them.

Transcontinental Corps (TCC) Directors:
These NTS officials will be involved only where traffic of a precedence higher than "routine" is to be handled between NTS Areas, or when extreme overloads are anticipated. TCC Directors are ready to alert TCC members and set up special out-of-net schedules as required. TCC Directors

Section 2: The Networks for Messages
Topic 11: Introduction to The National Traffic System

may be called upon by the Area Net Manager to set up "hotline" circuits between key cities involved in heavy traffic flow. TCC Directors know which of their TCC stations are located in, or close to, large cities to operate such circuits.

Area Staff Chair Responsibilities

The three Area Staff Chairpersons administratively oversee the NTS Officials and their operations above the Section level, and will advise their TCC Directors, and Area and Region Net Managers when appropriate. Their advice may be based on information forwarded by ARRL Headquarters. The chair maintains a high sensitivity to disasters and other emergencies that may develop. In a large-scale disaster, the chairperson should be able to contact one another via the International Assistance and Traffic Net and on other prearranged nets.

General Policy for all NTS Operators

NTS operators should be "self-alerting" to disaster conditions that might require their services, and should check-in to their regular net or perform assigned functions without being specifically called upon. Assignments should be worked out with the Net Manager in advance. If the operator cannot answer the question, "If I hear of a disaster, what should I do?" they should seek an answer through their Net Manager. It may be as simple as "report into the X Net on Y frequency."

If the operator concerned is highly specialized, it might be "report to your TCC director in the X net on Y frequency for a special assignment." Such an assignment might be an extra TCC function, or it might be as a functionary in a "hotline" point-to-point circuit needing special abilities or equipment.

Most NTS operators participate for one or two periods a week, and some are active daily. Although every net member should have a specific assignment, they must also remain flexible enough to change assignments when the need arises.

Read about Digital Communication and NTS:
Late in 2010 the Area Staff Chairs of the NTS approved updates to the ARRL **Public Service Communications Manual** (PSCM) Appendix B, Methods and Practices Guidelines, Chapter 6, NTSD and **Radio-email**. These revisions provide for a structure and guidance on how the ARRL Field Organization may use Radio-email to provide nation-wide messaging in the modern email format via Amateur Radio with near real-time delivery anywhere in the country, 24/7. It also provides for integration of the ARES®, NTS and NTSD efforts nation-wide.

The new **Radio-email** system uses the Winlink 2000 network, infrastructure independent local automatic email service modules, plus station-to-station, radio-all- the-way transport services provided by the NTS/D to support all Sections. The Winlink 2000 network also provides us with a firewall and white list protected interface with the public internet for handling welfare and agency messaging with internet addressees. New types of message formats are included, and guidance on handling ICS-213 and other similar message formats is included.

Section 2: The Networks for Messages
Topic 11: Introduction to The National Traffic System

As with any email system, it is necessary to know the addresses of stations on the network in order know how to address messages. **Radio-email** may be sent to multiple addressees with multiple copies and binary attachments. NTSD is assigning client Target Station addresses to be the outlet clients for messaging on the network. What this means for you, for example, is the ability to send public welfare emails from shelter victims directly to internet addressees, or at other shelters, and receive replies. You may also send Radiograms in the standard ARRL format, carried by **Radio-email**, directly to network stations in the NTS/D for handling. You may have agency and our own leadership officials, using their own computers, exchange **Radio-email** messages between all sites where amateur field stations are deployed. In each of those examples, no intermediate relaying manpower or nets are required within your "last mile" disaster area.

Section 2: The Networks for Messages
Topic 11: Introduction to The National Traffic System

Reference Links

For more on NTS, see Chapter 7 of The ARRL Operating Manual.

Additional details on ARES and NTS can be found in the Public Service Communications Manual at:
http://www.arrl.org/public-service-communications-manual

For local information, or to learn more about NTS net operation in your area, contact your Section Manager (SM) http://www.arrl.org/sections or Section Traffic Manager (STM).

For a list of ARES and NTS nets operating in your area see The ARRL Net Directory at http://www.arrl.org/arrl-net-directory.

Section 2: The Networks for Messages
Topic 11: Introduction to The National Traffic System

Review

The National Traffic System is a set of scheduled nets operating on a cycle that permits messages to be routed across the country in less than 24 hours. The cycles can be increased to allow for larger volumes of messages to be handled during an emergency. Nets operate at the local, Section, Region, and Area levels. The Transcontinental Corps can help expedite critical messages by bypassing the normal routes. Hotline circuits can be established between high-volume locations when needed. NTS nets provide a great venue for participants to practice using phonetics, and paying focused attention to details – which are required to take traffic and operate as an effective NCS.

Activities

1. List at least two resources for locating emergency nets that operate in your area.

2. Identify at least three emergency nets (days, times, frequencies) that operate in your area, including an NTS net if possible.

3. Contact the Net Control Station for at least one of the nets you have identified. Determine the requirements for joining the net.

Share your answers with your mentor.

Section 2: The Networks for Messages
Topic 11: Introduction to The National Traffic System

Welcome to Topic 11 Knowledge Review

In order to demonstrate mastery of the information presented in the topic, you will be asked a series of un-graded questions. There are approximately 5 questions on the following pages in multiple-choice or true/false format. Feedback will be offered to you based on the answer you provide.

Question 1:

Which of the following statements about the National Traffic System is *true*?

a) It is highly reliant upon CW.

b) It was designed within the last 25 years.

c) Each net within the System is an independent, "stand alone" entity.

d) It is a unique system for efficiently handling messages.

Question 2:

The Area Nets include which of the following?

a) The Eastern, the Central, the Canadian, and the Pacific.

b) The Eastern, the Central, the Mountain, and the Pacific.

c) The Central, the Mountain, and the Canadian.

d) The Eastern, the Central, and the Pacific.

Question 3:

Which is the purpose of a "hotline circuit?

a) To move a modest amount of routine traffic between two locations in small town.

b) To move a moderate amount of traffic between two served agencies across the country.

c) To move a high volume of traffic between two locations during a disaster.

d) To move a high volume of holiday traffic across the country.

Section 2: The Networks for Messages
Topic 11: Introduction to The National Traffic System

Question 4:

Which of the following statements is *true*?

a) NTS was designed to compete with independent traffic networks.

b) NTS generally encompasses five different levels of operation.

c) Section nets exclusively handle traffic between Local and Regional nets.

d) Regional Nets exclusively handle traffic among Sections within their Region.

Section 2: The Networks for Messages
Topic 12: Specialized Nets and Their Operations

TOPIC 12:

Specialized Nets and Their Operations

Objectives

Welcome to Topic 12.

After completing this Learning topic you will be able to provide a brief review of what "specialized nets" are, whom they are designed to serve and the differences between basic net operations and specialized nets.

Student Preparation required:

None.

Why We Have Specialized Nets

Specialized nets are created to serve specific agencies that are served by Amateur Radio emergency communications. These vary from region to region, as not all sections and districts will be serving the same agencies. From a general standpoint, the most common served agencies are The American Red Cross, The Salvation Army, the National Weather Service (NWS) and other such national organizations that have Memorandums of Understanding (MOUs) with the ARRL and its ARES program.

These nets are customized to fit the needs of an individual served agency, and are most often quite different in nature from the basic net, resource net or other general types of net operations that we have discussed so far.

Differences in Specific Specialized Nets

In the many sections and districts, we work for and with different served agencies. There are some that we do have in common however, and we will use examples of the most common among ARES operations, and how they differ.

For example: Many of us work with The American Red Cross (ARC) and local Emergency Operation Centers (EOC's). When we are conducting a net on behalf of the ARC, much of the information is relative to their functions such as communication between a local Chapter office and shelters that may be opened during a disaster. The information that they need varies depending on which type of disaster we are dealing with. If there is an evacuation due to fire or flood, then the Chapter will want to know detailed information about the number of "clients" who check in at the shelter and the provision of adequate supplies that are needed to accommodate them. While most of these nets can be operated by simplex voice, there are times when the

Section 2: The Networks for Messages
Topic 12: Specialized Nets and Their Operations

distance between locations would indicate that a repeater might best cover the area needed. Bear in mind that not only will the Chapter office need to communicate with EACH shelter, but the shelters will often need to talk to each other as well. For this reason a strong, well organized NCS will be needed so that the traffic will flow smoothly and in an orderly fashion.

Also you must remember that traffic that contains sensitive information must be confined to a SECURE communications method and never be transmitted through direct voice communication where proper names and/or health conditions are mentioned.

Amateur Radio is not a secure method of communication. Using various digital modes we can greatly decrease the possibility of interception, but these are also not secure nor should we ever allow a served agency to assume that they are. The most secure methods to be used for sensitive materials of course are telephone, fax, text message and email.

While digital modes such as Packet, D-Star and PSK-31 are MORE secure than voice, you must remember that they are not totally reliable as "secure" modes.

> Traffic that contains sensitive information must be confined to a SECURE communications method and never through direct voice communication where proper names and/or health conditions are mentioned. Amateur Radio is not a secure method of communication. Using various digital modes we can greatly decrease the possibility of interception, but it is not secure nor should we ever allow a served agency to assume it is.

After the first several hours of an event, Health and Welfare traffic may be the most valuable type of traffic for your served agency, so every communicator working with such a served agency will need to have a good supply of NTS forms (and other forms as required for your individual area) so that such traffic can be passed if and when called upon.

Working with a local EOC can be much different in nature, since most Emergency Managers are looking for different kinds of information to be passed during a callout. Since the creation of the Department of Homeland Security (DHS), the NIMS or ICS system has become more widely used. For this reason being familiar with the ICS 213 and other such forms used in that system is also good practice. We must be accustomed to the proper format and protocol that is dictated by the served agency, and not what we would elect to use. Again, we serve at their pleasure, so advance preparation would indicate that we become familiar with what their needs are so that when the time comes we are on the same page with them. This will vary from area to area, and the relationships formed between agency leaders and ARES leadership is vital.

> We must be accustomed to the proper format and protocol which is dictated by the served agency, and not what WE would elect to use.

As has already been discussed, an EOC is usually not the best place for a NCS to operate, since the chaos and noise factors can make such operation difficult. It is often better to have the NCS located off-site in a different location for best results. Also, an EOC will often require communications and tracking of information among a variety of different agencies they work with. Good advance preparation in your area of responsibility might consist of identifying and

Section 2: The Networks for Messages
Topic 12: Specialized Nets and Their Operations

appointing a specific person as liaison for each of the other agencies that an EOC works with.

Health-Oriented Served Agencies

During the last few years, many health organizations such as hospitals and health departments have discovered the value of amateur radio communications and have drawn an association with us into their emergency plans. Working with these types of served agencies can present some unique methods and challenges. For example, some elect to involve amateur radio for the relay of information while engaged in "Point of Dispensing or "PODs" for mass inoculation and vaccination. Often they will ask that we link to an area hospital, EOC and/or health department so that they can track how many doses have been expended and in what length of time. They would also need to know how many people have passed through a particular POD location and what remaining supplies are on hand. For this type of traffic a directed net usually works best. Each POD location would have communicators on hand to gather information then pass it on in regular intervals. NCS operators must be sensitive to accuracy of the information being relayed from each point. It can be noted that this application is also a good workout for packet and digital communication systems with specially assigned frequencies so that normal traffic does not conflict with the POD voice traffic in progress.

Are we alone?

Remember that your group may not be alone! The American Red Cross has a corps of Amateur Radio operators dedicated to them and who are their own ARC volunteers. How will you work with them? The Salvation Army has SATERN volunteers working ham radio. The Southern Baptist Men's Group also has volunteer Amateur Radio operators within their ranks as communicators. These groups may need to bring their full resources into your region depending on the severity of the situation. What is your plan to work cooperatively? How will your nets integrate with their needs?

Advance Planning and Drills

Working with different served agencies and providing nets to each can be difficult. In addition, the agencies often interact with each other, so advance planning and knowing assignments such as NCS operators can make a huge impact on the success of our operations with such agencies. Sitting down well in advance with agency leadership to determine their needs and requirements will help to make things flow smoothly during an actual event or emergency. One good way to handle such advance training would be a tabletop exercise during which demonstrations of Amateur Radio in action is shown, and interaction between agencies can

Section 2: The Networks for Messages
Topic 12: Specialized Nets and Their Operations

take place.

The BIG One!

One other specialized type of net needs to be discussed, even though we hope never to have to use it.

In a truly major disaster you cannot plan on your own local people being available. They may be victims. Help will come in from your neighboring sections and even from across the country.

But the task of the local or district ARES members is not over! Working with your SEC, DEC and others, they will need to form a special resource net which efficiently tracks needs and locations for operators, to whom they should report when they arrive, and what skills and equipment they bring to the task. In this case, the "served agency" is ARES itself!

With this in mind, it is necessary to form solid working relationships with neighboring sections and conduct drills and testing of a "Mutual Aid Net". These nets are conducted between sections to allow cohesion between SEC's, DEC's, EC's and others who would be working together should a disaster strike which could lead to such Mutual Aid or ARESMAT situations. It is good to establish a communications plan under which such requests are made and resources gathered.

Depending upon the geography, many different bands and modes may be chosen, depending on the individual situation. For example in the west where states and sections are spread out and larger, HF might be the best solution. Assuming that the Internet is not down, an IRLP, D-Star or Echolink node or system to link wide areas might be the mode of choice. If it is down, Winlink 2000, or similar mode of operation might help. In any event, this will be unique to your own area and situation, and advance planning and testing of such Mutual Aid scenarios is a must.

Working Together

Finally, remember that this is not the place for "my group, my repeaters, my plan" small mindedness. The NCS of a specialized net reports to both the EC and liaison directly involved with the agency for which the net was created and (usually via that liaison) to the leadership of the agency for which the net was created. We serve the public, not our egos, and the best service we can render in a truly major event is to provide and distribute a corps of trained operators into the right places of the scene in that first, critical 48 hours. Table-topping such a major event and developing a special resource net with your SEC - and even with neighboring sections - is excellent preparation. And, the same holds true at the local level. Working with neighboring ARES units during table top and even more extensive practice nets is a must.

Section 2: The Networks for Messages
Topic 12: Specialized Nets and Their Operations

Reference Links

For more information on any of the elements presented, please consult the following links: ARRL Public Service Communications Manual:
http://www.arrl.org/public-service-communications-manual

For more information on specialized nets in your area, which may be unique in your district or section, contact the Section Manager, Section Emergency Coordinator or District Emergency Coordinator for your ARRL Section. Also, you should consult the ARRL Operating Manual, chapters on emergency communications and traffic handling, and nets. See also the ARRL ARES Field Resources Manual:
http://www.arrl.org/ares-field-resources-manual

Section 2: The Networks for Messages
Topic 12: Specialized Nets and Their Operations

Review

Specialized Nets are specific to various served agencies and are not general nets. These nets are most often customized to fit the served agency involved and the types of communications and traffic relative to that individual agency, which vary in scope and type. Specialized Nets should be conducted away and apart from general, resource or tactical nets if run in conjunction with other nets and should use a frequency unique to this net. NCS operators must be versed in the operations of the specific agency for which the net is created.

Activities

Imagine that you have just been appointed the NCS for an inter-district American Red Cross Net following a major flood. Evacuation centers have been set up in several locations in your city and others nearby. Your mission is to see that 4 shelters are staffed, on frequency, and will form a net to provide coverage between the local chapter and the 4 shelters. For this scenario, the use of a repeater for optimum coverage may be needed. Share with your mentor a simple plan to accomplish this and list the tasks you would need to complete in order to be successful and provide the proper information and relay needed by the agency you are serving. How would you handle lists of clients? What if there were proper names to be transferred from shelters to the chapter headquarters?

Section 2: The Networks for Messages
Topic 12: Specialized Nets and Their Operations

Welcome to Topic 12 Knowledge Review

In order to demonstrate mastery of the information presented in the topic, you will be asked a series of un-graded questions. There are approximately 5 questions on the following pages in multiple-choice or true/false format. Feedback will be offered to you based on the answer you provide.

Question 1:

What is the purpose of a specialized net?

a) To work with a government agency or EOC.

b) To determine what resources are available for service.

c) To serve and be customized for a specific served agency.

d) For passing of health and welfare traffic only.

Question 2:

Which statement best describes a Specialized Net?

a) A net geared to a specific agency and its unique requirements.

b) A net for finding out which resources are available for service.

c) Communications with ARES personnel only.

d) Passing of Health & Welfare traffic only.

Question 3:

How should a NCS plan prior to a Specialized Net?

a) Work with the SEC, DEC and EC.

b) Meet and plan with the served agency itself.

c) Work with a liaison specially assigned to the actual agency.

d) All of the above.

Section 2: The Networks for Messages
Topic 12: Specialized Nets and Their Operations

Question 4:

To whom does the NCS of a specialized net report?

a) The EC or liaison directly involved with the agency for which the net was created, and also to the leadership of that agency.

b) The SM or SEC.

c) Only to the top leadership of the agency for which the net was created.

d) The ARES team leaders.

Section 2: The Networks for Messages
Topic 13: Severe Weather Nets

TOPIC 13:

Severe Weather Nets

Objectives

Welcome to Topic 13.

This Learning Topic will cover what every operator needs to understand about the basics of severe weather reporting programs and nets, including local or regional National Weather Service (NWS) SKYWARN® nets, and the wide-area Hurricane Watch Net.

Student Preparation required:

Review the Memorandum of Understanding (MOU) between the National Weather Service and the ARRL at:
http://www.arrl.org/files/file/Public%20Service/National%20Weather%20Service%20MOU.pdf
and the Hurricane Watch Net's Web site at: http://www.hwn.org

SKYWARN®

The name "Skywarn," like "ARES," is a registered name and cannot be used by other organizations. The SKYWARN® (note the registration mark ® - if you are using it in a publication, you need to include it) program is sponsored by the National Weather Service (NWS). Like ARES, it is a program and not a club or organization. Amateur Radio operators and other SKYWARN® volunteers report actual weather conditions in their own communities. These are sometimes called "ground truth" observations. Accurate information and rapid communication during extreme weather situations have proven to be indispensable to the NWS. Amateur Radio SKYWARN® operations have become integral to many communities' disaster preparedness programs.

Unlike most Amateur Radio operators, SKYWARN® observers are a "first-response" group, invaluable to the success of an early storm-warning effort. Weather spotting is popular because the procedures are easy to learn and reports can be given from the relative safety and convenience of a home or vehicle.

This learning unit concentrates primarily on the Amateur Radio nets themselves. While some

Section 2: The Networks for Messages
Topic 13: Severe Weather Nets

discussion of general spotting techniques is presented here, specific weather observation training for your area should be obtained locally from NWS.

To become a registered SKYWARN® volunteer, you must complete a short course of training in severe weather observation and reporting. Most courses are only a few hours long. Once completed, NWS personnel may assign you a spotter number and a toll-free number to call with your reports. Many amateurs are members and registered spotters and they provide a valuable service to NOAA and local NWS offices around the country. If there is no active program in your area, you might wish to find out more about starting one in conjunction with your local ARES group. For more information on SKYWARN® training, contact the local NWS office or your local emergency management agency.

What is generally reported

Reports on a severe-weather net are limited to specific critical weather observations, unless the NWS office requests other information. For this reason, amateurs without SKYWARN® training should monitor the net and transmit only when they can offer needed help. If they ARE members, they should report as requested and as needed by their local leadership and NWS office, and using their assigned SKYWARN® spotter number. Many areas open a net for the collection of such severe weather data.

Weather forecasters, depending on their geographical location, need specific types of data.

During the summer or thunderstorm season, SKYWARN® observers report:

- Tornadoes, funnel clouds, and wall clouds
- Hail – usually measured with a specific size
- Strong winds, usually 50 miles per hour or greater
- Flash flooding
- Heavy rain, with a sustained rate of 1 inch per hour or more
- Damage.
- Adverse traffic and driving conditions affecting travel

During the winter they report:

- High winds
- Heavy snowfall
- Freezing precipitation
- Sleet
- New snow accumulation of 2 or more inches per hour
- Damage caused by snow or ice.

Section 2: The Networks for Messages
Topic 13: Severe Weather Nets

Here is a four-step method to describe severe weather you see:

1. What: Tornadoes, funnel clouds, heavy rain, etc.

2. Where: Direction and distance from a well-known location; for example "3 miles south of Newington Center, on Route 15."

3. When: Time of observation.

4. Details: Storm's direction, speed of travel, size, intensity, and destructiveness. Include any uncertainty as needed e.g."Funnel cloud, but too far away to be certain if it is on the ground." Indicate if amounts are measured or estimated; i.e. wind gauge vs. visual estimate.

Activation

SKYWARN® observers are usually aware that the potential for severe weather has been forecast. As conditions begin to deteriorate, they should monitor the primary net frequency and the NOAA All Hazards Weather Radio (NWR), a system of VHF FM radio transmitters operated nationwide by the NWS on seven channels between 162.400 and 162.550 MHz. The SKYWARN® net may be formally activated upon the request of the local NWS office, or by net members if conditions warrant immediate action.

Operating the Weather Net

The format and operation of weather nets will vary from area to area, and should be designed to meet local needs. In areas with specific hazards, such as in "tornado alley," the net may be formal and well disciplined. In other areas with less sudden dangerous weather, the net may be less formal, and may not even have a NCS operator. When it is a directed net, the NCS maintains control over traffic being passed to NWS, and may organize liaison with other area repeaters. Often wide area, high level repeater systems will work best due to their coverage. Also, many ARES organizations designate an EC or AEC assigned to the NWS who become NCS during activation. Many of these also become Weather Net managers.

The Net Manager or NCS should designate one or more alternate frequencies in anticipation of an overload, the loss of a repeater, or if the net needs to split to handle different tasks or regions. If a disaster should occur during a severe-weather net, the net may take on disaster-relief operations in addition to tracking the progress of the storm. If the traffic on the net increases substantially, a separate net should be set up to handle relief operations to ensure that critical information gets through in a timely fashion. At least one station should be assigned as a liaison to monitor both nets and relay any critical messages or information between nets.

Section 2: The Networks for Messages
Topic 13: Severe Weather Nets

At the National Weather Service – In some areas, a permanent or temporary Amateur station is operated from the local NWS office. In other areas, an off-site station relays information to the local NWS office via telephone, fax, or email. In either case, this station receives, collates, and organizes the information being sent to NWS and passes it on to the forecasters as quickly as possible.

NWS personnel may request that a hand-held radio or scanner be placed at the severe-weather desk. In such cases, they need to be aware of which frequencies are to be monitored so that they may receive the most accurate and up to date information in real time. This arrangement allows them to monitor incoming traffic directly. Nevertheless, all traffic should be written on report forms and passed quickly to the forecasters.

The Hurricane Watch Net (HWN) - http://www.hwn.org

The Hurricane Watch Net serves as eyes and ears for the National Weather Service in the Caribbean, the Gulf of Mexico, and along the US Atlantic and Pacific coasts. Net members relay official weather bulletins to those monitoring the net in affected areas, and field observation reports back to NWS - primarily to the hurricane forecasters in the National Hurricane Center which has an on-site amateur radio station, WX4NHC. It also serves as a backup communication link between NWS forecast offices, National Specialized Centers, critical EOCs, and other disaster relief efforts.

HWN differs from SKYWARN® in two important ways. First, its volunteers are exclusively Amateur Radio operators. Second, its operations are primarily on HF-SSB rather than VHF or UHF-FM.

Membership in the net is not restricted to stations in hurricane areas. Amateur operators outside hurricane-prone areas can participate as relays or net control stations. The net has an urgent need for stations in the Midwest and on the west coast as propagation shifts westward. The net also has a need for stations that are available during the workday in all areas.

If you live in a hurricane-prone area, and your Amateur license class will not allow operation on the 20-meter band, you can still participate in the system. The National Hurricane Center monitors the APRS packet reporting system. You can submit your information manually via APRS, or better yet, connect a weather station to your packet station for automatic reporting. In some areas, local FM nets relay observations to NWS through HF operators on the HWN net.

Activation – The Hurricane Watch Net activates for all hurricanes that are a threat to land in the Atlantic and eastern Pacific Oceans. The net will normally activate when a hurricane is moving toward land at a range of 300 miles. On occasion, it may activate for tropical storms, or at any time when requested by the National Hurricane Center.

Before checking into the net, listen long enough to determine the nature and immediacy of events. If the storm is still hours from any serious impact, the net control will provide a window of opportunity to check in. If a hurricane is within an hour of landfall, check in ONLY if you are in the affected area, can assist with a specific relay, or supply information of immediate value to the net or Hurricane Center.

Section 2: The Networks for Messages
Topic 13: Severe Weather Nets

Net Operations – The Hurricane Watch Net, and WX4NHC at the National Hurricane Center in Miami, are staffed entirely by volunteers. While net operations are normally conducted on 14.325 MHz USB, the net may move to 3.950 MHz LSB if band conditions warrant.

The primary functions of the HWN are to:

1. Disseminate hurricane advisory information to marine interests, Caribbean island nations, emergency operations centers, maritime mobile Amateur stations, and other interests for the Atlantic and Eastern Pacific as released by the National Hurricane Center in Miami, Florida.

2. Obtain ground-level weather observations and damage reports from reporting stations and observers who are not part of the routine network for the National Weather Service, or the World Meteorological Organization, and forward it quickly and accurately to the National Hurricane Center.

3. Function as a backup wide-area communication link for the National Hurricane Center, Emergency Operation Centers, the National Weather Service, and other vital interests involved in the protection of life and property before, during, and after hurricane events.

4. Relay initial assessments of hurricane damage to the National Hurricane Center. Damage assessments come in about roads, power outages, structural damage, phone and communication problems, and of course, reports on the number of injuries and deaths. These non-weather report items are usually relayed to the appropriate agencies via other nets in operation on 20, 40, and 80 meters, or by the crew at WX4NHC (formerly W4EHW) to agencies that stay in regular contact with the National Hurricane Center.

Safety Concerns for All Weather Net Stations

As an Amateur Radio operator providing communications in the path of a dangerous storm, you need to be concerned for your own safety. Under no circumstances should you place yourself in physical danger in order to gather or report information. Remember, if the area is under an evacuation order, it is too dangerous for you as well. Antennas and supports should be placed so that winds will not carry them into power lines. Stations should be located as far from potential flood, flash flood, or storm surge areas, and as close to an escape route as possible. If setting up a portable station, choose buildings that were specifically designed to withstand storm winds. Stay away from unprotected windows, and make sure that you have more than one down-wind emergency exit should a fallen tree or other debris block the main exit. Park vehicles down-wind from buildings and structures to protect them from flying debris. Bring adequate supplies to remain in place for an extended time should evacuation or re-supply not be possible.

Section 2: The Networks for Messages
Topic 13: Severe Weather Nets

VoIP MODES

Radio amateurs using voice over Internet Protocol (VoIP) modes such as Echolink <http://www.echolink.org/ and IRLP http://www.irlp.net/ are also supporting forecasters tracking hurricanes.

The EchoLink and IRLP partnerships created for hurricanes and severe weather has seen upward of 100 VoIP connections during storm emergencies, many of which represent repeaters and conference rooms with many people listening.

The VoIP-WX Net http://www.voipwx.net/ also has a large number of Technician class operators who were not able to report via HF in the past. The HWN operates on 14.325 MHz--beyond reach of operators lacking at least a General ticket. Those connecting via VoIP modes often do so using VHF/UHF radios on battery power via an IRLP or EchoLink-equipped repeater.

For additional information, visit the WX4NHC Web site http://www.wx4nhc.org/.

Weather Net Operating Tips

For nets spanning more than one time zone, use UTC time in all reports, not local time. If you are not sure of the correct UTC time, use local time and be sure to notify the net control that you are using it.

If you are going to give a damage, injury, or casualty report and it is not based on your own personal observation, be prepared to provide the time, the name of the person providing it, their call sign or official position if any, and if possible, a telephone number, address or other means of contact so it can be confirmed later. Also be keenly aware that sensitive information should NOT be broadcast over general nets and must be kept to more secure modes such as telephone, Fax, or direct delivery if possible. This will avoid release of proper names and sensitive information to those who might be listening and not directly involved with disaster efforts.

Use "push-to-talk" – not VOX. Background noise in the room, from the storm, and from other radios may cause VOX to key your transmitter without you noticing and disrupt the net. Also, use headphones if possible at on site locations to ensure that you receive accurate information without disruption from such background noise.

Section 2: The Networks for Messages
Topic 13: Severe Weather Nets

Reference Links

- **National Weather Service:** http://nws.noaa.gov/
- **NOAA All Hazards Weather Radio (NWR):** http://www.weather.gov/nwr/
- **NWR Coverage Maps:** http://nws.noaa.gov/nwr/Maps/
- **NWS SKYWARN®:** http://www.weather.gov/skywarn/
- **SKYWARN®:** http://www.skywarn.net/ **(non-NWS commercial website)**
- **Hurricane Watch Net:** http://www.hwn.org/
- **For information on becoming a net control station of the Hurricane Watch Net, see:** http://www.hwn.org/home/membership-info.html
- **Blank HWN report forms are available at:** http://www2.fiu.edu/orgs/w4ehw/

Other wide-area Amateur Radio nets that deal with severe weather events:

- **The Maritime Mobile Service Net:** http://www.mmsn.org/
- **The Intercon Net:** http://www.interconnet.org/new_intercon/index.html
- **The SATERN Net:** http://www.satern.org/
- **The Waterway Net:** http://www.waterwayradio.net/

Section 2: The Networks for Messages
Topic 13: Severe Weather Nets

Review

The NWS SKYWARN® program and the Hurricane Watch Net compose the bulk of Amateur Radio weather nets. Both use Amateur Radio to relay real-time "ground-truth" weather information to the appropriate National Weather Service office. Amateurs participating in either type of net should take care not to expose themselves to dangerous weather conditions.

Activities

1. Determine if there are any weather nets operating in your State. For any such nets, and the Hurricane Watch Net, list the details of operation including:

    - Sponsoring or Served Agency
    - Qualifications for participating in the net
    - Next scheduled training event
    - Key contact personnel
    - Frequencies employed
    - Procedure(s) for activating the net

2. Suppose that you are placed in charge of training SKYWARN® participants in your area. What information would be critical for your participants to know?

Share your answers with your mentor.

Section 2: The Networks for Messages
Topic 13: Severe Weather Nets

Welcome to Topic 13 Knowledge Review

In order to demonstrate mastery of the information presented in the topic, you will be asked a series of un-graded questions. There are approximately 5 questions on the following pages in multiple-choice or true/false format. Feedback will be offered to you based on the answer you provide.

Question 1:

When is the Hurricane Watch Net normally activated?

a) Every morning at 1000 UTC during hurricane season only.

b) When a hurricane is within 300 miles of making landfall.

c) When a tropical storm approaches a populated land mass.

d) When a tropical wave develops west of Africa.

Question 2:

Who should check in to the Hurricane Watch Net an hour before a hurricane makes landfall?

a) All amateurs should check in.

b) Amateurs with weather stations only.

c) Only those stations on the net roster.

d) Only amateurs in the affected area, or amateurs with important information that would be needed by the net or the National Hurricane Center.

Question 3:

Does a station have to be located in a hurricane area to be a member of the Hurricane Watch Net?

a) Yes, the net is made up solely of stations in hurricane areas.

b) There is no membership in the Hurricane Watch Net. Anybody can check in at any time.

c) No. The net has a need for stations in Canada and on the west coast that can control the net as propagation shifts to the north and to the west.

d) No. The net has a need for stations in the Midwest and west coast that can control the net as propagation shifts to the west.

Section 2: The Networks for Messages
Topic 13: Severe Weather Nets

Question 4:

Which answer best describes the four step method to describe severe weather?

a) Who, What, When, Why.

b) What, Where, When, Details.

c) What, Where, Why, General Comments.

d) What, When, Why, Where.

Question 5:

SKYWARN® participants would generally not report which of the following?

a) Fog.

b) High winds.

c) Sleet.

d) Hail size.

Section 3: Message Handling
Topic 14: Basic Message Handling Part I

TOPIC 14:

Basic Message Handling Part I

Objectives

Welcome to Topic 14.

This topic is intended to provide basic knowledge for both formal and informal message handling, but is not intended to make you an "expert." Further study and practice on your own will be necessary.

Student Preparation required:

None.

Introduction

Consider the following scenario:

There are 330 hurricane evacuees in a Red Cross shelter. ARES is providing communications, working in 12-hour shifts. An elderly diabetic woman is brought in at 1400 hours. She will require her next dose of insulin by 2300 hours. The manager goes to the radio room. There is an operator wearing a red baseball hat with funny numbers and letters on it. He asks the operator to inform the county EOC of the medication need. The operator calls the Red Cross EOC and says, "Hey, we have a diabetic lady here who will need insulin by 2300 hours," but doesn't write the message down or log the request.

At 2030 hours the medication has still not been delivered. The shelter manager goes to the radio room to inquire about its status. There is now a different person with a blue baseball cap with a new set of funny letters and numbers.

He knows nothing of the earlier request, but promises to "check on it." In the meantime, EOC personnel have discarded the message because it was written on a scrap of paper and had no signature authorizing the order for medication. No one sent a return message requesting authorization.

If each operator had generated and properly logged a formal message, with an authorized signature, it would be a relatively simple matter to track. The informal message has no tracks to follow. Also, by sending a formal message, you are nearly guaranteeing that the receiving station will write it down properly (with a signature) and log it, greatly enhancing its chances of being delivered intact.

Section 3: Message Handling
Topic 14: Basic Message Handling Part I

Formal vs. Informal Messages

Both formal (written in a specific format, i.e. ARRL) and informal (oral or written but not in a specific format) messages have their place in emergency communication. In general, informal messages are best used for non-critical and simple messages, or messages that require immediate action, those are delivered directly from the author to the recipient.

Formal messages are more appropriate when two or more people will handle them before reaching the recipient, or where the contents are critical or contain important details. The most common formal message format is that used by ARRL's NTS, discussed on the following page.

Informal Oral Messages

Some emergency messages are best sent informally in the interest of saving precious seconds. If you need an ambulance for a severely bleeding victim, you do not have time to compose and send a formal message. The resulting delay could cause the patient's death. Other messages do not require a formal written message because they have little value beyond the moment. Letting the net control station know where you are or when you will arrive need not be formal. The message is going directly to its recipient, is simple and clear, and has little detail. Many of the messages handled on a tactical net fit this description.

Formal Written Message Formats

A standard written message format is used so that everyone knows what to expect. This increases the speed and accuracy with which you can handle messages. The ARRL message form, or "Radiogram," is a standard format used for passing messages on various nets, and is required for all messages sent through the National Traffic System. While this format may not be perfect for all applications, it serves as a baseline that can be readily adapted for use within a specific served agency. Regular practice with creating and sending messages in any standard format is recommended.

Components of a Standard ARRL Radiogram

The standard Radiogram format is familiar to most hams from the pads of yellow-green forms available from ARRL Headquarters. The form has places for the following information:

1. **The "Preamble"** sometimes referred to as "the header," consists of administrative data such as the message number, originating station, message precedence (importance) and date and time of origination. The combination of the message number and the originating station serves as a unique message identifier, which can be traced if necessary. We will discuss the Preamble in greater detail in a bit.

2. The **"Address"** includes the name, street address or post office box, city, state, and zip code of the recipient. The address should also include the telephone number with area code since many long distance Radiograms are ultimately delivered with a local phone call.

Section 3: Message Handling
Topic 14: Basic Message Handling Part I

3. **The "Text"** of the message should be brief and to the point, limited to 25 words or less when possible. The text should be written in lines of five words (ten if using a keyboard) to make it easier and faster to count them for the "check." Care should be taken to avoid word contractions, as the apostrophe is not used in CW. If a word is sent without the apostrophe, its meaning could be lost or changed. The contraction for "I will" (I'll) has a very different meaning when sent without the apostrophe! Contractions are also more difficult to understand when sent by phone, especially in poor conditions. Commas and other punctuation are also not used in formal messages. Where needed, the "period" can be sent as an "X" in CW and digital modes, and spoken as "X-RAY." The "X" may be used to separate phrases or sentences but never at the end of the text. Question marks are spelled out in text and spoken as "question mark," and sometimes as "query." Both the X and question mark should be used only when the meaning of the message would not be clear without them.

4. The "Signature" can be a single name, a name and call sign, a full name and a title, "Mom and Dad," and occasionally a return address and phone number – whatever is needed to ensure that the recipient can identify the sender and that a reply message can be sent if necessary.

[ARRL Radiogram form filled out as follows:]

The American Radio Relay League RADIOGRAM Via Amateur Radio

Number	Precedence	HX	Station of Origin	Check	Place of Origin	Time Filed	Date
207	P	E	W1FN	10	LEBANON NH	1200 EST	JAN 4

To: MARK DOE
RED CROSS DISASTER OFFICE
123 MAIN ST
RUTLAND VT 05701

Telephone Number: 802-555-1212

NEED   MORE   COTS   AND   SANITATION
KITS   AT   ALL   FIVE   SHELTERS

JOAN SMITH SHELTER MANAGER

Details of the Preamble:

The preamble or "header" is the section of the ARRL message form where all the administrative details of the message are recorded. There are **eight sections** or "blocks" in the preamble. Two of them, "time filed" and "handling instructions," are optional for most messages.

Section 3: Message Handling
Topic 14: Basic Message Handling Part I

Block #1 - Message Number:

This is any number assigned by the station that first puts the message into ARRL format. While any alphanumeric combination is acceptable, a common practice is to use a numeric sequence starting with the number "1" at the beginning of the emergency operation. Stations who are involved in day-to-day message handling may start numbering at the beginning of each year or each month.

Block #2 - Precedence:

The precedence tells everyone the relative urgency of a message. In all but one case, a single letter abbreviation is sent with CW or digital modes. On phone, the entire word is always spoken. Within the ARRL format, there are four levels of precedence:

Routine – abbreviated with the letter "R." Most day-to-day Amateur traffic is handled using this precedence - it is for all traffic that does not meet the requirements for a higher precedence. In a disaster situation, routine messages are seldom sent.

Welfare – abbreviated as "W." Used for an inquiry as to the health and welfare of an individual in a disaster area, or a message from a disaster victim to friends or family.

Priority – abbreviated as "P." For important messages with a time limit; any official or emergency-related messages not covered by the EMERGENCY precedence. This precedence is usually only associated with official traffic to, from, or related to a disaster area.

EMERGENCY – there is no abbreviation – the word EMERGENCY is always spelled out. Use this for any message having life or death urgency. This includes official messages from agencies requesting critical supplies or assistance during emergencies, or other official instructions to provide aid or relief in a disaster area. The use of this precedence should generally be limited to traffic originated and signed by authorized agency officials. Due to the lack of privacy on radio, EMERGENCY messages should only be sent via Amateur Radio when regular communication facilities are unavailable.

Block #3 - Handling Instructions:

This is an optional field used at the discretion of the originating station. The seven standard HX pro-signs are:

HXA – (Followed by number.) "Collect" telephone delivery authorized by addressee within (X) miles. If no number is sent, authorization is unlimited.

HXB – (Followed by number.) Cancel message if not delivered within (X) hours of filing time; service (notify) originating station.

HXC – Report date and "time of delivery" (TOD) to originating station.

Section 3: Message Handling
Topic 14: Basic Message Handling Part I

HXD – Report to originating station the identity of the station who delivered the message, plus date, time and method of delivery. Also, each station to report identity of station to which relayed, plus date and time.

HXE – Delivering station to get and send reply from addressee.

HXF – (Followed by date in numbers.) Hold delivery until (specify date).

HXG – Delivery by mail or telephone - toll call not required. If toll or other expense involved, cancel message, and send service message to originating station.

If more than one HX pro-sign is used, they can be combined like this: HXAC. However, if numbers are used, such as with HXF, the HX must be repeated each time. On voice, use phonetics for the letter or letters following the HX to ensure accuracy, as in "HX Alpha."

Block #4 - Station of Origin:

This is the FCC call sign of the first station that put the message into NTS format. It is not the message's original author. For instance, you are the radio operator for a Red Cross shelter. The fire station down the street sends a runner with a message to be passed and you format and send the message. You are the "Station of Origin," and fire station is the "Place of Origin," which will be listed in Block 6.

Block #5 - The Check:

The "check" is the number of words in the text section only. Include any "periods" (written as "X," spoken as "X-Ray"). The preamble, address and signature are not included. After receiving a message, traffic handlers count the words in the message and compare the word count to the "check" number in the preamble. If the two numbers do not agree, the message should be re-read by the sending station to verify that all words were copied correctly. If the message was copied correctly and an error in the check number exists, do not replace the old count with the new count. Instead, update the count by adding a "slash" followed by the new count. For example, if the old count was five, and the correct count was six, change the check to "5/6."

Block #6 - Place of Origin:

This is the name of the community, building, or agency where the originator of the message is located, whether a ham or not. This is not the location of the station that first handled the message, which is listed in Block 4, "Station of Origin."

Block #7 - Time Filed:

This is an optional field, unless handling instruction "Bravo" (HXB) is used. HXB means "cancel if not delivered within X hours of filing time." Unless the message is time sensitive, this field may be left blank for routine messages, but completing the time field is generally

Section 3: Message Handling
Topic 14: Basic Message Handling Part I

recommended for Welfare, Priority, and Emergency messages. Many hams use Universal Coordinated Time (UTC) for messages and logging. During emergencies, it is better to use local time and indicators such as PST or EDT to eliminate confusion by served agency personnel.

Block #8 - Date:

This is the date the message was first placed into the traffic system. Be sure to use the same date as the time zone indicated in Block 7.

Header Examples:

This is how a complete header might look for a CW or digital message:
NR207   P   HXE   W1FN   10
LEBANON NH   1200 EST   JAN 4

This is how the same header would be spoken:
"Number two zero seven Priority HX Echo Whiskey One Foxtrot November One Zero Lebanon NH One Two Zero Zero EST January four."

A brief pause is made between each block to help the receiving station separate the information. Note that the title of each block is not spoken, with the exception of the word "number" at the beginning, which tells the receiving station that you are beginning the actual message.

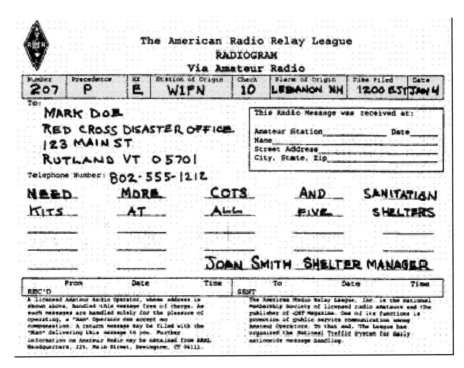

Section 3: Message Handling
Topic 14: Basic Message Handling Part I

Pro-Words and Pro-Signs

When sending formal traffic, standard "pro-words" or pro-signs" (CW) are used to begin or end parts of the message, and to ask for portions of the message to be repeated. In addition to adding clarity, the use of standard pro-words and pro-signs saves considerable time. Some pro-words and pro-signs tell the receiving station what to expect next in the address, text, and signature portions of the message – they are not used while reading the header, since the header follows a pre-determined format. Examples of commonly used pro-words are, "figures" sent before a group consisting of all numerals, "initial" to indicate that a single letter will follow, or "break" to signal the transition between the address and the text, and the text and the signature.

Message Handling Pro-Words, Prosigns and Abbreviations

*Two letters are sent as one character.

Pro-Word	Pro-Sign	Meaning or Example
BREAK	(CW)	Separates address from text and text from signature.
	BT*	
CORRECTION	HH*	"I am going to correct an error".
END	AR*	End of message.
MORE	B	Additional messages to follow.
NO MORE	N	No additional messages. In CW can also mean "negative" or "no"
FIGURES	Not Needed	Used before a word group consisting of all numerals
INITIAL	Not Needed	Used to indicate a single letter will follow.
I SAY AGAIN	IMI*	Used to indicate a single phrase will follow.
I SPELL	Not Needed	"I am going to spell a word phonetically".
LETTER	Not Needed	Several letters together in a group will follow. Example: ARES, SCTN.
MIXED GROUP	Not Needed	Letters and numbers combined in a group will follow. Example: 12BA6
X-RAY	X	Used to indicate end of sentence, as with a "period".
BREAK	BK*	Break; break-in; interrupt current transmission on CW
CORRECT	C	Correct, yes
CONFIRM	CFM	Confirm (please check me on this)
THIS IS	DE	Used preceding identification of your station
HX	HX	Handling instructions, single letter to follow – optional part of preamble
GO AHEAD	K	Invitation for specific station to transmit
ROGER	R	Message understood. In CW, may be used for decimal point in context
WORD AFTER	WA	"Say again word after…"
WORD BEFORE	WB	"Say again word before…"
BETWEEN	-	"Say again between … and …"
ALL AFTER	AA*	Say again all after …"
ALL BEFORE	AB	"Say again all before…"

Section 3: Message Handling
Topic 14: Basic Message Handling Part I

Sending a Message with Voice

When the receiving station is ready to copy, read the message at a pace that will allow the receiving station to write it down. Once you are done, if the receiving station has missed any portion of the message they will say, "say again all after____," "say all before," or "say again all between____ and ____." In some nets, the practice is to say "break" and then unkey between sections of the message so that a station can ask for missing words to be repeated before going on (these repeated words are also known as "fills"). In many nets the entire message is read first before any fills are requested, to save time. All numbers in groups are spoken individually, as in "three two one five," not "thirty-two fifteen," or "three thousand two hundred and five."

Here is an entire message as it should be spoken:

> Refer to video file 5

Time Savers

What NOT to say: When passing formal traffic, do not add unnecessary words. Since the parts of the header are always sent in the same order, there is no need to identify each of them. The only exception is the word "number" at the beginning of the header. Here is an example of how not to read the header of a message on the air:

"Number two zero seven precedence, Priority handling instructions, HX Echo station of origin W1FN check one zero place of origin, Lebanon NH time one two zero zero EST date, January 4. Going to Mark Doe Red Cross Disaster Office Address figures one two three Main Street Rutland VT, ZIP figures zero five seven zero one. Telephone Figures eight zero two five five five one two one two"

This example added many unneeded words to the message, including "station of origin," "check," "time," "going to," "address," "ZIP," and "telephone" and other block titles. If there is something about the message that deviates from the standard format, or if an inexperienced operator is copying the message without a pre-printed form, then some additional description may be necessary, but in most cases it just wastes time. (The pro-word "figures" is used correctly, and "number" is always spoken before the message number.)

Section 3: Message Handling
Topic 14: Basic Message Handling Part I

Reference Links

For a list of ARES and NTS nets in your area, see the ARRL Net Directory at:
http://www.arrl.org/arrl-net-directory

ARRL Precedence and Handling Instructions:
http://www.arrl.org/public-service-communications-manual

ARES and NTS Forms:
http://www.arrl.org/public-service-field-services-forms

Much more information on formal message handling and forms is available at:
http://www.arrl.org/files/file/Public%20Service/MPG104A.pdf

Section 3: Message Handling
Topic 14: Basic Message Handling Part I

Review

Formal messages are more likely to be delivered intact than oral comments. Using a standard format for formal messages makes it easier and faster for both sending and receiving stations to handle. Frequent practice with any formal message format is essential if you are to be able to use it accurately and quickly.

Activities

1. Discuss formal vs. informal messages with your mentor.

2. Discuss with your mentor the components of a standard ARRL Radiogram.

3. Compose four complete ARRL formatted messages, one example for each Precedence, in written form. Use Handling Instructions and include the time and date sent. Provide samples to your mentor.

Click here or copy and paste the following URL into your browser to download an interactive form to use for assignment 3. (You will need to have Adobe® reader installed on your computer.)
http://www.arrl.org/files/file/Intro%20to%20Emcomm%20Course/RADIOGRAM2011_Interactive.pdf

Section 3: Message Handling
Topic 14: Basic Message Handling Part I

Welcome to Topic 14 Knowledge Review

In order to demonstrate mastery of the information presented in the topic, you will be asked a series of un-graded questions. There are approximately 5 questions on the following pages in multiple-choice or true/false format. Feedback will be offered to you based on the answer you provide.

Question 1:

The preamble to an ARRL Radiogram message contains a block called "Precedence." Which of the following represents the correct precedence for an EMERGENCY message?

a) "URGENT."

b) "U."

c) "EMERGENCY."

d) "E."

Question 2:

The preamble to an ARRL Radiogram message contains a block called "Handling Instructions." What is the meaning of the handling instruction "HXE"?

a) Delivering station to get and send reply from addressee.

b) Report date and time of delivery to originating station.

c) Cancel message if not delivered within (X) hours of filing time.

d) Collect telephone delivery authorized.

Question 3:

ARRL Radiogram messages contains a block called "Time Filed." Which of the following is true of entries in that block?

a) This field is always completed.

b) Time entries are always Universal Coordinated Time.

c) During emergencies its best to use and indicate "local time.

d) During emergencies "local time" along with the local date is used.

Section 3: Message Handling
Topic 14: Basic Message Handling Part I

Question 4:

ARRL Radiogram messages contain a block called "The Check." Which of the following is true of entries in that block?

a) The check contains a count of the words in the entire message.

b) The check contains a count of the words in the preamble and the text of the message.

c) The check contain a count of the words in the preamble, address and text of the message.

d) The check contains a count of the words in the text of the message.

Question 5:

Which of the following statements is true of punctuation within an ARRL Radiogram?

a) Punctuation is always helpful; it should be used whenever possible.

b) Punctuation is rarely helpful; it should never be used.

c) Punctuation should be used only when it is essential to the meaning of the message.

d) The comma and apostrophe are the most common punctuation signs used in NTS messages.

Section 3: Message Handling
Topic 15: Basic Message Handling, Part II

TOPIC 15:
Basic Message Handling Part II

Objectives

Welcome to Topic 15.

This topic is a continuation of the previous learning unit - Basic Message Handling Part I.

Student Preparation:

No additional preparation is required.

Message Handling Rules

Do not speculate on anything relating to an emergency! There may be hundreds of people listening to what you say (other Amateurs, and the media and general public using scanners) and any incorrect information could cause serious problems for the served agency or others. You do not want to be the source of any rumor. If your served agency requests an estimate, you can provide that information as long as you make it very clear that it is only an estimate when you send it. For example, saying "The estimated number of homes damaged is twelve" would be acceptable.

Pass messages exactly as written or spoken. Even more important than speed, your job as a communicator is to deliver each message as accurately as possible. Therefore, you must not change any message as you handle it. If it is longer than you would like, you must send it anyway. Apparently misspelled words or confusing text must be sent exactly as received. Only the original author may make changes. If you note an inaccurate word count in a NTS format message, you must maintain the original count and follow it with the actual count received at your station, i.e.: "12/11."

Should you return a message to the author before first sending it if it seems incorrect or confusing? This is a judgment call. If the apparent error will affect the meaning of the message and the author is easily contacted, it is probably a good idea. Whenever possible, it is a good practice to read each message carefully in the presence of the author before accepting it. This way, potential errors or misunderstandings can be corrected before the message is sent.

Section 3: Message Handling
Topic 15: Basic Message Handling, Part II

Non-Standard Format Messages

Much of the tactical information being passed during a major emergency will not be in ARRL format. It may have much of the same information, but will be in a non-standard format or no format at all. These messages should also be passed exactly as received. If necessary, use the ARRL format and place the entire non-standard message in the "text" section.

The Importance of the Signature

During an emergency, the messages you handle can easily contain requests for expensive supplies that have a very limited "shelf life" (such as blood for a field hospital), or for agencies that will only respond to properly authorized requests (i.e.: for medevac helicopters). For this reason, it is critical that you include the signature and title of the sender in every message.

ARRL Numbered Radiograms

ARRL Numbered Radiograms are a standardized list of often-used phrases. Each phrase on the list is assigned a number. There are two groups: Group One is for emergency relief and consists of 26 phrases numbered consecutively from "ONE" to "TWENTY SIX," and proceeded by the letters "ARL." For example, "ARL SIX" means "will contact you as soon as possible." Group Two contains 21 routine messages, including number "FORTY SIX" and from "FIFTY" through "SIXTY NINE."

In the text of the message, the numbered radiogram is inserted by using the letters "ARL" as one word, followed by the number written out in text, not numerals. For example: "ARL FIFTY SIX."

When using numbered radiograms, the letters "ARL" are placed in the "check" block of the preamble, just prior to the number indicating the word count, as in "ARL7."

"ARL FIFTY SIX" is counted as three words for the "check" block. Two common receiving errors are to write "ARL-56" and count it as one word, or "ARL 56" and count it as two words. It is important to spell out the numbers letter by letter when sending using voice. This allows the receiving station to correctly copy what is being sent, and not inadvertently write the figures out as "FIVE SIX" instead of "FIFTY SIX."

Some numbered messages require a "fill in the blank" word in order to make sense. Two examples are provided. See below for the first one:

ARL SIXTY TWO: Greetings and best wishes to you for a pleasant ___ holiday season.

ARL SIXTY FOUR: Arrived safely at _____.

Go to the next page for another example.

Section 3: Message Handling
Topic 15: Basic Message Handling, Part II

Here's an example of a message to convey a Christmas greeting, indicate safe arrival and send regards from family members.

```
57  R  W1AW  ARL 16  PUEBLO CO DECEMBER 10
RICHARD RYAN
3820 S SUNNYRIDGE LANE
NEW BERLIN WISCONSIN 53151
414 555 1234
BREAK
ARL FIFTY ARL SIXTY TWO CHRISTMAS ARL SIXTY FOUR HOME
MOM AND DAD SEND THEIR LOVE BREAK
BOB AND ALICE
```

Note that no "XRAY" is used between parts of this message. The numbered radiogram assumes a period at the end of the phrase.

Important: Be sure to decode a message containing an ARL text into plain language before delivering it! Chances are good that the recipient will not know the meaning of the ARL code number. In one real situation, a recipient thought that an un-decoded ARL radiogram delivered by telephone was actually a spy message, and contacted the FBI.

Copying Hints

When copying the text of a message by hand, receiving stations should write five words on each line, (or ten words per line if using a keyboard). The standard ARRL Radiogram form is set up for hand copying with spaces for each word, but even if you are writing on whatever happens to be handy, grouping the words five to a line allows for a very quick count after the message is received. Once complete, the receiving operator compares the word count with the check. If okay, the message is "Rogered" – if not, the message is repeated at a faster reading speed to locate the missing or extra words.

Modified Message Form for Disasters

While ARRL format messages can handle many different types of information flow, there can be requirements for formats that are unique to an individual agency or type of emergency. Your emcomm group should work with each served agency before the emergency to see which format will best fulfill their needs. A good example is the popular Incident Command System (ICS) form ICS-213 used by most government agencies.

Service Messages

A "service message" is one that lets the originating station know the status of a message they have sent. A service message may be requested by a handling instruction (HX), or may be sent by any operator who has a problem delivering an important message. During emergencies, service messages should only be sent for Priority and Emergency messages.

Section 3: Message Handling
Topic 15: Basic Message Handling, Part II

Logging and Record Keeping

An accurate record of formal messages handled and various aspects of your station's operation can be very useful, and is required by law in some cases. Lost or misdirected messages can be tracked down later on, and a critique of the operation afterward can be more accurate. All logs should include enough detail to be meaningful later on, especially the date and an accurate time. With some agencies, your log becomes a legal document and may be needed at some later time should an investigation occur. In this case, logs should be completed and turned in to the appropriate person for safekeeping and review.

What to Log

Log all incoming and outgoing messages. Record the name of the sender, addressee, the station that passed the message to you, the station to whom the message was sent, the message number, and the times in and out. Keep the written copy of each message in numerical order for future reference.

Also, log which operators are on duty for any given period, and record any significant events at your station. These might include changes in conditions, power failures, meals, new arrivals and departures, equipment failures, and so on.

In addition to the log, copies of all messages should be kept and catalogued for easy retrieval if needed later for clarification or message tracking. Many operators make notes about when the message was received and sent, and to and from whom, directly on the message form itself. This helps speed up tracking later on. Never rely on your memory.

Should informal messages be logged? This is usually up to the stations involved, and depends on the circumstances. Even informal messages can contain important details that may need to be recalled later. Emergency or Priority messages of any kind, even unwritten messages, should always be logged. Some net control operators like to log every message or exchange, no matter how inconsequential. Others like to log only those with potentially important details.

Log Formats

At a station with little traffic, all information can be included in one chronological log. However, if a large number of messages are being handled and you have a second person to handle logging, separate logs can make it faster and easier to locate information if it is needed later. You might keep one log for incoming messages, one for outgoing messages, and a third for station activities. The NCS will also need to keep a log of which operators are assigned to each station, and the times they go on and off duty.

Section 3: Message Handling
Topic 15: Basic Message Handling, Part II

Who Should Log

At the net level, logging can be handled in several ways. If activity is low, the net control operator can handle logging. In busy nets, a second person can keep the log as the net's "secretary" and act as a "second set of ears" for the NCS. The logger can be at the NCS, or they might be listening from a different location.

If an "alternate NCS" station has been appointed, they should keep a duplicate log. If they need to "take over" the net at any point, all the information will be at hand, preserving the continuity of the net.

In addition to logs kept at the net level, each individual operator should keep his or her own log. This will allow faster message tracking and provides duplicate information should one station's logs become lost or damaged.

In a fast moving tactical net, keeping a log while on the move may be impossible for individual stations. In this case, the net control station may decide to keep one log detailing the various informal messages passed on the network.

Logging is a good position for a trainee with limited experience, or an unlicensed volunteer. Two experienced and licensed operators can also alternate between on-air and logging duties to help combat fatigue.

Writing Hints and Techniques for Message Copying and Logging

Your logs should be clear and legible to be of any use. If only you can read your handwriting, the log will be of little value to the operator who takes the next shift or to the served agency as a legal document. Print in neat block letters on lined paper or a pre-printed log form. A firm writing surface with support for your forearm will reduce fatigue and improve legibility. Keep both pens and pencils on hand since each works better under different conditions. Logs that will become legal documents should always be written in permanent ink. Some operators prefer special "diver's" pens that will write on wet surfaces at any angle.

Logs should be kept in notebooks to prevent pages from becoming lost. In the case of pre-printed log sheets, use a three-ring binder. If more than one log is kept, each should be in its own notebook to prevent confusion and accidental entries. Logs that will become legal documents should be kept in hard-bound books with pre-numbered pages so that missing pages will be obvious.

In fast-moving situations, it can be difficult or impossible to keep a log of any kind. If a message, exchange, or event should be logged, try to do it as soon as possible afterwards, or ask the NCS to add it as a notation in his log. If there are enough operators to do so, one may be assigned the sole task of logging the net's operations, thus freeing up other net participants to handle messages more quickly.

Section 3: Message Handling
Topic 15: Basic Message Handling, Part II

Message Authoring – Them or Us?

One of the oldest arguments in emcomm is the question of whether or not emcomm personnel should author (create) agency-related official messages. If your job is strictly communication, and the message is not about the communication function you are providing, the best answer is "no." "Pure" communicators are not generally in a position to create messages on behalf of the served agency. They have no direct authority and usually lack necessary knowledge. However, you should always work with a message's author to create text that is clear, to the point, and uses the minimum number of words necessary. Once you do this with most agency personnel, they will be happy to send you appropriate messages, since it saves them time, too. If the author tells you to "just take care of the wording for me," it is still a good idea to get their final approval and signature before sending the message.

If you have additional training for an agency- specific job that involves message origination, this is quite different from the situation of a "pure" communicator. In this case, you may be able to generate an official message if you have been given the authority to do so.

Other messages that can and should be generated by all emcomm operators are those that deal solely with communication. Examples would be messages about net operations and frequencies, and requests for relief operators, radio equipment, supplies, food, and water for emcomm personnel.

Message Security & Privacy

Information transmitted over Amateur Radio can never be totally secure, since FCC rules strictly prohibit us from using any code designed to obscure a message's actual meaning. Anyone listening in with a scanner can hear all that is said on voice nets. The federal Communications Privacy Act does not protect Amateur Radio communications, and anything overheard may be legally revealed or discussed. Reporters in disaster-prone areas have been known to purchase digital-mode decoding software for laptops in order to intercept ham radio communications during disasters.

However, this does not mean that you can discuss any message you send with others. Messages sent via Amateur Radio should be treated as privileged information, and revealed only to those directly involved with sending, handling, or receiving the message. This must be done to offer at least a minimum level of message security. You cannot prevent anyone from listening on a scanner, but you can be sure they do not get the information directly from you.

Section 3: Message Handling
Topic 15: Basic Message Handling, Part II

Your served agency should be made aware of this issue, and must decide which types of messages can be sent via Amateur Radio, and using which modes. The American Red Cross has strict rules already in place. In general, any message with personally identifiable information about clients of the served agency should be avoided – this is a good policy to follow with any agency if you are in doubt. Messages relating to the death of any specific person should never be sent via Amateur Radio. Sensitive messages should be sent using telephone, landline fax, courier, or a secure served-agency radio or data circuit. While we can never guarantee that a message will not be overheard, there are ways to reduce the likelihood of casual listeners picking up your transmissions.

Here are some security ideas:

Use a digital mode: packet, PSK31, fax, RTTY, AMTOR, digital phone, etc. Pick an uncommon frequency – stay off regular packet nodes or simplex channels. Do not discuss frequencies or modes to be used openly on voice channels. Avoid publishing certain ARES or RACES net frequencies on web sites or in any public document. Some agencies use a system of "fill in the blank" data gathering forms with numbered lines. To save time on the radio, all that is sent is the line number and its contents. A casual listener might hear, "Line 1, 23; line 5, 20%; line 7, zero." The receiving station is just filling in the numbered lines on an identical form. Without the form, a casual listener will not have any real information. As long as encryption is not the primary intent, this practice should not violate FCC rules.

Informal Messages

When we send a written ARRL-format message, we do it to preserve accuracy no matter how many people pass the message along. Informal or "tactical" messages are not written out in ARRL format, or not written at all. However, this does not mean that accuracy is any less important. If someone gives you a short message to relay to someone else, you should repeat it as closely to the original as possible. Messages that will be relayed more than once should always be sent in ARRL format to prevent multiple modifications.

Here is an example of what might happen if you are not careful to maintain the precise meaning of the original message:

The original message: "The shelter manager says she needs fifty cots and blankets at Hartley Hill School by tonight." After being passed through several people: "He says they need a bunch more cots and blankets at that school on the hill."

Section 3: Message Handling
Topic 15: Basic Message Handling, Part II

Reference Links

Much more information on formal message handling and forms is available at:

http://www.arrl.org/files/file/Public%20Service/MPG104A.pdf

Section 3: Message Handling
Topic 15: Basic Message Handling, Part II

Review

In this unit you learned how to format, send, and receive a formal ARRL style message, and the importance of the signature, logging, and accuracy. Formal message formats make message handling more efficient and accurate. Not every situation requires a formal message, but where the accuracy of specific information is critical, the formal message is the best method.

Amateur Radio is not a secure mode, but you can take steps to protect messages. You should never discuss the contents of messages with anyone else. Officials of a served agency normally originate messages, but if you have additional training in a job for your served agency, you may also be authorized to originate messages. Whenever possible, you should work with a message's author to create a clear text using the minimum number of words necessary.

Activities

1. Create a formal ARRL style message using an ARL numbered radiogram text. Be sure the word count is correct. Provide an example to your mentor.

2. Volunteer, if possible, to receive traffic from the NTS and deliver it to the addressees. Describe your experience to your mentor.

3. Assume that you are helping a served agency staffer condense a lengthy message. Edit the following message text to reduce the number of words to a minimum, without losing any clarity. Provide your mentor with examples.

   "We need 50 additional cots and blankets at the Fudd School shelter, and we also need more food since 20 new people just arrived and we are told another 30 may be coming soon. Please call me and tell me when these supplies will arrive."

4. Go to the ARRL website and look up ARRL Numbered Radiograms: http://www.arrl.org/fsd-3-arrl-numbered-radiograms
   When you have located the list of Numbered Radiograms, answer the questions that follow and share the results with your mentor.
   Which of the Radiograms:

   A. Indicates that a medical emergency exists?
   B. Requests additional radio operators?
   C. Offers congratulations on a new baby?
   D. Offers greetings for a merry Christmas and happy New Year
   E. Indicates safe arrival.

Section 3: Message Handling
Topic 15: Basic Message Handling, Part II

Welcome to Topic 15 Knowledge Review

In order to demonstrate mastery of the information presented in the topic, you will be asked a series of un-graded questions. There are approximately 5 questions on the following pages in multiple-choice or true/false format. Feedback will be offered to you based on the answer you provide.

Question 1:

As part of an EMCOMM group handling message traffic in an emergency, you are asked to forward a message that contains typographical errors. Which of the following is your best course of action?

a) Delay sending the message.

b) Forward the message exactly as received.

c) Return the message to the originating station.

d) On your own, correct the error in the message and forward it.

Question 2:

As part of an Emcomm net handling message traffic in an emergency, you are asked to forward a message in a non-standard format. Which of the following is your best course of action?

a) Delay sending the message until you have conferred with the originator.

b) Return the message to the originator.

c) On your own, rewrite the message in proper format and forward it.

d) Forward the message exactly as received.

Question 3:

You have been asked to send an ARRL Radiogram dealing with birthday greetings. Which of the following is the correct way to write it in the message text?

a) ARRL 46.

b) ARL 46.

c) ARL FORTY SIX.

d) ARRL FORTY SIX.

Section 3: Message Handling
Topic 15: Basic Message Handling, Part II

Question 4:

When delivering an ARRL numbered radiogram, which should be done?

a) Deliver the message exactly as received.

b) Deliver the message exactly as received but add your own written explanation.

c) Decode the message into plain language before delivery.

d) Deliver the message exactly as received but add your own verbal explanation.

Question 5:

During an emergency, service messages should only be sent for which of the following categories of message?

a) Emergency, Priority, Welfare and Routine.

b) Emergency, Priority and Welfare.

c) Priority and Welfare.

d) Emergency and Priority. In answer key at end of book, B is indicated as the correct answer. Needs to be changed to D.

Section 4: What Happens When Called
Topic 16: The Incident Command System

TOPIC 16:

The Incident Command System

Objectives

Welcome to Topic 16.

Following completion of this Learning Topic, you will understand the Incident Command System (ICS) concept and the National Incident Management System (NIMS) and how they are used to coordinate and unify multiple agencies during emergencies.

Student Preparation required:

None.

Introduction

In the early 1970s, a disorganized and ineffective multi-agency response to a series of major wild fires in Southern California prompted municipal, county, state and federal fire authorities to form an organization known as Firefighting Resources of California Organized for Potential Emergencies (FIRESCOPE). California authorities had found that a lack of coordination and cooperation between the various responding agencies resulted in over-lapping efforts, and gaps in the overall response. Many specific problems involving multi-agency responses were identified by FIRESCOPE. These included poor overall organization, ineffective communication between agencies, lack of accountability, and the lack of a single, universal, and well-defined command structure.

Their efforts to address these difficulties resulted in the development of the original Incident Command System. Although developed for wild fires, the system ultimately evolved into an "all-risk" system, appropriate for all types of fire and non-fire emergencies.

There are other versions of the ICS in use, but the Incident Command System (ICS), as developed by the National Fire Academy (NFA), has been widely recognized as a model tool for the command, control, and coordination of resources and personnel at the scene of an emergency and is used by most fire, police, and other agencies around the country. The use of the ICS is now required by various federal laws for all hazardous material incidents, and in other situations by many state and local laws. The ICS has also been adopted for use in many other countries.

Looking at a larger scale, the success of the ICS also led to development of protocols that would guide whole regions of the country, including non-government responders. This became NIMS – the National Incident Management System.

Section 4: What Happens When Called
Topic 16: The Incident Command System

NIMS

The National Incident Management System (NIMS) provides a systematic, proactive approach to guide departments and agencies at all levels of government, nongovernmental organizations, and the private sector to work seamlessly to prevent, protect against, respond to, recover from, and mitigate the effects of incidents, regardless of cause, size, location, or complexity, in order to reduce the loss of life and property and harm to the environment.

NIMS works hand in hand with the National Response Framework (NRF). NIMS provides the template for the management of incidents, while the NRF provides the structure and mechanisms for national-level policy for incident management.

What is the ICS?

The Incident Command System is a management tool designed to bring multiple responding agencies, including those from different jurisdictions, together under a single overall command structure. Before the use of the ICS became commonplace, various agencies responding to a disaster often fought for control, duplicated efforts, missed critical needs, and generally reduced the potential effectiveness of the response. Under ICS, each agency recognizes one "lead" coordinating agency and that person will handle one or more tasks that are part of a single overall plan, and interact with other agencies in defined ways.

The Incident Command System is based upon simple and proven business management principles. In a business or government agency, managers and leaders perform the basic daily tasks of planning, directing, organizing, coordinating, communicating, delegating and evaluating. The same is true for the Incident Command System, but the responsibilities are often shared among several agencies. These tasks, or functional areas as they are known in the ICS, are performed under the overall direction of a single Incident Commander (IC) in a coordinated manner, even with multiple agencies and across jurisdictional lines. The ICS also features common terminology, scalability of structure and clear lines of authority.

What the ICS is Not

Many people who have not studied the full details of the Incident Command System have a variety of erroneous perceptions about what the system means to them and their agencies. To set the record straight, the Incident Command System is not:

- A fixed and unchangeable system for managing an incident.

- A means to take control or authority away from agencies or departments that participate in the response.

- A way to subvert the normal chain of command within a department or agency.

- Always managed by the fire department or the first agency to arrive on-scene.

- Too big and cumbersome to be used in small, everyday events.

Section 4: What Happens When Called
Topic 16: The Incident Command System

- Restricted to use by government agencies and departments.

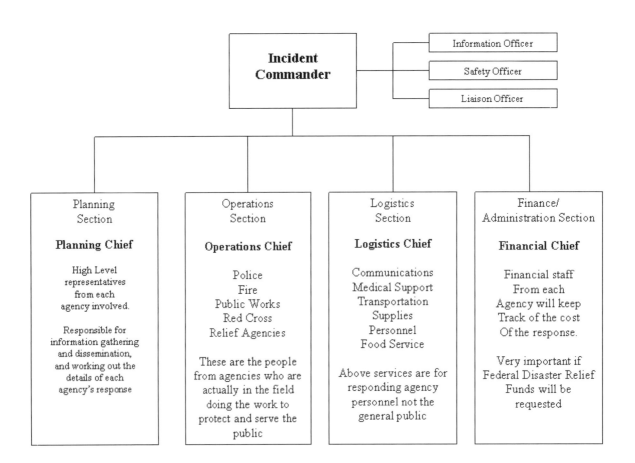

The ICS Structure

The Incident Command System has two interrelated parts. They are "**management by objectives**," and the "**organizational structure**."

Management by objectives:

Four essential steps are used in developing the response to every incident, regardless of size or complexity:

- Understand the policies, procedures and statutes that affect the official response.

- Establish incident objectives (the desired outcome of the agencies' efforts).

- Select appropriate strategies for cooperation and resource utilization.

- Apply tactics most likely to accomplish objectives (assign the correct resources and

Section 4: What Happens When Called
Topic 16: The Incident Command System

onitor the results).

The complexity of the incident will determine how formally the "management by objectives" portion will be handled. If the incident is small and uncomplicated, the process can be handled by oral communication between appropriate people. As the incident and response become more complex, differences between the individual agencies' or departments' goals, objectives, and methods will need to be resolved in writing.

The ICS Structure: Organizational Structure

The ICS supports the creation of a flexible organizational structure that can be modified to meet changing conditions. Under the ICS, the one person in charge is always called the "Incident Commander" (IC). In large responses, the IC may have a "Command Staff" consisting of the Information, Safety and Liaison Officers. In a smaller incident, the IC may also handle one, two or all three of these positions, if they are needed at all.

Various other tasks within the ICS are subdivided into four major operating sections: Planning, Operations, Logistics and Finance/ Administration. Each operating section has its own "chief," and may have various branches or units working on specific goals. The Logistics section handles the coordination of all interagency communication infrastructures involved in the response, including Amateur Radio when it is used in that capacity.

These operating sections may be scaled up or down, depending on the needs of the situation. In a small, single agency response, the IC may handle many or all functions. As the size and complexity of a response increase, and as other agencies become involved, the various tasks can be re-assigned and sub-divided. For instance, if the only responding agency is the fire department, communications will be handled according to existing department policies. If the incident expands, more agencies become involved, and other communication assets are required, a Logistics Chief may handle communication decisions along with other tasks, or assign the job to a "communication unit leader" directly or through a service branch director as his own workload increases.

The Incident Commander

The initial IC is usually the most senior on- scene officer from the first responding agency. The IC is responsible for the management of the incident and starts the process by helping to set initial incident objectives, followed by an "Incident Action Plan" (IAP). In a small incident, the IC may perform all the ICS functions without aid, but in a larger incident, he or she will usually delegate responsibilities to others. The IC still has overall responsibility for the incident, regardless of any duties delegated.

The persons filling certain ICS positions may change several times during an incident as the needs of the response change. For instance, in the early stages of a hazardous materials spill, the Incident Commander may be a fire department officer. As the Coast Guard or other federal agency arrives to begin cleanup efforts, one of their officers will become the Incident Commander.

Section 4: What Happens When Called
Topic 16: The Incident Command System

How Does an Emcomm Group "Fit Into" The ICS?

Involvement in any incident where ICS is used is by "invitation only"—there is no role for off-the-street volunteers. The relationship of an emcomm group to the ICS structure will vary with the specific situation. If your group is providing internal communication support to only one responding agency, and has no need to communicate with other agencies that are part of the ICS, you may not have any part in the ICS structure itself except through your served agency. If your group is tasked with handling inter-agency communications, or serves more than one agency's internal communication needs, it is likely your group will have a representative on the Logistics Section's "communication unit." In certain situations, an emcomm group might serve one or more agencies simultaneously. As the responsibility for managing the incident shifts from one agency to another, the emcomm group's mission may shift to assisting the new lead agency, or simply end. In some cases, your group might begin by supporting your own served agency, and end up supporting a new and unfamiliar agency. The choice of whether to use your emcomm group's services may be made by the served agency, Communication Unit Leader, Service Branch Director, Logistics Chief, or Incident Commander, depending on the specific situation and the degree of ICS structure in use.

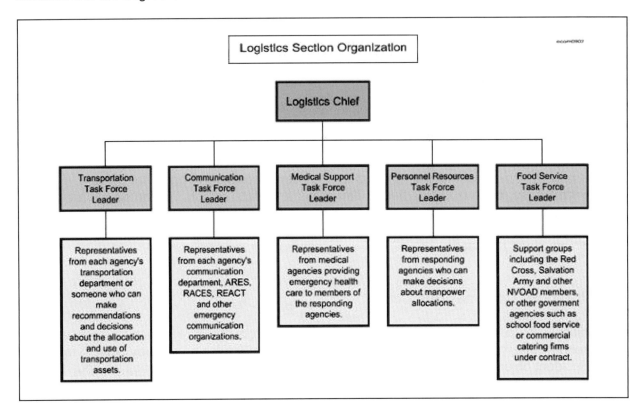

Section 4: What Happens When Called
Topic 16: The Incident Command System

Reference Links

Incident Command System courses can be found at:

http://www.fema.gov/emergency/nims/NIMSTrainingCourses.shtm

NIMS information can be found at:

http://www.fema.gov/emergency/nims/AboutNIMS.shtm

And http://www.fema.gov/pdf/emergency/nims/NIMS_core.pdf

Information about the National Response Framework can be found at:

http://www.fema.gov/pdf/emergency/nrf/nrf-core.pdf

Section 4: What Happens When Called
Topic 16: The Incident Command System

Review

The ICS is a management tool that preserves the command structure of each responding agency, while bringing them all together under a common plan and leader. Emcomm groups often operate as part of the Logistics section of the ICS. If the emcomm group serves the internal communication needs of only one agency, it may not be a formal part of the ICS structure.

Activities

1. Contact a leader of your local emcomm group. Ask the leader:

    A. If the emcomm group is affiliated with a specific agency.

    B. If there is a local, planned ICS structure and if so, how the emcomm group fits into the local ICS structure.

    C. Ask the leader if the emcomm group has ever been activated. If so, what were the lessons learned from operating with local agencies?

2. Suppose that during an emergency activation, you find yourself to be the leader of the local emcomm group. To which agency would you report? To whom within the agency would you report? What would your duties be as leader of the emcomm group?

Share answers to both activities with your mentor.

Section 4: What Happens When Called
Topic 16: The Incident Command System

Welcome to Topic 16 Knowledge Review

In order to demonstrate mastery of the information presented in the topic, you will be asked a series of un-graded questions. There are approximately 5 questions on the following pages in multiple-choice or true/false format. Feedback will be offered to you based on the answer you provide.

Question 1:

What do the letters "ICS" stand for?

a) International Correspondence School.

b) Incident Command System.

c) Institutional Control System.

d) Internal Control Sequence.

Question 2:

What is ICS?

a) A management tool for coordinating the resources of several agencies within a single command structure.

b) A fixed and unchangeable system for managing an incident.

c) A means of subverting the normal command structure within an agency or department.

d) A management system restricted to use by government agencies and departments.

Question 3:

The ICS has two interrelated parts. What are they?

a) A mission statement and management objectives.

b) Management by objectives and organizational structure.

c) Organizational structure and a financial plan.

d) A financial plan and an operational plan.

Section 4: What Happens When Called
Topic 16: The Incident Command System

Question 4:

Aside from the Incident Commander, there are four other major operating sections within an ICS. What are they?

a) Planning, Operations, Logistics and Public Relations.

b) Personnel, Planning, Operations and Finance/Administration.

c) Planning, Operations, Logistics, and Finance/Administration.

d) Payroll, Finance/Administration, Logistics and Operations.

Question 5:

What is an emcomm group's relationship to the ICS structure during an incident?

a) The emcomm group always serves within the Logistics area.

b) The emcomm group may or may not be a formal part of the ICS structure.

c) The emcomm group always serves the Task Force leader directly.

d) The emcomm group always serves the Incident Commander directly.

Section 4: What Happens When Called
Topic 17: Preparing for Deployment

TOPIC 17:

Preparing for Deployment

Objectives

Welcome to Topic 17.

In this Lesson Topic you will learn about the steps an emcomm volunteer should take to be ready to respond quickly, and be fully prepared to handle their emcomm assignment.

Student Preparation required:

None.

Prepared for What?

Remember the Boy Scout motto, "Be Prepared"? Nearly one hundred years ago, a young British Boy Scout asked Sir Robert Baden- Powell, the founder of Scouting, what exactly it was he should be prepared for. B-Ps famous answer was, "Why, for any old thing, of course!"

The same should be true of emcomm volunteers. You never know which challenges an emergency situation will offer. You might have ac power, or just the batteries you bring along. Safe drinking water may be available, or you may have only your canteen. Sometimes you can find out in advance what sort of conditions are likely for your assignment, but many times no one will know— particularly during the early stages of an emergency.

Being prepared for an emergency communication deployment involves a wide range of considerations, including radio equipment, power sources, clothing and personal gear, food and water, information, and specialized training. No two deployments are the same, and each region offers its own specific challenges. What is appropriate for rural Minnesota in January probably won't work for urban southern California in any season.

Jump Kits

The last thing you should need to do when a call for assistance comes is think of and locate all the items you might need. Any experienced emergency responder knows how important it is to keep a kit of the items they need ready to go at a moment's notice. This is often called a "jump kit" or "go kit." Without a jump kit, you will almost certainly leave something important at home, or bring items that will not do the job. Gathering and packing your equipment at the last moment also wastes precious time. It is important to think through each probable deployment ahead of time, and the range of situations you might encounter.

Section 4: What Happens When Called
Topic 17: Preparing for Deployment

Here are a few basic questions you will need to answer:

- Which networks will you need to join, and which equipment will you need to do so?
- Will you need to be able to relocate quickly, or can you bring a ton of gear?
- Will you be on foot, or near your vehicle?
- Is your assignment at a fixed location or will you be mobile?
- How long might you be deployed—less than 48 hours, or even a week or more?
- Will you be in a building with reliable power and working toilets, or in a tent away from civilization?
- What sort of weather or other conditions might be encountered?
- Where will food and water come from?
- Are sanitary facilities available?
- Will there be a place to sleep?
- Do you need to plan for a wide variety of possible scenarios, or only a few?
- Can some items do "double duty" to save space and weight?

Other questions may occur to you based on your own experience. If you are new to emcomm or the area, consult with other members of your group for their suggestions.

Most people seem to divide jump kits into two categories: one for deployments under 24 hours, and one for up to 72 hours. For deployments longer than 72 hours, many people will just add more of the items that they will use up, such as clothing, food, water and batteries. Others may add a greater range of communication options and backup equipment as well.

Jump Kit Idea List

- Something to put it in—one or more backpacks, suitcases, plastic storage tubs, etc.
- Package individual items in zip-lock bags or plastic kitchen containers

Section 4: What Happens When Called
Topic 17: Preparing for Deployment

Radios and Accessories:

- Hand-held VHF or dual-band radio (some people also like to bring a spare)
- Spare rechargeable batteries for handhelds
- Alkaline battery pack for handhelds
- Alkaline batteries
- Speaker-mic and earphone for handhelds
- Battery chargers, ac and dc for handhelds
- Mobile VHF or dual-band radio
- HF radio
- Multi-band HF antenna, tuner, heavy parachute cord or nylon mason's twine
- VHF/UHF gain antennas and adapters (roll-up J-Pole, mobile magnetic mount, etc)
- Coaxial feed lines, jumpers
- Ground rod, pipe clamp and wire
- Ac power supplies for VHF/UHF mobile and HF radios, accessories
- Large battery source for VHF/UHF mobile and HF radios, with charger
- All related power, data, audio and RF cables and adapters
- Small repair kit: hand tools, multi-meter, connectors, adapters, fuses, key parts
- Materials for improvisation: wire, connectors, small parts, insulators, duct tape, etc.
- Photocopies of manuals for all equipment
- Headphones, for noisy areas and privacy with proper connector, adaptors
- Specialized gear for packet, ATV or other modes
- Multi-band scanner, weather radio
- Personal cell phone, pager, spare batteries and chargers
- Pencils, legal pads, pencil sharpener

Personal Gear:

- Clothing for the season, weather, and length of deployment
- Toilet kit: soap, razor, deodorant, comb, toilet paper
- Foul-weather or protective gear, warm coats, hats, etc. as needed
- Sleeping bag, closed-cell foam pad, pillow, earplugs
- High-energy snacks
- Easily prepared dried foods that will store for long periods
- Eating and cooking equipment if needed
- Water containers, filled before departure
- First aid kit, personal medications and prescriptions for up to one week
- Money, including a large quantity of quarters for vending machines, tolls, etc.
- Telephone calling card

Information:

- ID cards and other authorizations
- Copy of Amateur Radio license
- Frequency lists and net schedules
- Maps, both street and topographic
- Key phone numbers, e-mail and Internet addresses
- Contact information for other members in your group, EC, DEC, SEC and others

Section 4: What Happens When Called
Topic 17: Preparing for Deployment

- Copy of emergency plans
- Resource lists: who to call for which kinds of problems
- Log sheets, message forms
- Operating Supplies
- Preprinted message forms
- Log sheets or books
- Standard forms used by the served agency
- Letter or legal size notepads
- Sticky notes
- Paper clips and rubber bands
- Blank envelopes
- Stapler, spare staples

Sub-Dividing Your Kits

You may want to divide your jump kit into smaller packages. Here are some ideas:

- Quick deployment kit: hand-held radio kit, personal essentials, in a large daypack
- VHF/UHF, HF kits for fixed locations
- Accessory and tool kit
- Emergency power kit
- Short and long term personal kits in duffel bags
- Field kitchen and food box in plastic storage tubs
- Field shelter kit (tents, tarps, tables, chairs, battery/gas lights) in plastic storage tubs

You may not want to pre-pack some items for reasons of expense or shelf life. Keep a checklist of these items in your jump kit so that you will remember to add them at the last minute.

Section 4: What Happens When Called
Topic 17: Preparing for Deployment

Pre-Planning

When the time comes, you need to know where to go, and what to do. Having this information readily available will help you respond more quickly and effectively. It will not always be possible to know these things in advance, particularly if you do not have a specific assignment. **Answering the following basic questions may help**.

- Which frequency should you check in on initially?
- Is there a "backup" frequency?
- If a repeater is out of service, which simplex frequency is used for the net?
- Which nets will be activated first?
- Should you report to a pre-determined location or will your assignment be made as needed?

Learn about any place to which you may be deployed to familiarize yourself with its resources, requirements and limitations. For instance, if you are assigned to a particular shelter, you might ask your emcomm superiors to schedule a visit, or talk to others who are familiar with the site.

- Will you need a long antenna cable to get from your operating position to the roof?
- Are antennas or cables permanently installed, or will you need to bring your own?
- Will you be in one room with everyone else, or in a separate room?
- Is there dependable emergency power to circuits at possible operating positions?
- Does the building have an independent and dependable water supply?
- Is there good cell phone or beeper coverage inside the building?
- Can you reach local repeaters reliably with only a rubber duck antenna,
- or do you need a more efficient antenna or one with gain?
- If the repeaters are out of service, how far can you reach on a simplex channel?
- Will you need an HF radio to reach the net?

If you will be assigned to an EOC, school, hospital or other facility with its own radio system in place, learn under what conditions you will be required or able to use it, where it is and how it works. In addition to radios, consider copiers, computers, fax machines, phone systems and other potentially useful equipment.

Consider escape routes. If you could be in the path of a storm surge or other dangerous condition, know all the possible routes out of the area. If you will be stationed in a large building such as a school or hospital, find the fire exits, and learn which parking areas will be the safest for your vehicle.

Section 4: What Happens When Called
Topic 17: Preparing for Deployment

Training & Education

If the served agency offers emcomm volunteers job-specific training in areas related to communication, take it. Your emcomm managers should help you to learn how the served agency's organization works. Learn their needs and how you can best meet them. Work within your own emcomm organization to get any additional training or information you might need. For instance, the American Red Cross offers self-study or classroom courses in mass care, damage assessment and other areas that either directly involve or depend upon effective communication. Many emergency management agencies offer additional training in areas such as radiological monitoring, sheltering, mass casualty response and evacuation. The Federal Emergency Management Agency's Emergency Management Institute offers a wide range of courses, some of which may be related to your agency's mission.

Your own group may offer general or agency- specific training in message handling and net operations under emergency conditions. If your group has its own equipment, it should offer opportunities for members to become familiar with its setup and operation in the field. On your own, set up and test your personal equipment under field conditions to be sure it works as expected.

Participate in any drills or exercises offered in your area. Some are designed to introduce or test specific skills or systems, others to test the entire response. ARRL's Field Day and Simulated Emergency Test are two good nation-wide examples, but local organizations may have their own as well.

Section 4: What Happens When Called
Topic 17: Preparing for Deployment

Reference Links

Federal Emergency Management Agency:

http://www.fema.gov/emergency/nims/NIMSTrainingCourses.shtm

More about preparation can be found in the ARES Field Resources Manual

http://www.arrl.org/ares-field-resources-manual

Section 4: What Happens When Called
Topic 17: Preparing for Deployment

Review

Pre-planning and physical preparation are essential to an effective and timely emergency response. Know in advance where you are going, and what you will do when you get there. Keep a stocked and updated "jump kit" ready to go at a moment's notice. Be sure your kit is adequate for the types of deployments you are most likely to encounter. Information is as important as equipment. Keep updated lists of other volunteers and contact information, frequencies, and other resources on hand as well as copies of all emcomm pre-plans.

Activities

1. Make a list of items suitable for a jump kit for your area and assignment. Share this list with your mentor

2. Share with your mentor a list of contacts and resources to keep in your jump kit.

3. Using the list you created above, put together a basic jump kit. It need not be complete, as you will be updating the kit in time.

Optional Activities

1. Go to the FEMA Emergency Management Institute website. (See Reference links.) List five offerings from the Emergency Management Institute that you feel might be useful to emergency volunteers in your area.

Section 4: What Happens When Called
Topic 17: Preparing for Deployment

Welcome to Topic 17 Knowledge Review

In order to demonstrate mastery of the information presented in the topic, you will be asked a series of un-graded questions. There are approximately 5 questions on the following pages in multiple-choice or true/false format. Feedback will be offered to you based on the answer you provide.

Question 1:

Of the following, which is the *best* reason for preparing a jump kit in advance?

a) You will not leave something important at home or waste valuable time.

b) You are spared the added expense of shopping for something after an emergency arises.

c) You can be fully rested on the day of the emergency.

d) You can test the batteries on your hand-held VHF before leaving home.

Question 2:

Which of the following would you omit from a jump kit prepared for a 12-hour deployment?

a) Hand-held VHF or dual-band radio.

b) Spare batteries for the hand-held radio.

c) High energy snacks.

d) Camp cot and tent.

Question 3:

Among the following, which are the most important items of information to include in your jump kit?

a) ID cards and other authorizations.

b) Field cookbook.

c) Automobile repair manual.

d) Instruction book for your chain saw.

Section 4: What Happens When Called
Topic 17: Preparing for Deployment

Question 4:

Among the following, which is the least important item of personal gear to include in your jump kit?

a) Frequency lists and net schedules.

b) Contact information for other members of your group, EC, DEC, and SEC.

c) Key phone numbers, email and Internet addresses.

d) A deck of playing cards.

Question 5:

If you are assigned in advance to a particular location for emcomm operations, what is the *least* important thing to know in advance?

a) The escape routes from the facility itself.

b) The regular business hours maintained at the facility.

c) The availability of radio equipment at the facility.

d) The location of your operating position and the planned location of the antenna.

Section 4: What Happens When Called
Topic 18: Equipment Choices for Emergency Communication

TOPIC 18:

Equipment Choices for Emergency Communication

Objectives

Welcome to Topic 18.

There is no one "best" set of equipment that will ensure success for every assignment, but the principles outlined in this Learning Topic will help you make intelligent choices.

Student Preparation required:

None.

ARRL – ARES® Branded Apparel Standard

There are many articles of ARES branded clothing on the market. Some is from ARRL itself, but much more is from other manufacturers and sellers with the ARES logo added.

HOWEVER…When on actual deployments, there is a great need for a uniformed look to ARES volunteers. Other organizations have instituted standards for volunteers that provide identity, support public relations and comply with new emcomm standards (the American Red Cross is an excellent example of this). ARES people, however, continue to appear in all sorts of garb, are not easily recognized, and may fail to meet the increasing clothing and ID requirements of NIMS applications.

Section 4: What Happens When Called
Topic 18: Equipment Choices for Emergency Communication

This recommended standard (specifics in following pages) does not affect or change the availability or marketing of ARES branded clothing in non-deployed uses. It refers only to periods when ARES volunteer personnel are deployed for public service or emergency response situations. The result is easier identification, better recognition of the services that ARES performs by and for the public, more professional and peer acceptance, and an esprit de corps across ARES groups that surpass localized identities.

Apparel: The Specifics

Garment colors

Safety Green (many people call it yellow) with silver reflective tape that meets ANSI Class 2 standards.

Garment Types

3 types to accommodate climate conditions:

1. Tee shirts - long and short sleeve, 50/50 cotton/poly.
2. Vests - Velcro or zip front, break away, 100% polyester, solid or mesh.
3. Jacket or coat

Apparel: The Specifics: The Back

All garments shall be imprinted on the back with 2 inch tall Arial Black font, black in color, three lines, center justified:

AMATEUR RADIO

EMERGENCY

COMMUNICATIONS

If the size of the vest does not allow for that size font, the next closest Arial Black font size that fits should be used.

Those in a leadership position may add their title (SEC, DIRECTOR, EC, PIO, etc) below Emergency Communications in not less than 3" tall Serpentine font, black.

Apparel: The Specifics: The Front

Front left chest shall be imprinted with the ARES logo, no less than 3.5", and black in color. If the vest size is such that it does not allow room for that size logo, the closest size to it that fits there shall be used.

Section 4: What Happens When Called
Topic 18: Equipment Choices for Emergency Communication

The right chest area of the garment shall be left blank to allow wearer to affix their name/call badge or official ID badge.

Apparel: The Specifics: Adding Organizational Names

Local jurisdictions may elect to add their organization name in the either or both of two places:

1. On the front below the ARES logo, Arial Black, black color, in not larger than 1/2" lettering.

2. On the back by adding their organization name (such as SUSSEX COUNTY, DELAWARE ARES) above Amateur Radio Emergency Communications with no larger than 1" Arial Black lettering, color black.

Apparel: The Specifics: Implementation

A three year period has been given for the attrition of deployment clothing purchased before these standards were recommended. Over these years older deployment clothing should be replaced by clothing meeting the standards above.

Beginning January 1, 2013, ARES volunteers in deployments, both emergency and community service related, will be encouraged to wear outermost garments meeting these standards.

Clubs and other groups are encouraged to make group buys through ARRL which may provide discounts for such purchases for ARRL affiliated clubs and groups. Garments available through the ARRL store are described at http://www.arrl.org/shop/Emergency-Communications/.

ARES members who may note merchants still selling ARES deployment clothing (intended for outerwear while on actual deployment) not meeting these standards are requested to politely inform the merchant of the new standards.

Transceivers: VHF/UHF

The most universal choice for emcomm is a dual band FM 35-50 watt mobile transceiver. Radios in this class are usually rugged and reliable, and can operate at reasonably high duty cycles, although an external cooling fan is always a good idea if one is not built-in. Handheld transceivers should be used only when extreme portability is needed, such as when "shadowing" an official or when adequate battery or other dc power is not available. Handheld radios should not be relied upon to operate with a high duty-cycle at maximum power, since they can overheat and fail.

Both portable and mobile dual-band radios can be used to monitor more than one net, and some models allow simultaneous reception on more than one frequency on the same band (Sometimes known as "dual watch" capability). Some mobiles have separate external speaker outputs for each band. For high traffic locations, such as a Net Control or Emergency

Section 4: What Happens When Called
Topic 18: Equipment Choices for Emergency Communication

Operations Center, a separate radio for each net is a better choice since it allows both to be used simultaneously by different operators. (Antennas must be adequately separated to avoid "de-sensing.")

Many dual-band transceivers also offer a "cross-band repeater" function, useful for linking local portables with distant repeaters, or as a quickly deployable hilltop repeater. True repeater operation is only possible if all other mobile and portable stations have true dual-band radios. Some so-called "dual" or "twin" band radios do not allow simultaneous or cross-band operation—read the specifications carefully before you purchase one.

Transceivers: HF

Operation from a generator equipped Emergency Operations Center can be done with an ac powered radio, but having both ac and dc capability ensures the ability to operate under all conditions. Most 12 Volt HF radios fall in either the 100-watt or QRP (less than 5 watts) categories. Unless power consumption is extremely important, 100-watt variable output radios should be used. This gives you the ability to overcome noise at the receiving station by using high power, or to turn it down to conserve battery power when necessary.

Do not use dc to ac inverters to power HF radios. Most use a high-frequency conversion process that generates significant broad-spectrum RF noise at HF frequencies that is difficult to suppress. Direct dc powering is more efficient in any case.

Voltage Tolerance and Current Drain

Some transceivers nominally powered using 12 volts DC actually have a rather narrow range of voltage (e.g., 13.0 to 13.8 volts) over which they will operate properly, and even a high-quality battery part way through its discharge cycle can easily fall below such a tolerable range. Transceivers with a wide range of acceptable input voltages (e.g., 11.5 to 15 volts) are preferable in limited-power situations; they will keep operating as the external battery discharges.

Similarly, some transceivers draw much more power than others during receive. If your chosen rig has a current drain on the high side, look for menu settings that will lower the overall drain, especially if you will be operating from a limited power source.

Radio Receiver Performance

For radios on all bands, several aspects of a radio receiver's performance can affect its suitability for emcomm. These include sensitivity (ability to receive weak signals), selectivity (ability to reject signals on adjacent frequencies) and intermodulation rejection (ability to prevent undesired signals from mixing within the receiver and causing interference). If you are inexperienced at comparing radio specifications, be sure to ask for guidance from another, more experienced, ham. An in-depth discussion of radio performance specifications is beyond the scope of this learning topic.

Section 4: What Happens When Called
Topic 18: Equipment Choices for Emergency Communication

When operating near public service and business radio transmitters, an FM receiver's "intermodulation rejection" is important. Mobile radios generally have better intermodulation rejection than handheld radios, but you should review each individual radio's specifications. External intermodulation (band pass) filters are available, but they add to the expense, complexity, size and weight of the equipment. Bandpass filters will also prevent you from using a broadband radio to monitor public service frequencies. Some older "ham bands only" FM mobile radios have better front-end filtering than newer radios with broadband receive capability, making them more immune to intermodulation and adjacent channel interference. Receiver filters are important for effective HF operation. Choose appropriate filters for the types of operations you are most likely to use, including CW, RTTY and phone.

Digital Signal Processing (DSP) may be the single most important filtering feature available. Internal or external DSP circuits can allow clear reception of signals that might not otherwise be possible in situations with heavy interference.

"Noise blankers" are used to reduce impulse noise from arcing power lines, vehicle and generator ignition systems, and various other sources. While most all HF radios have some form of noise blanker, some work better than others. Test your radio in suitably noisy environments before designating it for emcomm use.

Please read the article below for more information regarding ARRL Product Reviews:

> Find *QST Product Reviews, In Depth, In English* in the Appendix to this course transcript.

Antennas

VHF/UHF:

A good antenna, mounted as high as possible without incurring large feedline losses, is more important than high transmitter power. Not only does it provide gain to both the transmitter and receiver, but a higher gain antenna may also allow output power to be reduced, thus prolonging battery life. In relatively flat terrain, use a mast-mounted single or dual- band antenna with at least 3dBd gain. If you are operating in a valley, the low angle of radiation offered by a gain antenna may actually make it difficult to get a signal out of the valley. Low or "unity" gain antennas have "fatter" radiation lobes and are better suited for this purpose. Unity gain J-poles are rugged, inexpensive and easily built. For directional 2-meter coverage with about 7-dBd gain, a three or four element Yagi can be used. Collapsible and compact antennas of this type are readily available. For permanent base station installations, consider a more rugged commercial 2-way collinear antenna, such as the well-known "Stationmaster" series. Most 2-meter versions will also perform well on 70cm. Commercial open dipole array antennas will work well for a single band, and are more rugged than a fiberglass radome encased collinear antenna.

A magnetic mount mobile antenna is useful for operating in someone else's vehicle. They can also be used indoors by sticking them to any steel surface, such as filing cabinets, beams or ductwork, even up-side down.

Hand-held radio antennas, known as "rubber duckies," have negative gain. Use at least a 1/4

Section 4: What Happens When Called
Topic 18: Equipment Choices for Emergency Communication

wave flexible antenna for most operations, and consider a telescoping 5/8-wave antenna for long- range use in open areas where the extra length and lack of flexibility will not be a problem. "Roll-up J-pole" antennas made from 300 ohm television twin-lead wire can be tacked up on a wall or hoisted into a tree with heavy-duty string. In addition to unity gain, the extra height can make a big difference. Even a mobile 1/2 wave magnetic mount antenna can be used with hand-helds when necessary.

HF: There is no single perfect antenna for HF operation. Your choice depends on the size and terrain of the area you need to cover, and the conditions under which you must install and use it.

For local operations (up to a few hundred miles), a simple random wire or dipole hung at a less than ¼ wavelength above the ground works well and is easy to deploy. This is known as a "Near Vertical Incidence Skywave" (NVIS) antenna. The signal is radiated almost straight up and then bounces off the ionosphere directly back downward. During periods of high solar activity, NVIS propagation works best on 40 meters during the day, switching to 80 meters around sunset. During low parts of the sunspot cycle, 80 meters may be the most usable daytime NVIS band, and 160 meters may be needed at night. The new 60-meter band is also ideal for NVIS operation.

An antenna tuner is necessary for most portable wire antennas, (especially for NVIS antennas), and is a good idea for any HF antenna. The antenna's impedance will vary with its height above ground and proximity to nearby objects, which can be a real problem with expedient installations. An automatic tuner is desirable, since it is faster and easier to use, and many modern radios have one built in. Include a ground rod, clamps and cable in your kit since almost all radios and tuners require a proper ground in order to work efficiently.

For communication beyond 200 miles, a commercial trapped vertical may work, although it has no ability to reject interfering signals from other directions. Mobile whip antennas will also work, but with greatly reduced efficiency. The benefits of a mobile antenna are its size and durability.

Directional (beam) antennas offer the best performance for very wide area nets on 10 to 20 meters, since they maximize desired signals and reduce interference from stations in other directions. This ability may be critical in poor conditions. Beam antennas also have a number of limitations that should be considered. They are usually expensive, large, and difficult to store and transport. In field installations, they can be difficult to erect at the optimum height, and may not survive storm conditions. One strategy is to rely on easily installed and repaired wire dipole antennas until conditions allow the safe installation of beam antennas.

Feedlines: Feedlines used at VHF and UHF should be low-loss foam dielectric coaxial cable. For short runs of 30 feet or less, RG-58 may be suitable. For longer runs consider RG-8X or RG-213. RG-8X is an "in-between" size that offers less loss and greater power handling capability than RG-58 with far less bulk than RG-213. If you wish to carry only one type of cable, RG-8X is the best choice.

On HF, the choice between coaxial cable and commercial (insulated—not bare wire) "ladder" line will depend on your situation. Ladder line offers somewhat lower loss but more care must be taken in its routing, especially in proximity to metal objects, or where people might touch it. Coaxial cable is much less susceptible to problems induced by routing near metal objects or other cables.

Section 4: What Happens When Called
Topic 18: Equipment Choices for Emergency Communication

Operating Accessories

Headphones are useful anywhere, and are mandatory in many locations. Operators in an Emergency Operations Center or a Command Post where multiple radios are in use must use headsets. They are also beneficial in locations such as Red Cross shelters, to avoid disturbing residents and other volunteers trying to get some rest.

Some radios and accessory headsets provide a VOX (voice operated transmit) capability. During emcomm operations this should always be turned off and manual "push-to-talk" buttons used instead. Accidental transmissions caused by background noise and conversations can interrupt critical communications on the net. As an alternative to VOX, consider using a desk or boom microphone and foot switch to key the transmitter. A microphone/headset combination and foot switch also works well.

Batteries

Battery power is critical for emcomm operations. Ac power cannot usually be relied upon for any purpose, and portable operation for extended periods is common. Batteries must be chosen to match the maximum load of the equipment, and the length of time that operation must continue before they can be recharged.

NiCad, NiMH and Li-Ion: For handheld transceivers, the internal battery type is determined by the manufacturer. NiMH batteries store somewhat more energy than NiCad batteries for their size. Many smaller radios are using Lithium Ion (LIon) batteries, which have much higher power densities, without the so-called "memory effect" of NiCads. Many handhelds have optional AA alkaline battery cases, and are recommended emcomm accessories. Common alkaline batteries have a somewhat higher power density than NiCad batteries, are readily available in most stores and may be all you have if you cannot recharge your other batteries. Most handheld radios will accept an external 13.8Vdc power connection for cigarette lighter or external battery use.

External batteries of any type can be used with a handheld, as long as the voltage and polarity are observed. Small 12-15 volt gel cells and some battery packs intended for power tools and camcorders are all possibilities. For maximum flexibility, build a dc power cable for each of your radios, with suitable adapters for each battery type you might use. Molex plugs work well for power connections, but Anderson power poles can withstand repeated plugging and unplugging without deterioration and have become the standard used by most ARES units. This standardization allows easier swapping and sharing of equipment if needed.

Lead Acid

There are three common types of lead-acid batteries: flooded (wet), VRLA (Valve Regulated Lead Acid), and SLA (Sealed Lead- Acid). Wet batteries can spill if tipped, but VRLA batteries use a gelled electrolyte or absorptive fiberglass mat (AGM technology) and cannot spill. SLA batteries are similar to VRLA batteries, but can be operated in any position—even up-side down. All lead-acid batteries are quite heavy.

Section 4: What Happens When Called
Topic 18: Equipment Choices for Emergency Communication

Lead acid batteries are designed for a variety of applications. "Deep-cycle" batteries are a better choice than common automotive (cranking) batteries, which are not designed to provide consistent power for prolonged periods, and will be damaged if allowed to drop below approximately 80% of their rated voltage. Deep cycle batteries are designed for specific applications and vary slightly in performance characteristics. For radio operation, the best choice would be one specified for UPS (uninterruptible power source) or recreational vehicle (RV) use. For lighting and other needs, a marine type battery works well. For best results, consult the manufacturer before making a purchase.

Sealed lead acid (SLA) or "gel cells," such as those used in alarm or emergency lighting systems, are available in smaller sizes that are somewhat lighter. These batteries are also the ones sold in a variety of portable power kits for Amateur Radio and consumer use. Typical small sizes are 2, 4, and 7Ah, but many sizes of up to more than 100Ah are available. SLA batteries should never be deeply discharged. For example, a 12 volt SLA battery will be damaged if allowed to drop below 10.5 volts. Excessive heat or cold can damage SLA batteries. Storage and operating temperatures in excess of 75 degrees F. or below 32 degrees F. will reduce the battery's life by half. Your car's trunk is not a good place to store them. Storage temperatures between 40 and 60 degrees will provide maximum battery life.

Battery "Power Budgeting"

The number of ampere/hours (Ah—a rating of battery capacity) required, called a "power budget," can be roughly estimated by multiplying the radio's receive current by the number of hours of operation, and then adding the product of the transmit current multiplied by the estimated number of hours of transmission and by the duty cycle for that mode. For a busy net control station, the transmit current will be the determining factor because of the high percentage of transmit time. For low-activity stations, the receiver current will dominate. The value obtained from this calculation is only a rough estimate of the ampere/hours required. The Ah rating of the actual battery or combination of batteries should be up to 50% higher, due to variations in battery capacity and age.

Don't confuse the percent of time transmitting with "duty cycle," which is mode-specific (e.g., 100% for FM and digital, 50% for CW and 30% for uncompressed SSB).

Estimated 24-hour power budget example:

Receive current: 1 amp x 24 hours = 24 Ah
Transmit current: 8 amps x 6 hours = 48 Ah (figuring 6 hours as the 25% transmit time)

Total AH: 72 Ah estimated actual consumption
Actual battery choice 72 x 1.5 = **108** Ah figuring 50% higher due to variations

Chargers, Generators and Solar Power

Battery Chargers:

You should have two or more batteries so that one can be charging while another is in use.

Section 4: What Happens When Called
Topic 18: Equipment Choices for Emergency Communication

NiCad and NiMH batteries: The type of charger required depends on the battery—for instance; most NiCad chargers will also charge NiMH, but not Li-Ion batteries. Several aftermarket "universal" chargers are available that can charge almost any battery available. A rapid-rate charger can ensure that you always have a fresh battery without waiting, although rapid charging can shorten a battery's overall lifespan.

Lead-acid batteries: Always consult the battery's manufacturer for precise charging and maintenance instructions, as they can vary somewhat from battery to battery. It is best to slow-charge all batteries, since this helps avoid over-heating and extends their over-all life span.

In general, automotive and deep cycle batteries can be charged with an automobile and jumper cables, an automotive battery charger, or any constant-voltage source. If a proper battery charger is not available, any dc power supply of suitable voltage can be used, but a heavy-duty isolation diode must be connected between the power supply and the battery. (This is important, since some power supplies have a "crowbar" overvoltage circuit, which short-circuits the output if the voltage exceeds a certain limit. If a battery is connected, the crowbar could "short-circuit" the battery with disastrous results.) The output voltage of the supply must be increased to compensate for the diode's voltage drop. Take a measurement at the battery to be sure.

Wet Batteries: These should be charged at about 14.5 volts, and VRLA batteries at about 14.0 volts. The charging current should not exceed 20% of the battery's capacity. For example, a 20-amp charger is the largest that should be used for a battery rated at approximately 100 Ah. Consult the battery's manufacturer for the optimum charging voltage and current whenever possible.

Deep cycle batteries do not normally require special charging procedures. However, manufacturers do recommend that you use a charger designed specifically for deep cycle batteries to get the best results and ensure long life.

SLA or "gel- cell": Gel-Cell batteries must be charged slowly and carefully to avoid damage. All batteries produce hydrogen gas while recharging. Non-sealed batteries vent it out. SLA batteries do what is called "gas recombination." This means that the gas generated is "recombined" into the cells. SLA batteries actually operate under pressure, about 3 psi. for most. If the battery is charged too quickly, the battery generates gas faster than it can recombine it and the battery over-pressurizes. This causes it to overheat, swell up, and vent, and can be dangerous and will permanently damage the battery. The charging voltage must be kept between 13.8 and 14.5 volts. Wherever possible, follow the battery manufacturer's instructions. Lacking these, a good rule of thumb is to keep the charging current level to no more than 1/3 its rated capacity. For example, if you have a 7Ah battery, you should charge it at no more than 2 amps.

The time it takes for a SLA battery to recharge completely will depend on the amount of charge remaining in the battery. If the battery is only 25% discharged then it may recharge in a few hours. If the battery is discharged 50% or more, 18-24 hours may be required.

Solar panels and charge controllers: These are readily available at increasingly lower costs. These provide yet another option for powering equipment in the field when weather and site conditions permit their use. When choosing solar equipment, consult with the vendor regarding the required size of panels and controller for your specific application.

Section 4: What Happens When Called
Topic 18: Equipment Choices for Emergency Communication

DC to AC inverters: While direct dc power is more efficient and should be used whenever possible, inverters can be used for equipment that cannot be directly powered with 12Vdc. Not all inverters are suitable for use with radios, computers or certain types of battery chargers. The best inverters are those with a "true sine-wave" output. Inverters with a "modified sine-wave" output may not operate certain small battery chargers, and other waveform-sensitive equipment. In addition, all "high-frequency conversion" inverters generate significant RF noise if they are not filtered, both radiated and on the ac output. Test your inverter with your radios, power supplies and accessories (even those operating nearby on dc) and at varying loads before relying upon it for emcomm use.

Effective filtering for VHF and UHF can be added rather simply (using capacitors on the dc input, and ferrite donuts on the ac output), but reducing HF noise is far more difficult. Inverters should be grounded when in operation, both for safety and to reduce radiated RF noise.

As an alternative to an inverter, consider a mid- sized 12V computer UPS (uninterruptible power source). Smaller, square-wave UPS units are not designed for continuous duty applications, but larger true sine-wave units are. Most true sine-wave units use internal batteries, but with minor modifications can be used with external batteries. The larger commercial UPS units run on 24 or 48 volts, and require two or four external batteries in series. UPS units will have a limit on the number of depleted batteries they can re-charge, but there is no limit to the number of batteries that can be attached to extend operating time.

Generators are usually required at command posts and shelters for lighting, food preparation and other equipment. Radio equipment can be operated from the same or a separate generator, but be sure that co-located multiple generators are bonded with a common ground system for safety. Not all generators have adequate voltage regulation, and shared generators can have widely varying loads to contend with. You should perform a test for regulation using a high-current power tool or similar rugged device before connecting sensitive equipment. A voltmeter should be part of your equipment any time auxiliary power sources are used.

Section 4: What Happens When Called
Topic 18: Equipment Choices for Emergency Communication

Noise levels can be a concern with generators. Some are excessively noisy and can make radio operations difficult and increase fatigue. A noisy generator at a shelter can make it difficult for occupants to rest, and can result in increased levels of stress for already stressed people. Unfortunately, quieter generators also tend to be considerably more expensive. Consider other options such as placing the generator at a greater distance and using heavier power cables to compensate. Placing a generator far from a building can also prevent fumes from entering the building and causing carbon monoxide poisoning, an all-too-common problem with emergency generators.

Several other devices may be helpful when dealing with generators or unstable ac power sources. High quality surge suppressors, line voltage regulators and power conditioners may help protect your equipment from defective generators. Variable voltage transformers ("Variacs") can be useful to compensate for varying power conditions.

Equipment for Other Modes

If you plan to operate one of the digital modes (packet, APRS, AMTOR, PSK31, etc), then you will also need a computer and probably a TNC or computer sound card interface. Some newer radios have built-in TNCs. Be sure to identify all the accessories, including software and cables, needed for each mode. Include the power required to operate all of the radios and accessories when you are choosing your batteries and power supply. The internal battery in your laptop computer will probably not last long enough for you to complete your shift. Be prepared with an external dc power supply and cable, or a dc to ac inverter. If you need hard copy, then you will also need a printer, most of which are ac powered.

Scanners and Other Useful Equipment

In addition to your Amateur Radio equipment, you may find a few other items useful.

- Multi-band scanning radio (to monitor public service and media channels)
- FRS, GMRS (separate license required) or MURS handhelds
- Cellular telephone (even an unregistered phone can be used to call 911)
- Portable cassette tape recorder with VOX (for logging, recording important events)
- AM/FM radio (to monitor media reports)
- Portable television (to monitor media reports)
- Weather Alert radio with "SAME" feature (to provide specific alerts without having to monitor the channel continuously)
- Laptop computer with logging or emcomm- specific packet software

Section 4: What Happens When Called
Topic 18: Equipment Choices for Emergency Communication

Testing the Complete Station

After making your equipment selection (or beforehand if possible), field test it under simulated disaster conditions. This is the fundamental purpose of the annual ARRL Field Day exercise in June, but any time will do. Operations such as Field Day can add the element of multiple, simultaneous operations on several bands and modes over an extended period. Try to test all elements of your system together, from power sources to antennas, and try as many variations as possible. For instance, use the generator, and then switch to batteries. Try charging batteries from the solar panels and the generator. Use the NVIS antenna while operating from batteries and then generator. This procedure will help reveal any interactions or interference between equipment and allow you to deal with them now—before proper operation becomes a matter of life and death.

Section 4: What Happens When Called
Topic 18: Equipment Choices for Emergency Communication

Reference Links

Deep cycle battery tips:

http://www.batteryfaq.org/

Anderson PowerPole connectors:

http://www.andersonpower.com/

Molex 1545 Series connector data:

http://www.molex.com/molex/

Section 4: What Happens When Called
Topic 18: Equipment Choices for Emergency Communication

Review

All equipment chosen should be flexible and easy to use, rugged, and capable of being battery powered. Antennas should be compact, rugged, and easily erected. Directional or omni-directional gain antennas for VHF and UHF are essential in many locations, and the higher they are mounted, the better as long as feedline losses are kept low. Battery power is essential, as is a means of charging batteries. Testing equipment under field conditions before assigning it to emcomm uses ensures fewer surprises in an actual deployment. All equipment should be tested periodically for proper operation, and inspected for damage or deterioration.

Activities

Evaluate the equipment you now own to see if it is suitable for emcomm operation. Make a list of equipment you already own, and a second list of the items you will need to complete a basic emcomm package appropriate to your needs. Discuss this evaluation with your mentor.

Section 4: What Happens When Called
Topic 18: Equipment Choices for Emergency Communication

Welcome to Topic 18 Knowledge Review

In order to demonstrate mastery of the information presented in the topic, you will be asked a series of un-graded questions. There are approximately 5 questions on the following pages in multiple-choice or true/false format. Feedback will be offered to you based on the answer you provide.

Question 1:

In considering power sources for HF radios, which of the following is *true*?

a) DC to AC inverters are often used to power HF radios.

b) Standard automotive batteries last longer than deep cycle batteries.

c) AC powered HF radios are suitable for all emcomm use.

d) Whenever possible, use deep cycle batteries to power HF radios.

Question 2:

In considering antennas for VHF/UHF radios, which is the *best* rule?

a) High transmitter power is more important than having a good antenna.

b) Transmitter power and antenna selection are equally important.

c) A good antenna is more important than high transmitter power.

d) If properly used, "rubber ducky" antennas can compensate for low transmitter power.

Question 3:

Beam antennas have many advantages. Which of the following is the *best* reason for selecting a beam antenna?

a) They are inexpensive and easy to transport.

b) They are easy to erect and very stable in storm conditions.

c) They are compact and easy to store.

d) They maximize desired signals and reduce interference from other stations.

Section 4: What Happens When Called
Topic 18: Equipment Choices for Emergency Communication

Question 4:

Which of the following statements about ARES deployment clothing is true?

a) Three years (until January 1, 2013) are being given to "wear out" and replace older clothing.

b) The recommended standards increase recognition and acceptance of ARES units.

c) The recommended standards apply only to clothing worn on actual ARES deployments.

d) All of the above.

Question 5:

In comparing the 30 amp Anderson power pole connector with the 10 amp Molex connector, which of the following statements is *true*?

a) The Molex is better for high power applications.

b) The Molex is better for heavy duty cycles.

c) The Anderson handles only low power applications.

d) The Anderson is capable of being plugged and unplugged a greater number of times without deterioration.

Section 4: What Happens When Called
Topic 19: Emergency Activation

TOPIC 19:

Emergency Activation

Objectives

Welcome to Topic 19.

This Learning Topic outlines some of the methods used to activate an emcomm group when an emergency occurs. After reading the material you will be able to use the methods outlined as you work in an emergency activation setting.

Student Preparation required:

None.

How Will I know?

The actual method by which emcomm volunteers are notified of activation will be determined locally, but this lesson outlines some of the most popular methods. To begin with, you must be registered with a local emcomm group in advance in order to be on their notification list. "Last minute" volunteers are extremely difficult to integrate into an already confusing emergency response. Join the group well in advance of any emergency, get any training they offer, and be ready when a call comes.

Every emcomm group should have developed a formal, written plan with its served agency to activate their members when needed. The plan should be developed in detail and then reduced to a simple "checklist" that both served agency officials and emcomm managers can keep nearby at all times. It should detail the circumstances under which emcomm activation might occur, who will call whom, and the various methods that can be used to contact them. The checklist can also list the actual telephone numbers and other contact information for each individual listed in the order that it is to be used. This information should be verified and updated on a regular schedule. Each member should know the plan and follow it closely.

Initial Notification by the Served Agency

In most cases, three or more members serve as "activation liaisons" to the served agency. When the emcomm volunteers are needed, it is one of these members who is called first. **Never rely on a single point of contact**. If that person is unavailable for any reason, the served agency should have one or more alternatives to try. They may be called by phone at work or at home, but the most reliable primary method is commercial radio paging (beepers). In the event that the paging system or an individual pager is not operating, the served agency should have

Section 4: What Happens When Called
Topic 19: Emergency Activation

all possible telephone numbers, including fax and mobile, and even e-mail addresses.

Group Alerting Systems

Once a liaison has been notified, a number of group alerting methods may be used. The most common ones are described below. No one method should be relied upon, since emergency conditions may render it useless. Commercial paging systems and ham repeaters might be off the air, phone lines down, and Internet service disrupted. Again, a written plan and checklist should be developed well in advance, and updated periodically.

Telephone Tree: In this system, the liaison calls two members, who each call two other members and so on until the entire group has been notified. If any one person cannot be reached, the person calling must then call the members that person would have called had they been reached. This method insures that the "tree" is not broken. Messages should always be left on all answering machines and voice mailboxes.

Text Messaging: Even when voice cell phone systems are overloaded, there may be text messaging capabilities. Depending on your cell phone, it may be possible to create lists of contacts and quickly send text messages to each person on the list. Recognize, however, that text messages sent over cellular phone systems can be delayed for several hours or more in times of heavy use.

Paging: If commercial digital pagers are used, the liaison or someone he designates calls each member's pager telephone number and sends a specific numeric emcomm activation code. The code might indicate the six-digit frequency of a local repeater, followed by a three-digit "action" code (e.g.: 911 for an emergency, 000 for test). Some groups use a two-tone, POCSAG (digital), or similar paging signal on a local Amateur repeater with wide coverage, activating commercial voice or digital pagers that have been modified to monitor the repeater's frequency.

A low-cost method of "paging" a group using an Amateur repeater uses a specific Continuous Tone Coded Squelch System (CTCSS) tone. Members leave their radios turned on in the "CTCSS decode" mode when they are not actively listening to the repeater. When the correct CTCSS tone is turned on for emcomm activation, everyone can hear the transmissions.

Since many newer radios include CTCSS decoding as a standard feature or low-cost option, this method is generally simple to implement. The tones may need to be generated by the repeater itself, since many repeaters will not "pass through" received tones. If the repeater is not operating, a mobile operating simplex on the repeater's output frequency from a high or central location can often work quite well.

E-mail: While e-mail might not immediately reach members anywhere they happen to be, it is a good backup method as long as it continues to function. Many people have full time high-speed Internet connections at home and the office, and most people check their e-mail frequently. Someone who has otherwise been unreachable may check their e-mail even several hours later, just as they might check an answering machine or voicemail box.

Self-Activation: If you become aware of an incident or situation that might require the

Section 4: What Happens When Called
Topic 19: Emergency Activation

activation of your emcomm group, you should take immediate steps to make yourself available. Depending on your group's activation plan, this might mean monitoring the assigned net or served agency frequencies, or making contact with one or more appropriate persons in the emcomm group or served agency. SKYWARN members might also monitor National Weather Radio. Remember, if you are not specifically authorized to directly contact served agency personnel or travel to an incident location, do not do it. Know your plan and follow it.

I Have Been Notified—Now What?

Your group's activation plan should tell each member what steps to take immediately after learning of emcomm activation. In most cases, the first step should be to check in on a specific frequency or repeater. If a repeater is used as the primary gathering point for members, a back-up simplex frequency (the repeater's output frequency works well) should be specified in the event that the repeater is no longer operating. In other cases, some members may also have specific assignments. These might include making contact with the served agency, going directly to a specific location such as an EOC, or making certain preparations. These members should quickly check into the "activation" net to let emcomm managers know that they have been reached and are responding.

One of the liaison stations should be available on the net to provide additional information from the served agency and directions to members as they check in. If a member is pre-assigned to act as NCS for the "activation" net, that person should take over the task as soon as possible to free up the liaison to work with the served agency or take other action. Some groups simply have the first person signing on act as a temporary NCS until an assigned NCS checks in. Again, it is important to have more than one person assigned to take on the NCS duties in the event that anyone is unavailable.

En Route

While you are headed home to pick up your jump kit or other gear, or while you are on your assigned location, there are several things you may need to do. Check into and continue to monitor the activation net for further information or instructions. Fill your vehicle with fuel and pick up any supplies you may need, including alkaline batteries for radios and lights, food, water, and other supplies on your checklist. Contact your spouse, children or other family members to let them know what is happening and where you will be. Give them any instructions they will need to be safe. Tell them when you will next try to contact them, and how to contact you if necessary. Knowing that everyone is OK can let you do your job without needless worry, and, of course, the same is true for them.

Section 4: What Happens When Called
Topic 19: Emergency Activation

Review

The "emcomm activation liaisons" are several people who can be contacted by the served agency to activate the emcomm group. Notification systems that can be used are telephone trees, commercial or amateur paging systems, email, or simple CTCSS receiver activation. Regardless of which primary notification method your group uses, there should be several backup methods as well. Each member should know where to go, what frequencies to monitor, and what nets to check into immediately after notification.

Activities

1. List the strengths and weaknesses of the telephone tree as an alerting system.

2. List the strengths and weaknesses of paging as an alerting system.

3. List the strengths and weaknesses of self- activation as an alerting system.

4. Share your answers to activities 1, 2, and 3 with your mentor.

5. Design an emcomm activation system for a seven member team. Be sure to include back up methods. Share your design with your mentor.

Section 4: What Happens When Called
Topic 19: Emergency Activation

Welcome to Topic 19 Knowledge Review

In order to demonstrate mastery of the information presented in the topic, you will be asked a series of un-graded questions. There are approximately 5 questions on the following pages in multiple-choice or true/false format. Feedback will be offered to you based on the answer you provide.

Question 1:

When a telephone tree is activated, what should be done when a caller cannot reach one of their assigned contacts?

a) Call all those assigned to the person who cannot be reached.

b) Call the liaison to report the difficulty.

c) Ignore that person and go on to the next assigned contact.

d) Stop calling at that point to "break" the tree.

Question 2:

What is an "emcomm activation liaison" for a served agency?

a) A phone answering service employed by the agency.

b) An automatic paging service employed by the agency.

c) An agency employee who arrives early to turn on the equipment.

d) A member of an emcomm group who is alerted first by the agency.

Question 3:

Regarding emcomm alerting systems, which of the following is true?

a) All systems are equally useful.

b) As an alerting system, commercial paging is clearly superior to all others.

c) As an alerting system, the telephone tree is clearly superior to all others.

d) It is best not to rely exclusively upon any single alerting system.

Section 4: What Happens When Called
Topic 19: Emergency Activation

Question 4:

Which of the following is true of e-mail as an alerting system?

a) With e-mail, emcomm members can be reached immediately anywhere they happen to be.

b) With e-mail, high-speed Internet connections guarantee that messages will be received very quickly.

c) E-mail is best used as a backup alerting system.

d) With e-mail, the CTCSS tone assures that all members will be quickly alerted.

Question 5:

Which of the following statements is true about the NCS?

a) The NCS is so important that it should never be assigned on a temporary basis.

b) The NCS is so important that temporary assignment as NCS should be limited to only one member of the group.

c) The NCS is so important that several members should be trained to take on the duties until the assigned NCS checks in.

d) The first member to sign on to a net is always the NCS for the duration of the incident.

Section 4: What Happens When Called
Topic 20: Setting Up, Initial Operations and Shutdown

TOPIC 20:

Setting Up, Initial Operations and Shutdown

Objectives

Welcome to Topic 20.

Following completion of this Learning Topic, you will be able to implement the steps necessary to set up, begin, and end operations in temporary locations, such as shelters in schools or churches, or temporary command centers at any location.

Student Preparation required:

None.

Responding After the Activation

If you already have your assignment, confirm that it is being activated by monitoring and checking into the local activation net. If you do not have a standing assignment, you should check into an activation net and make yourself available for an assignment. It might be a "resource" logistics net if one is active, or the general "tactical" command activation net. (Since local procedures vary widely, you should get to know your group's specific plans and procedures well in advance.)

After you have gathered your equipment and supplies, filled the gas tank and are ready to respond, you may need to do several things, depending on local plans and the nature of the emergency. You may be asked to check in to a specific net to let them know you are en route, and then periodically to report your progress, particularly if travel is hazardous.

In some cases, you may be asked to proceed to a "staging" or "volunteer intake" area to wait for an assignment. This could take some time, especially if the situation is very confused. Often, the development of the response to the emergency is unclear and it will take some time to develop a cohesive and uniform response plan for that incident. You should expect the situation to be fluid as each incident is unique and to respond accordingly. Be prepared to wait patiently for a determination to be made and an assignment to be given. In other cases, such as the immediate aftermath of a tornado or earthquake, you may be forced to make expedient arrangements as you go. Travel may be difficult or impossible, so you may need to do what you can, where you can. Nets may be established on an ad-hoc basis using whatever means are available.

Section 4: What Happens When Called
Topic 20: Setting Up, Initial Operations and Shutdown

Who Is In Charge?

At each station, the EC or other emcomm manager should appoint one member of the emcomm group to take a leadership role as "station manager," with full responsibility for all operations at that site. This person serves as a point of contact, information and decisions for the team with the incident commander and with other groups aiding in the response. This helps avoid confusion and arguments.

When you accept a position as an emcomm volunteer, you do so knowing that you will often need to follow the directions of another person. Cooperation and good teamwork are key elements that result in an efficient and effective emcomm operation. As the situation arises, you may have to step into a role of a leader to keep the operation moving forward. Expect to work with others. Expect that there are times you are the follower. Expect that other times, you may be the leader.

Arriving at the Site

If you are assigned to a facility operated by the served agency, such as a shelter, introduce yourself to the person in charge as an "emergency communicator" assigned to serve that location. They will be busy, so get right to the point:

Identify yourself and explain that you have been assigned to set up a communication station for that location, and by whom.

Inform them that you would like to set up your equipment and get on the air. Ask if another communicator has already arrived. Ask if they have a preference for the station's location and explain your needs.

If you are the first communicator to arrive, be prepared to suggest an appropriate location—one that can serve as both an operating and message desk, has feed line access to a suitable antenna location, access to power and telephone, and is just isolated enough from the command center to avoid disturbing each other.

Ask if there are any hazards or considerations in the immediate area that you should be aware of, or cause you to relocate later.

If no building or other suitable shelter is available, you may need to set up your own tent, or work from your car. Choose a location that provides shelter from wind, precipitation and other hazards, and is close enough to the served agency's operations to be convenient but not in each other's way.

Being a Good Guest

In many cases, you will be occupying a space that is normally used by someone else for another purpose. Respect and protect their belongings and equipment in every way possible. For instance, if you are in a school and will be using a teacher's desk, find a way to remove all the items from its surface to a safe place for the duration of operations. A cardboard box, sealed

Section 4: What Happens When Called
Topic 20: Setting Up, Initial Operations and Shutdown

and placed under the desk usually works well. Do not use their office supplies or equipment, or enter desk drawers or other storage areas without specific permission from a representative of the building's owners. Some served agencies will seal all filing cabinets, drawers and doors to certain rooms with tamper-evident tape upon arrival to protect the host's property and records.

When installing antennas, equipment and cables, take care not to damage anything. For instance, avoid using "duct" tape to fasten cables to walls or ceilings, since its removal will usually damage the surface. If damage is caused for any reason, make note of it in your log and report it to the appropriate person as soon as possible.

Initial Set Up and Information Gathering

In most cases, your first priority will be to set up a basic station to establish contact with the net. Pack that equipment in your vehicle last so that you can get to it first. If you arrive as a team of two or more, station setup can begin while others carry in the remaining equipment.

Set up and test the antenna for proper SWR, and then check into the net. Test to find the lowest power setting that produces reliable communication, especially if you are operating with battery or generator power, to conserve power for extended operations. High power should also be avoided whenever lower power will work just as well to prevent interference with other radio systems, telephones and electronic equipment.

Once your basic station is on the air, you can begin to work on other needs:

- Check for working telephones, faxes, Internet and other means of communications
- Learn about the served agency's operations and immediate needs at that site
- Install additional stations or support equipment
- Make a list of stations within simplex range
- Identify possible alternative message paths
- Find sanitary facilities
- Determine water and food sources, eating arrangements
- Review overall conditions at the site, and how they will affect your operations
- Find a place to get some occasional rest

As soon as possible, ask a member of the served agency's staff to spend a few moments to discuss the agency's operational needs. What are the most critical needs? Whom do they need to communicate with, and what sort of information will need to be transmitted? Will most messages be short and tactical in nature, or consist of long lists? Will any messages be too confidential for radio? Are phones and fax still working? What will traffic needs be at different times of day? How long is the site anticipated to be open? Will there be periodic changes in key agency staff?

You may also need to provide agency staff with some basic information on how to create a message, show them how to use message forms, and instruct them on basic procedures to follow. Be sure to let them know that their communications will not be private and "secure" if sent by Amateur Radio, and discuss possible alternatives.

Section 4: What Happens When Called
Topic 20: Setting Up, Initial Operations and Shutdown

Ending Operations

Emcomm operations may end all at once, or be phased out over time. Several factors may affect which operations end, and when:

- Damaged communication systems are restored and returned to service
- Traffic loads are reduced and can be handled with normal systems
- Shelters and other locations are closed

How you are notified to end operations will depend on the policies of your emcomm group and served agency, and the specific situation. For instance, even though a shelter manager has been told to shut down by the served agency, your orders may normally come from a different person who may not be immediately aware of the shelter's closing. In this case, you might need to check with the appropriate emcomm manager before closing your station. Once the decision to close your station has been received and verified, be sure that the person in charge of the location is aware that you are doing so, and if necessary, why.

File and package all messages, logs and other paperwork for travel. Return any borrowed equipment or materials. Carefully remove all antennas and equipment, taking care to package and store it correctly and safely. Avoid the temptation to toss everything into a box with the intention to "sort it out later," unless you are under pressure to leave in a hurry. In the event you are re-deployed quickly, this will save time in the end.

Departure

Several actions may be necessary when leaving. First, be sure to leave the space you used in as good a condition as possible. Clean up any messes, remove trash and put any furniture or equipment back where it was when you arrived. If you sealed desktop items in a box for safekeeping, simply place the box on the cleaned desk. Do not unpack the items and attempt to replace them on the desk. This will provide proof to the desk's owner that you took steps to protect their belongings, and helps keep them secure until their owner takes possession again. Do not remove tamper evident tape or similar seals placed by others unless told to do so by the appropriate person, or in accordance with the agency's policy.

Thank all those who worked with you. Even a simple "thanks" goes a long way, compared to hearing not a single word. Do not forget the building's owners or staff, the served agency staff or others you worked with, and any other emcomm personnel. This is also the time for any apologies. If things did not always go well, or if any damage was caused, do your best to repair the relationship before departing. These simple efforts can go a long way toward protecting relationships between all groups and individuals involved.

The Debriefing

After each operation, your emcomm group, and perhaps even the served agency, will probably want to hold a meeting to review the effectiveness of the operation. There may be issues that occurred during operations that you will want to discuss at this meeting. Events may have occurred within the served agency that involved communications you handled. If you try to rely

Section 4: What Happens When Called
Topic 20: Setting Up, Initial Operations and Shutdown

entirely on your memory or logbooks, you will probably forget key details or even forget certain events altogether.

To prevent this from happening, keep a separate "de-briefing" diary, specifically for use during this meeting. Some entries might only refer briefly to specific times and dates in the station operating log, or they may contain details of an issue that are not appropriate in the station log.

If you will be required to turn over your station logs immediately at the end of operations, your de-briefing diary will need to contain full details of all events and issues for discussion. Such information might include:

- What was accomplished?
- Is anything still pending? Note unfinished items for follow-up.
- What worked well? Keep track of things that worked in your favor.
- What needed improvement?
- Ideas to solve known problems in the future.
- Key events
- Conflicts and resolutions

During the de-briefing, organize the session into (a) what worked well, and (b) what could be improved for the next operation. Change criticisms and judgment statements into a constructive manner by saying, "This method might have worked better if…" rather than "This method was stupid." Also, avoid personal attacks and finger pointing. In most cases, interpersonal issues are dealt with most effectively away from the group meeting.

Section 4: What Happens When Called
Topic 20: Setting Up, Initial Operations and Shutdown

Reference Links

For information about ARRL Public Service Communications:

http://www.arrl.org/public-service-communications-manual

For specific information on ARES, see the ARES Field Resources Manual:

http://www.arrl.org/ares-field-resources-manual

Section 4: What Happens When Called
Topic 20: Setting Up, Initial Operations and Shutdown

Review

The process of setting up, operating, and taking down your station should be an orderly and thoughtful one. A little advance planning can save considerable time. From the very first minute, work closely with served agency personnel to pick a location for your station, and learn what their operational needs are. Protect the building and its contents in every way possible. Log all events and issues for discussion in the post-event debriefing.

Activities

1. Suppose that you were given the assignment of coaching a new member of your emcomm group. Describe to your mentor six rules would you teach the new member regarding behavior at a served agency.

2. It is always a good idea to pack the equipment needed to get on the air right away in your vehicle last, so that you can get to it first. Consider all the gear that you might need for a three-day emcomm assignment. Describe to your mentor how you might load your gear in a vehicle.

3. Develop a checklist of actions you should take upon arrival if you were assigned to a different served agency during an emcomm event. Share the checklist with your mentor.

4. Develop a checklist of actions you should take before departing a served agency at the conclusion of an emcomm event. Describe these actions to your mentor.

Section 4: What Happens When Called
Topic 20: Setting Up, Initial Operations and Shutdown

Welcome to Topic 20 Knowledge Review

In order to demonstrate mastery of the information presented in the topic, you will be asked a series of un-graded questions. There are approximately 5 questions on the following pages in multiple-choice or true/false format. Feedback will be offered to you based on the answer you provide.

Question 1:

Suppose that you have been activated during an emergency and have been told to report to an agency that is different from your usual assignment. Which of the following is your best course of action upon arriving at the new agency?

a) Take charge and set up a communication center right away.

b) Check around the site and find the best place to set up a communication center.

c) Ask the receptionist about the best location for setting up a communication center.

d) Introduce yourself to the person in charge as the emergency communicator assigned to that location.

Question 2:

You are to brief the staff of a served agency about privacy on Amateur Radio. Which of the following is the most accurate statement you can make?

a) Speaking quietly into a microphone assures that no one will overhear private information.

b) It is permissible to use code words to assure privacy on the air.

c) There is no privacy with Amateur Radio voice communications.

d) There are NO methods by which the security of any message can be assured on Amateur Radio.

Question 3:

Suppose that you have been assigned to a site and the emergency ends. If the site manager asks you to close your station, what is your best course of action?

a) Do as the site manager tells you and close down your station immediately.

b) Ignore the site manager and await further instructions from higher authority.

c) Check in with the emcomm manager or NCS before closing down.

d) Have your emcomm manager or NCS speak directly with the site manager before you take

Section 4: What Happens When Called
Topic 20: Setting Up, Initial Operations and Shutdown

any action.

Question 4:

In preparing to leave a site after an emcomm event, which of the following actions is NOT appropriate?

a) Clean up any mess, discard trash, and move furniture back to its original position.

b) Unpack all desk items that you have placed in boxes and put them back in their original locations.

c) Thank all of those who worked with you.

d) Repair any relationships that may have been strained during the event.

Question 5:

A debriefing should be scheduled after each emcomm event. What is the primary purpose of the debriefing?

a) It provides an occasion to swap "war stories."

b) It serves as a legitimate forum for complaints.

c) It serves to improve future emcomm activities.

d) It provides an occasion for resolving interpersonal issues.

Section 5: Considerations
Topic 21: Operations & Logistics

TOPIC 21:

Operations & Logistics

Objectives

Welcome to Topic 21.

This Learning Topic will help familiarize you with and deal with some of the operating and logistical issues that arise during emergency relief and communication operations.

Student Preparation required:

None.

Choosing Phone Net Frequencies

Unlike commercial and public safety radio users, Amateurs have a vast amount of radio spectrum to use in meeting the needs of an emergency. Most local and regional emcomm communication takes place on 2 meter or 70 centimeter FM, or on 40, 60 or 80 meter SSB/ CW. The choice made is based on the locations to be covered, the availability of repeaters, distance, terrain, and band conditions.

VHF and UHF FM are preferred for most local operations because the equipment is common, portable, has a clear voice quality and the coverage is extended by repeater stations. VHF and UHF communication range is determined by terrain, antenna height and the availability of repeaters.

For larger areas or in areas without repeaters, HF SSB may be needed. Most local emcomm operation is on the 40 or 80-meter bands using Near Vertical Incidence Skywave (NVIS) propagation. For long-haul communication needs and international operations, 15 or 20-meter nets may be the best option. Many emcomm groups will have pre-selected a number of frequencies for specific purposes. The complete list of these frequencies should be in your jump kit, and pre-programmed into your radios.

Section 5: Considerations
Topic 21: Operations & Logistics

Know Your Resources In Advance

Become familiar with the coverage and features of each permanent repeater and digital message system in your area, and pre-program your radios with the frequencies, offsets and CTCSS tones. Ask your EC or AEC which repeaters are used for emergency communication in your area. Will they be available for exclusive emcomm use, or must they be shared with other users? Information to find out includes:

- How does it identify itself?

- Are there any "dead spots" in critical areas?

- How much power is required to reach the repeater with a clear, quiet, signal from key locations?

- Does the repeater have a courtesy tone, and what does it sound like? Do the tones change depending on the repeater's mode?

- How long is the "time-out timer"?

- Is it part of a linked system of repeaters?

- What features does it have, and which touch-tone commands or CTCSS tones activate them?

For net frequencies that support digital communication systems, such as packet radio bulletin board messaging systems, PACTOR, PSK31 and RTTY:

- Which software do they use? ARESPACK, Fnpack, FNpsk?

- Do the digital systems have mailboxes or digipeater functions?

- Which other nodes can they connect to?

- Can traffic be passed over an Internet link automatically or manually?

- How many connections can they support at once?

Network Coverage Concerns

Most emcomm managers rely on simplex operation when planning their VHF or UHF FM nets for one reason—repeaters often do not survive disasters or are overwhelmed with the amount of traffic. Repeaters that do survive and are usable are considered a bonus. Since simplex range is limited by terrain, output power, antenna gain and height, operation over a wide area can be a challenge. Almost any structure or hills can block signals to some degree. Don't overlook SSB on our VHF or UHF bands; it can support communication over surprising distances and over rough terrain.

Section 5: Considerations
Topic 21: Operations & Logistics

To avoid last minute surprises, your group should pre-test all known fixed locations in your area for coverage. For instance, if you are serving the Red Cross, test simplex coverage from each official shelter to the Red Cross office and the city's EOC or other key locations, and mobile coverage in the same areas. If needed, there are several ways to improve simplex range:

- Use an antenna with greater gain

- Move the antenna away from obstructions

- Use a directional antenna

- Increase antenna height

- Increase transmitter output power as a last resort.

- In a fast moving situation with poor simplex coverage and no repeater, it can be helpful to place a mobile station on a hilltop or office building where they can communicate with, and relay for, any station in the net. A mobile relay station can also allow communications to follow a moving event, such a wildfire or flash flood. That station becomes, in effect, a "human repeater."

Although an expedient "work-around," this slow and cumbersome process can reduce net efficiency by more than half. A modern aid to this kind of operation is the "simplex repeater." This device automatically records a transmission, and immediately re-transmits it on the same frequency. Remember that FCC rules do not allow unattended operation of simplex repeaters, and that you must manually identify it.

A better solution is a portable duplex repeater that can be quickly deployed at a high point in the desired coverage area. The coverage of this repeater does not have to be as good as a permanent repeater—it just has to reach and hear the stations in your net. Portable repeaters have been used successfully from the back seat of a car, using a mobile antenna, and parked on a ridge or even the top floor of a parking garage. Portable masts and trailer-mounted towers have also been used successfully. Check with your local frequency-coordinating body if your plans include portable repeaters.

If all stations in the net have dual-band radios or scanners, a strategically located mobile radio may be operated in "cross-band repeater" mode. If you use your dual-band mobile in this manner for an extended period, use the low or medium power setting to avoid overheating and damaging your radio. Consider using a fan to further reduce the likelihood that your radio will be damaged from overheating.

For a permanent repeater to be useful in a disaster, it must have emergency power and be in a location and of such construction that it can survive the disaster. Agreements with repeater owners should be in place to allow emergency operations to the exclusion of regular users.

Section 5: Considerations
Topic 21: Operations & Logistics

Frequency and Net Resource Management

While we may have a large amount of frequency resources, in actual practice our choices are limited to the available operators and their equipment. Net managers may occasionally need to "shift" resources to meet changing needs. In the early stages of an emergency, the tactical nets may require more operators, but in later stages, the health and welfare traffic might increase.

In addition to the main net frequency, each net should have several alternate frequencies available. These should include one or more "back up" frequencies for use in the event of interference, and one or two frequencies to be used to pass traffic "off net."

Message Relays

When one station cannot hear another, a third station may have to "relay" the messages. Although this is a slow and cumbersome process, it is often the only way to reach certain stations. If relays must be used, move the stations involved off the main net frequency to avoid tying up the channel for an extended period.

Radio Room Security

To protect your equipment and the messages you handle, and prevent unnecessary distractions, it is best to allow only the operators who are on duty to be in the room. Avoid leaving the radio room and equipment unattended and accessible. It is never a good idea to allow members of the press to be in the room without specific permission from the served agency.

Record Keeping

Most served agencies will expect you to keep records of your operations. These records will certainly include original copies of any messages sent, station logs, memos, and official correspondence. Some may even require you to keep "scratch" notes and informal logs. Depending on agency policy, you may be required to keep these records in your own possession for a time, or to turn some or all records over to the agency at the end of operations. In some agencies, your station records are permanent and important legal documents and must be treated as such. It is important to know your served agency's policy on recordkeeping in advance so that you can comply from the very beginning of operations.

Your station operating logs should probably contain the following information:

- Your arrival and departure times
- Times you check in and out of specific nets
- Each message, by number, sender, addressee and other handling stations
- Critical events—damage, power loss, injuries, earth tremors, other emergencies
- Staff changes—both emcomm and site management, if known
- Equipment problems and issues

Section 5: Considerations
Topic 21: Operations & Logistics

Every individual message or note should be labeled with a time and date. In the case of scratch notes, place dates and times next to each note on a sheet, so that information can be used later to determine a course of events.

If you expect to operate from the location for more than a day or two, establish a message filing system so that you can retrieve the messages as needed. A "portable office" type file box, expanding file or any other suitable container can be used to organize and file the messages. This is also an efficient way to allow another operator to pick up where you left off, even if they arrive after you leave. Effective record keeping allows them to come up to speed quickly.

Dealing With Stress and Egos

Any unusual situation can create personal stress—disasters create incredible amounts of it. Most people are not used to working under extreme stress for long periods, and do not know how to handle it. They can become disoriented, confused, unable to make good decisions or any decisions at all, lose their tempers, and behave in ways they never would any other time. Nervous breakdowns are common among those who get overwhelmed and have not learned to manage stress and stress-causing situations.

Especially in the early hours of a disaster, the tendency is to regard every situation or need as an "emergency," requiring an immediate response. You might get a barrage of requests for action. You might not have the extra seconds it requires to fully consider the options, and to prioritize your actions. The result is an overload of responsibility, which can lead to unmanageable levels of stress. While you cannot eliminate disaster-related stress, you can certainly take steps to reduce or control it.

Tips to help manage stressful situations:

- Delegate some of your responsibilities to others.

- Only take on those tasks that you can handle.

- Prioritize your actions—the most important and time-sensitive ones come first.

- Do not take comments personally—mentally translate "personal attacks" into "constructive criticism" and a signal that there may be an important need that is being overlooked.

- Take a few deep breaths and relax. Do this often, especially if you feel stress increasing. Gather your thoughts, and move on.

- Watch out for your own needs—food, rest, water, medical attention.

- Do not insist on working more than your assigned shift if others can take over.

- Get rest when you can so that you will be ready to handle your job more effectively later on.

- Take a moment to think before responding to a stress-causing challenge—if needed, tell them you will be back to them in a few minutes.

Section 5: Considerations
Topic 21: Operations & Logistics

- If you are losing control of a situation, bring someone else in to assist or notify a superior.

- Do not let a problem get out of hand before asking for help.

- Keep an eye on other team members, and help them reduce stress when possible.

Some within the emergency response community have "big egos," and still others with a need to be in full control at all times. Both personality types can be problematic anytime but far worse under stress. Take time now to consider how you will respond to the challenges they present. If your automatic response to certain behaviors is anger, make a conscious decision to come up with a different and more positive response strategy. Depending on the official position of the "problem" person, you might:

- Do your job as best you can, and deal with it after the emergency is over

- Politely decline and state your reasons

- Refer the issue to a superior

- Choose in advance to volunteer in another capacity and avoid that person altogether

Long Term Operations

As soon as it becomes clear that the situation is not going to return to normal for a while, you and your group should make plans for extended emcomm operations. Hopefully, your emcomm group and served agency have prepared contingency plans for this, and all you will have to do is put them into action. If not, here are some potential needs to consider:

- Additional operators to allow for regular shift changes, and those who go home.
- Replacement equipment, as operators leave with their own gear or gear fails.
- Food and water.
- A suitable place to sleep or rest.
- Generator fuel.
- Fresh batteries, sanitation facilities (bring your own TP), shelter.
- Message handling supplies, forms.
- Alternate NCS operators, backups.
- Additional net resources to handle message traffic.

Section 5: Considerations
Topic 21: Operations & Logistics

Battery Management

If you are operating on battery power, you will eventually need to recharge your batteries. As discussed earlier, some batteries need more time to recharge than others, and this time needs to be taken into account in your planning. Deep cycle marine batteries, for instance, can require a full day or longer to fully recharge. Sealed lead-acid (SLA) batteries, also known as "gel-cells," require up to 18 hours to recharge depending on the size of the battery. NiCad, Li-Ion and similar batteries can be recharged quite quickly, although repeated rapid charge cycles can reduce overall battery life.

If you are using slow-charging batteries, you may need to have enough on-hand to last the entire length of the operation. If your batteries can be charged quickly, some means must be provided for doing so. Some chargers can be powered from a vehicle's 12-volt system, and are a good choice for emcomm. If no local means of charging is available, your logistics team may need to shuttle batteries back and forth between your position and a location with power and chargers.

Generator and Power Safety

Take some care in the placement of generators so that they will not be a problem for others. Engine noise can make it difficult for shelter residents and volunteers to get much needed rest. Exhaust fumes should not be allowed to enter the building or nearby tents or vehicles. Carbon monoxide tends to settle, so exhaust components should be carefully located so that fumes cannot settle into inhabited basements or other enclosed areas below the generator. A position "down- wind" of any occupied location is best. Even when vehicles are not included, internal combustion engines are still the number one cause of carbon monoxide poisoning in the United States. Propane powered engines produce as much or more CO as gasoline or diesel engines. Earth grounding of portable or vehicle- mounted ac generators is not required as long as only plug and cord connected equipment is used, and the generator meets National Electrical Code (NEC) standards listed in Article 250-6. The main exception is for generators that will be connected, even temporarily, to a building's permanent electrical system. For further details on grounding ac electrical systems, please refer to Article 250 of the NEC.

Ground Fault Interrupters (GFIs) add a further degree of safety when working with generators and portable power systems. GFIs detect any difference between the currents flowing on the hot and neutral conductors, and open the circuit. Also, be sure to test any GFI device to be used with or near HF radios to be sure that the GFI will function properly while the radio is transmitting.

Ac extension cords used to connect to generators or other power sources should be rated for the actual load. Consider radios, lights, chargers and other accessories when calculating the total load. Most extension cords are rated only for their actual length, and cannot be strung together to make a longer cord without "de- rating" the cord's capacity.

For example, a typical 16-gauge, 50 foot orange "hardware store" cord is rated for 10 amps. When two are used to run 100 feet, the rating drops to only 7 amps. Choose a single length of cord rated for the load and the entire distance you must run it. If this is not possible, you can also run two or more parallel cords to the generator in order to reduce the load on any single cord. For more information on portable power cord requirements, consult Article 400 of the

Section 5: Considerations
Topic 21: Operations & Logistics

NEC.

While some groups have used "Romex" type wire for long extension cords, this is actually a violation of the National Electrical Code, and a dangerous practice. Repeated bending, rolling and abrasion can cause the solid copper conductors and insulation to break, resulting in a fire and electrocution hazard. Use only flexible insulated extension cords that are UL rated for temporary, portable use.

Equipment—Leaving Yours Behind?

You are exhausted, and ready to head for home, but the emcomm operation is far from over. You brought along a complete station, and when you leave, the next operator is not nearly as well equipped. Should you leave your equipment behind for the next operator?

You have several options here—and they are all yours to choose from. No one can, or should, tell you to leave your equipment behind. If you feel comfortable that someone you know and trust will look after your gear, you may choose to leave some or all of it behind. If you do, be sure every piece is marked with at least your name and call sign. Do not leave behind anything the next operator does not truly need. Also, remember that even if you leave the equipment in the possession of someone you know, you still have the ultimate responsibility for its operation and safety. Emergency stations are difficult places to control and monitor. If your equipment is stolen, lost or damaged, you should not hold anyone responsible but yourself. Conversely, if someone leaves their equipment in your care, treat and protect it better than you would your own, and be sure it is returned safely to its owner.

Accepting Specialized Assignments

In the world of modern emcomm, you may be asked to handle other assignments for the served agency that may or may not include communicating. At one time, most emcomm groups had strict policies against doing other tasks, and this is still true of some. In the days when radios were difficult to operate under field conditions and required constant attention, this was important. The other common reason given is that you have volunteered to be a communicator, not a "bed pan changer." It is true that some agency's staff will abuse the situation when they are short of help, but if both the agency's staff and emcomm group are clear about any limits beforehand, the problem should not arise.

Today, most emcomm groups will permit their members to be cross-trained for, and perform, a variety of served-agency skills that also include communicating. Examples are SKYWARN weather spotting, Red Cross damage assessment and many logistics jobs. If your group still has a "communication only" policy, are you really meeting your agency's needs? Is it necessary to have a damage assessment person and a communicator to do that job? What would happen to your agency if each driver also had to bring along a dedicated radio operator? Can one person do both jobs?

Section 5: Considerations
Topic 21: Operations & Logistics

Reference Links

For information about ARRL Public Service Communications, please see The Public Service Communications Manual:

http://www.arrl.org/public-service-communications-manual

For specific information on ARES, see the ARRL ARES Field Resources Manual at:

http://www.arrl.org/ares-field-resources-manual

Section 5: Considerations
Topic 21: Operations & Logistics

Review

Simplex operation is often preferred over repeaters because repeaters may fail in a disaster situation. Frequencies and operators are a resource that should be managed for maximum efficiency and effectiveness. Record keeping is essential to an effective emcomm operation. It allows messages to be tracked, and preserves continuity when personnel change. Demanding situations like disasters can breed disagreements, especially when strong egos and short-fused tempers are introduced. Take steps to reduce the level of stress on yourself, and do not respond in kind to an angry person. When an operation looks like it will be an extended one, begin immediately to prepare for the additional people and resources necessary to sustain the operation. Arrange to charge batteries as needed. Use generators and power distribution equipment safely. Leaving your equipment behind is a choice only you can make. Think about this well in advance to be sure other arrangements are made before you leave with all your equipment. Modern emcomm groups often accept other agency tasks beyond just communications.

Activities (choose two)

1. Describe to your mentor how you would help a new emcomm group member deal with stress during an emergency.

2. Develop a list of at least five possible served agency jobs that would also require your communication skills and share the list with your mentor.

3. Discuss with your mentor five safety rules pertaining to generators and electrical lines in and near a radio room.

Section 5: Considerations
Topic 21: Operations & Logistics

Welcome to Topic 21 Knowledge Review

In order to demonstrate mastery of the information presented in the topic, you will be asked a series of un-graded questions. There are approximately 5 questions on the following pages in multiple-choice or true/false format. Feedback will be offered to you based on the answer you provide.

Question 1:

Which of the following will *NOT* limit VHF simplex range?

a) Terrain.

b) Output Power.

c) Antenna Gain.

d) Digipeaters.

Question 2:

Which of the following actions will *NOT* improve simplex reception?

a) Increase the antenna height.

b) Switch to a non-directional antenna.

c) Increase transmitter output power at both stations.

d) Move the antenna away from obstructions.

Question 3:

Which of the following is true about a simplex repeater?

a) The FCC rules do not permit unattended operation of simplex repeaters.

b) They work best in the "cross band repeater" mode.

c) They require the use of two radios.

d) Is the same as a "human repeater."

Section 5: Considerations
Topic 21: Operations & Logistics

Question 4:

Which of the following is a good means of dealing with stress during an emcomm event?

a) Take every comment personally.

b) Pay no attention to other team members; let them handle their own problems.

c) To reduce personal stress, insist on working more than your own shift.

d) Prioritize your actions - the most important and time sensitive ones come first.

Section 5: Considerations
Topic 22: Safety & Survival

TOPIC 22:

Safety & Survival

Objectives

Welcome to Topic 22.

This Learning Topic will help you make informed decisions that will protect your own health and safety in a disaster environment, and that of your family as well.

Student Preparation required:

None.

Introduction

Disaster relief volunteers sometimes become so involved with helping others that they forget to take care of their own families and themselves. The needs of disaster victims seem so large when compared with their own that volunteers can feel guilty taking even a moment for their own basic personal needs. However, if you are to continue to assist others, you need to keep yourself in good condition. If you do not, you risk becoming part of the problem. If your family is not safe and all their needs are not taken care of, worrying about them may prevent you from concentrating on your job.

Home and Family First

Before leaving on an assignment, be sure you have made all necessary arrangements for the security, safety and general well being of your home and family. Family members, and perhaps friends or neighbors, should know where you are going, when you plan to return, and a way to get a message to you in an emergency. If you live in the disaster area or in the potential path of a storm, consider moving your family to a safe location before beginning your volunteer duties. Take whatever steps you can to protect your own property from damage or looting, and let a neighbor or even local police know where you are going, when you plan to return, and how to reach you or your family members in an emergency.

In addition to your emcomm deployment checklists, you might want to create a home and family checklist. It should cover all their needs while you are gone. Here are some ideas to get you started:

House Checklist –
- Board up windows if you are in a storm's path
- Put lawn furniture and loose objects indoors if high winds are likely

Section 5: Considerations
Topic 22: Safety & Survival

- Move valuables to upper levels if flooding is possible
- Heating fuel tanks should be filled
- Drain pipes if below-freezing temperatures and power loss are possible
- Shut off power and gas if practical and if structural damage is possible
- If you live in earthquake country, have an automatic shutoff valve on the gas line

Family Checklist –
- Designate a safe place to stay if needed, preferably with friends or relatives
- Reliable transportation, with fuel tank filled
- Adequate cash money for regular needs and emergencies (not ATM or credit cards)
- House, auto, life and health insurance information to take along if evacuated
- Access to important legal documents such as wills, property deeds, etc.
- Emergency food and water supply. AM/FM radio and extra batteries
- Flashlight and extra batteries, bulbs
- Generator, fuel and safe operating knowledge
- Adequate supply of prescription medications on hand
- List of emergency phone numbers
- Pet supplies and arrangements (shelters will not take pets)
- List of people to call for assistance
- Maps and emergency escape routes
- A way to contact each other
- A plan for reuniting later

Should You Leave At All?

There are times when your family may need you as much or more than your emcomm group. Obviously, this is a decision that only you and your family can make. If a family member is ill, your spouse is unsure of their ability to cope without you, if evacuation will be difficult, or any similar concern arises, staying with them may be a better choice. **If there is ever any doubt, your decision must be to stay with your family.** This is also something you should discuss, and come to an agreement with your spouse about well before any disaster, in order to avoid any last minute problems.

You First—the Mission Second

Once you are working with your emcomm group, you will need to continue to take care of yourself. If you become over-tired, ill or weak, you cannot do your job properly. If you do not take care of personal cleanliness, you could become unpleasant to be around. Whenever possible, each station should have at least two operators on duty so that one can take a break for sleep, food and personal hygiene. If that is not possible, work out a schedule with the emcomm managers or your NCS to take periodic "off-duty" breaks.

Food

Most people need at least 2000 calories a day to function well. In a stressful situation, or one with a great deal of physical activity you may need even more. Experienced emcomm managers

Section 5: Considerations
Topic 22: Safety & Survival

and served agency personnel will usually be aware of this issue and take steps to see that their volunteer's needs are met. If you are at a regular shelter, at least some of your food needs may be taken care of. In other situations, you may be on your own, at least for a while. High calorie and high protein snacks will help keep you going, but you will also need food that is more substantial. You may need to bring along some freeze-dried camping food, a small pot, and a camp stove with fuel, or some self-heating military-style "Meal, Ready to Eat" (MRE) packages.

Water

Safe water supplies can be difficult to find during and after many disasters. You will probably use 3-5 gallons of water each day just for drinking, cooking and sanitation. In extremely hot or cold conditions, or with increased physical activity, your needs will increase significantly. Most disaster preparedness checklists suggest at least one gallon per person, per day.

Many camping supply stores offer a range of water filters and purification tablets that can help make local water supplies safer. However, they all have limitations you should be aware of.

Filters may or may not remove all potentially harmful organisms or discoloration, depending on the type. Those with smaller filter pores (.3 microns is a very tight filter) will remove more foreign matter, but will also clog more quickly. Iodine- saturated filters will kill or remove most harmful germs and bacteria, but are more expensive and impart a faint taste of iodine to the water. Most filters will remove Giardia cysts. All water filters require care in their use to avoid cross-contamination of purified water with dirty water.

Purification tablets, such as Halazone, have a limited shelf life that varies with the type, and give the water an unpleasant taste. The tablets will do nothing for particulate (dirt) or discoloration in the water. Be sure to read and understand the information that comes with any water purification device or tablet before purchasing or using it.

The CDC says you can use unscented household chlorine bleach. After filtering out any particulates by pouring the water through several layers of densely woven cloth, put 1/8 teaspoon of bleach in a gallon of water, mix well, and allow it to sit for thirty minutes. If it still smells slightly of bleach, you can still use it.

If you have no other means, boiling for at least five minutes will kill any bacteria and other organisms, but will not remove any particulate matter or discoloration. Boiling will leave water with a "flat" taste that can be improved by pouring it back and forth between two containers several times to reintroduce some oxygen.

Section 5: Considerations
Topic 22: Safety & Survival

Sleep & Personal Hygiene

Sleep

Try to get at least six continuous hours of sleep in every twenty-four hour period, or four continuous hours and several shorter naps. Bring fresh soft foam earplugs and a black eye mask to ensure that light and noise around you are not a problem. An appropriate sleeping bag, closed-cell foam pad or air mattress, and your own pillow will help give you the best chance of getting adequate rest. If caffeine keeps you awake, try to stop drinking coffee, tea, or other beverages containing caffeine at least four hours before going to bed. Allowing yourself to become over- tired can also make falling asleep difficult.

Personal Hygiene

If you pack only a few personal items, be sure they include toothpaste and toothbrush, a comb, and deodorant. If possible, bring a bar of soap or waterless hand cleaner, a small towel and washcloth, and a few extra shirts. Waterless shampoo is available from many camping stores. After two or three days without bathing, you can become rather unpleasant to be around—think of others and make an attempt to stay as clean and well-groomed as you can under the circumstances.

Safety in an Unsafe Situation

Many disaster assignments are in unsafe places. Natural disasters can bring flying or falling debris, high or fast moving water, fire, explosions, building collapse, polluted water, disease, toxic chemicals, and a variety of other dangers. While you may focus on the job assigned you, never lose "situational awareness." You should always be aware of your surroundings and the dangers they hold. Never place yourself in a position where you might be trapped, injured or killed. Try to anticipate what might happen and plan ahead. Always have an escape plan ready in the event that conditions suddenly become dangerous. Do not allow yourself to become "cornered"—always have **more than one** escape route from buildings and hazardous areas.

Wear appropriate clothing. Depending on the weather, your gear might include a hard hat, rain gear, warm non-cotton layers, work gloves and waterproof boots. In sunny climates, include a shade hat, long sleeved shirt, long pants and sunscreen. Always bring several pairs of non-cotton socks and change them often to keep your feet clean and dry. Create seasonal clothing lists suitable for your climate and the types of disasters you might encounter. As a volunteer communicator, you will not generally be expected to enter environments that require specialized protective clothing or equipment. Do not worry about purchasing these items unless required by your served agency.

Avoid potentially dangerous areas. Industrial buildings or facilities may contain toxic chemicals, which can be released in a disaster. Dams can break, bridges can wash out and buildings can collapse. Areas can become inaccessible due to flooding, landslides, collapsed structures, advancing fires or storm surges. If you can avoid being in harm's way, you can also prevent yourself from becoming part of the problem rather than part of the solution.

Be prepared to help others find or rescue you should you become trapped or isolated. Carry a

Section 5: Considerations
Topic 22: Safety & Survival

police or signal whistle and a chemical light stick or small flashlight in your pocket. Let others know where you are going if you must travel anywhere, even within a "safe" building. Try not to travel alone in dangerous conditions—bring a "buddy."

Shelter

In most cases, you will not need your own shelter for operating or sleeping. You may be able to stay or work in the emergency operations center, evacuation shelter or even your own vehicle. However, in some cases a tent, camp trailer, motor home or other suitable shelter may be necessary. Your choice will depend on your needs and resources.

Tents should be rated for high winds, and should be designed to be waterproof in heavy weather. Most inexpensive family camping tents will not survive difficult conditions. Dome tents will shed wind well, but look for published "wind survival" ratings since not all dome designs are equal. Your tent should have a full-coverage rain fly rather than a single waterproof fabric. The tent's bottom should be waterproof, extending up the sidewalls at least six inches in a "bath-tub" design, but bring an extra sheet of plastic to line the inside just in case. (Placing a plastic ground cloth under a tent will allow rain to quickly run under and through a leaky tent floor.) Bring extra nylon cord and long ground stakes to help secure the tent in windy conditions. If you are not an experienced foul weather camper, consider consulting a reputable local outfitter or camping club for advice on selecting and using a tent.

Medical Considerations

If you have a medical condition that could potentially interfere with your ability to do your job, it is a good idea to discuss this with your physician ahead of time. For instance, if you are a diabetic, you will need to avoid going for long periods without proper food or medication, and stress may affect your blood sugar level. Persons with heart problems may need to avoid stressful situations. Even if your doctor says you can participate safely, be sure you have an adequate supply of appropriate medications on hand, and a copy of any prescriptions. Let your emcomm manager and any work partners know of your condition so that they can take appropriate actions if something goes wrong. Wear any medical ID jewelry you have. Keep a copy of any special medical information and emergency phone numbers in your wallet at all times. We know you want to help, but your EC needs to know and then can make an appropriate assignment.

Protect Your Eyes and Sight

If you wear eyeglasses or contact lenses, bring at least one spare pair. If you use disposable contact lenses, bring more than enough changes to avoid running out. Some contact lens wearers may want to switch to glasses to avoid having to deal with lens removal and cleaning under field conditions. If you have any doubts, consult your eye doctor ahead of time. Bringing a copy of your lens prescription along may also be a good idea, especially if you are likely to be some distance from home for a while.

Sunglasses may be a necessity in some situations and should always be carried in sunny

Section 5: Considerations
Topic 22: Safety & Survival

climates. Working without them in bright sun can cause fatigue, and possibly eye damage. If you are in an area with large expanses of snow or white sand, prolonged periods of exposure can cause the retina to be burned, a very painful condition commonly known as "snow blindness." Since no painkiller will help with retinal burns, it is best to use good quality UV blocking sunglasses at all times, and avoid prolonged exposure. If you do not normally wear eyeglasses, consider a pair of industrial safety glasses or goggles to protect your eyes from smoke and ash, wind-blown water, dust and debris. Keep all spare eyeglasses or safety glasses/goggles in a felt-lined hard-shell storage case to prevent scratching and breakage.

Sample Personal Survival and Comfort Needs Checklist

(Modify according to your own situation)

- ✓ Suitable size backpack or duffel bag for clothing and personal gear
- ✓ Plastic storage tub for food, cooking gear
- ✓ Toilet kit—soap, comb, deodorant, shampoo, toothbrush, toothpaste
- ✓ Toilet paper in zipper-lock freezer bag
- ✓ Small towel and washcloth
- ✓ Lip balm
- ✓ Facial tissues
- ✓ Sunscreen
- ✓ Insect repellent
- ✓ Prescription medications (1 week supply) Copies of medication and eyeglass/contact lens
- ✓ Prescriptions
- ✓ Spare eyeglasses or contact lenses and supplies
- ✓ Hand lotion for dry skin
- ✓ Small first aid kit
- ✓ Non-prescription medications, including painkiller, antacids, anti-diarrheal, etc.
- ✓ Extra basic clothing—shirts, socks, underwear
- ✓ Gloves, for protection or warmth
- ✓ Pocket flashlight
- ✓ Folding pocketknife
- ✓ Sleeping bag, closed-cell foam pad or air mattress, pillow
- ✓ Ear plugs (soft foam type in sealed package)
- ✓ Opaque eye mask
- ✓ Outer clothing for season and conditions (rain gear, parka, hat, face mask, etc)
- ✓ Hardhat
- ✓ Reflective vest, hat
- ✓ Travel alarm clock
- ✓ Chemical light sticks Police or signal whistle Dust masks
- ✓ Phone/e-mail/address list for family, friends, neighbors, physician, pharmacy
- ✓ Emergency contact/medical information card in your wallet
- ✓ Spare car and house keys
- ✓ High energy or high protein snacks
- ✓ Food—Freeze-dried or MREs
- ✓ Coffee, tea, drink mixes
- ✓ Plate or bowl, knife, fork and spoon, insulated mug
- ✓ Camp stove, small pot, fuel and matches

Section 5: Considerations
Topic 22: Safety & Survival

- ✓ Battery or other lantern
- ✓ Water, in heavy plastic jugs
- ✓ Water purification filter or tablets
- ✓ Magnetic compass, maps
- ✓ Duct tape, parachute cord

Pack individual items or kits in zipper-lock freezer bags to keep dry, clean, & neat.

Section 5: Considerations
Topic 22: Safety & Survival

Reference Links

CDC: http://www.cdc.gov/

FEMA Disaster Safety Information: http://www.fema.gov/

FEMA Disaster Preparedness for kids: http://www.fema.gov/kids/

American Red Cross – Disaster Safety:
http://www.redcross.org/portal/site/en/menuitem.d8aaecf214c576bf971e4cfe43181aa0/?vgnextoid=72c51a53f1c37110VgnVCM1000003481a10aRCRD

Food: http://www.fsis.usda.gov/factsheets/basics_for_handling_food_safely/index.asp

Water: http://www.fema.gov/plan/prepare/watermanage.shtm

Protecting Family & Property: http://www.fema.gov/plan/index.shtm

Preparedness: http://www.ready.gov/

Section 5: Considerations
Topic 22: Safety & Survival

Review

As important as the mission might seem, you must first take steps to protect your own home, family, and health. Plan well ahead, and include other members of your family in your planning. Let others know where you will be and how to reach you. To avoid becoming part of the problem, bring along the items you will need to be comfortable, clean, and safe. Take time to meet your own needs during your deployment so that you do not become part of the problem.

Activities

1. Discuss with your mentor how you would provide for your own home, family, and health during an emergency.

2. Prepare a personal-needs checklist for yourself and share this list with your mentor.

3. Describe to your mentor two major disaster threats in your area. For each threat, list five actions you would take as a precaution to protect your home and family.

Section 5: Considerations
Topic 22: Safety & Survival

Welcome to Topic 22 Knowledge Review

In order to demonstrate mastery of the information presented in the topic, you will be asked a series of un-graded questions. There are approximately 5 questions on the following pages in multiple-choice or true/false format. Feedback will be offered to you based on the answer you provide.

Question 1:

Which of the following statements concerning water purification is FALSE?

a) Boiling water for a full 5 minutes will kill most harmful bacteria.

b) Boiling water to purify it can leave it with a flat taste.

c) Filters may or may not remove harmful bacteria.

d) Purification tablets will remove bacteria and particulate matter (dirt).

Question 2:

Which of the following is TRUE about using unscented household chlorine bleach to purify water?

a) It is best to use 8 tablespoons of chlorine bleach per gallon of water.

b) Adding the proper amount of chlorine bleach to water will improve the taste.

c) After adding bleach, water must sit for 3 hours before drinking.

d) It is best to use 1/8 teaspoon of plain chlorine bleach per gallon of water.

Question 3:

Which of the following is TRUE about the personal gear you bring to a long-term incident?

a) Include several pairs of warm cotton socks.

b) Lightweight summer clothing is all you will ever need.

c) Keep spare eyeglasses or safety glasses/goggles in a hard-shell, felt-lined storage case.

d) As a volunteer communicator, you will need to bring specialized protective clothing.

Section 5: Considerations
Topic 22: Safety & Survival

Question 4:

Many disaster assignments are in unsafe places. Which of the following is TRUE about such locations?

a) Always plan an escape route from buildings and hazardous areas.

b) Always plan more than one escape route from buildings and hazardous areas.

c) The only dangers that you need be concerned with in any location are fire, flood, and falling debris.

d) Dams, bridges and buildings can generally be thought of as "safe zones."

Question 5:

Which of the following statements about safety and survival is TRUE?

a) The mission takes priority over everything else.

b) A person requires at least four gallons of water per day just for drinking.

c) If caffeine keeps you awake, stop drinking caffeinated beverages at least ten minutes before going to bed.

d) Your personal safety and well-being are a higher priority than the mission.

Section 5: Considerations
Topic 23: ARES PIO: The Right Stuff

TOPIC 23:

ARES PIO: The Right Stuff

Objectives

Welcome to Topic 23.

After reading this Learning Topic students will acquire the basic understanding of their role and that of a PIO when attached to a deployed ARES unit. The topic is meant to encourage further training in this specific activity area.

Student Preparation required:

None.

Introduction

More and more sections are appointing ARES-specific Public Information Officers (PIOs). These PIOs are specialists in covering media relations when ARES units are deployed in an emergency or community service operation. While general PIOs may also do this work, the entire emergency field is becoming more and more complex and special training is not only advisable, but strongly encouraged.

The goal of a PIO in an emergency is:

"Providing the Right information
 to the Right people
 at the Right time
 so they can make the Right decisions."
 - FEMA Advanced PIO Course

In addition to the regular PIO duties and tasks of establishing media relationships, informing the public and attracting new members, the ARES PIO has the opportunity to become an integral part of the Incident Command System (ICS).

The public needs to know what is happening, how big is the emergency, what is being done about it and what they themselves may need to do. Silence or errors on any of these topics breed rumors – and some rumors get very interesting indeed! The ICS has standardized ways to coordinate this information in a unified voice. Short-circuiting that process will only make you unwelcome at best.

As the gravity of a situation unfolds and more responders and agencies become involved, a

Section 5: Considerations
Topic 23: ARES PIO: The Right Stuff

Unified Command is activated. The UC comprises a group of trained and qualified individuals that work together to lead and orchestrate the effort. One component of forming the Unified Command is that of a group of Public Information Officers (PIOs) representing the various responders, agencies and disciplines will come together to form a Joint Information Center (JIC). It is the duty of the JIC to establish a unified message and become the voice of the event, providing consistent and unified information, dispel rumors, as well as providing a central location for media to receive information and ask questions. A trained ARES PIO is very likely to be invited to represent Amateur Radio within the JIC.

As an ARES PIO, your job is to be the "expert" on Amateur Radio efforts involved (number of ARES personnel involved, locations of ARES stations, etc.) You may be assigned multiple additional duties within the JIC to assist the Lead PIO. You will be expected to perform these additional duties as well as your ARES PIO duties simultaneously. Should the media inquire about ARES or Amateur Radio involvement, the Lead PIO will call on you to provide the facts and figures. Your job will be to answer any questions regarding Amateur Radio and ARES.

The ARES PIO will also be the person who guides reporters to meet and talk with other ARES members. For example, if a TV reporter wants to interview an ARES operator, the PIO will set it up, stay close to make sure it goes well, aid the operator if the interview gets "sticky," and frame it in the best possible way. The PIO is also responsible for seeing that the operator makes a good impression with appropriate clothing and appearance – not a stained, dirty T shirt with inappropriate logos on it! (It happens.)

UNDER NO CIRCUMSTANCES SHOULD YOU EVER SPECULATE AS TO THE OUTCOME OF THE SITUATION, OR PROVIDE ANY INFORMATION AS TO VICTIM NAMES, CONDITION OF INDIVIDUALS OR GRAVITY OF THE SITUATION TO THE MEDIA!

This is the job of others, not an ARES operator nor an ARES PIO. The PIO may be asked to speak to the media about Amateur Radio involvement, number of ARES personnel involved and the kinds of communications being supported by ARES, but even the PIO can only talk about ARES' own work and must refer other topics to more appropriate personnel.

And always remember…especially during an emergency situation with risk of life and property, **there is no such thing as "off the record."** Anything you say directly or within earshot of the media, even in jest, can lead to disastrous results that could jeopardize the entire operation, cause your dismissal and risk exclusion of Amateur Radio from future incidents.

Section 5: Considerations
Topic 23: ARES PIO: The Right Stuff

Can an EC also be the PIO?

Not really. Each role, if being done right, is a full time job. The best media relations are done by specifically designated and trained people whose singular function is to work with media, allowing EC's and others to do their job. While the EC and the PIO should work closely together, they are different roles calling for different people.

Why can't just anyone talk to the press?

While there will always be people who want their 15 seconds of fame in the media, they usually only end up (at best) promoting themselves, not ARES and Amateur Radio. In many cases they don't have accurate information, numbers, and a larger perspective on the situation. In the worst cases, they start guessing rather than admit that they do not have the real information.

Your job as an ARES **operator** is to relay messages for the served agency. Refer the media to your ARES PIO, the Lead PIO or the JIC.

Some Rules You Need to Know

Amateur Radio must NOT be used to assist news media in gathering information **when telephones or other normal means of communication are available**.

Amateur Radio operators may assist news media representatives in their efforts to gather information for relay to the public **from areas where normal communications have been disrupted**. Amateurs may ask questions of, or relay media questions to, other amateurs in the emergency area and their responses be recorded by media representatives.

Who Can Record and Transmit What

One constant area of confusion is in the recording and re-transmission of Amateur Radio messages.

- Amateur Radio operators can NOT record and re-transmit commercial radio and TV broadcasts.

- Commercial radio and TV reporters CAN record and then broadcast Amateur Radio messages.

Section 5: Considerations
Topic 23: ARES PIO: The Right Stuff

Reference Links

There are Basic and Advanced PIO classes offered both via online and in classrooms by many state Emergency Management Agencies as well as the FEMA Emergency Management Institute in Emmetsburg, MD.

Recommended additional NIMS/ICS training:

- NIMS 700-800
- ICS 100, 200
- Basic PIO
- Advanced PIO

Amateur Radio specific PIO training is offered through the ARRL's PR-101 course available at: http://www.arrl.org/shop/PR-101-Course-on-CD-ROM

Section 5: Considerations
Topic 23: ARES PIO: The Right Stuff

Activities

Talk to your local EC and learn who the designated PIO is for ARES in your group or locality. If possible, contact this person and interview him or her as to their duties. Discuss the role of the PIO with your mentor.

Section 5: Considerations
Topic 23: ARES PIO: The Right Stuff

Welcome to Topic 23 Knowledge Review

In order to demonstrate mastery of the information presented in the topic, you will be asked a series of un-graded questions. There are approximately 5 questions on the following pages in multiple-choice or true/false format. Feedback will be offered to you based on the answer you provide.

Question 1:

A Joint Information Center is established to:

a) Formulate a unified voice and message.

b) Dispel rumors.

c) Provide a central location for media questions.

d) All of the above.

Question 2:

As an ARES PIO you will be expected to:

a) Get coffee for the Lead PIO.

b) Provide relevant information to media regarding Amateur Radio involvement.

c) Give timely updates regarding the overall emergency effort and participants.

d) Provide a victim list including names and conditions.

Question 3:

You are involved in an ARES deployment but not as a PIO. A reporter shows up at your location and starts to ask you questions. What should you do?

a) If possible, refer them to the JIC, designated Lead PIO or ARES PIO.

b) If possible, refer them to the EC and DEC.

c) Refer them to the Unified Commander.

d) Be friendly, tell them what you are doing and how the operation is going.

Section 5: Considerations
Topic 23: ARES PIO: The Right Stuff

Question 4:

There's a flood in progress. A reporter for the local TV station comes to your location and asks you to get on the radio and talk to someone at the levees to find out if they think the sandbags will hold. What things need to be considered in this request?

a) Are other means of communication still available.

b) Amateurs can ask questions of other amateurs – not just "someone".

c) The question is speculating about things not specific to the Amateur Radio operation.

d) All of the above.

Section 5: Considerations
Topic 24: Alternative Communication Methods

TOPIC 24:

Alternative Communication Methods

Objectives

Welcome to Topic 24.

After reading this Learning Topic the emcomm volunteer will know the pros and cons of using alternate communication systems. This topic discusses a variety of communication options that do not depend on Amateur Radio, and some circumstances where they might be used.

Student Preparation required:

Read the FCC Rules (http://www.arrl.org/part-97-amateur-radio) on emergency communications *before beginning this lesson*.

Introduction

Amateur Radio may not always be the only or best radio service for the job. Sometimes it is better to hand an official a radio he can use to stay in contact with the ARES team on site, and not saddle him or her with a ham radio "shadow." This is particularly true for officials who must regularly deal with sensitive issues. Other voluntary agencies may use these radio services in their own operations.

The radio services discussed in this chapter are commonly available at low cost and are in general use. Other volunteers may already own radio equipment in these services, and amateur emergency communication groups should be equipped to communicate with them.

Legal Considerations

Some radio services require licenses, and others do not. However, in a true emergency as defined by the FCC, this may not be a problem. FCC rules permit the use of "any means necessary" to communicate in order to protect life and property—but only when no other normal means of communication is possible. Please do not assume that this means you can just modify your radio and call for help on the local police frequency the next time you see a car crash on the highway. Law enforcement agencies are not bound by the FCC's rules. Hams who have called for "help" on police frequencies have been convicted of "interfering with a police agency" under state and local laws, even though the FCC had taken no enforcement action. In one case, the judge ruled that by modifying his radio in advance, the amateur had committed "premeditated" interference, a serious charge. If you are in a position to save someone's life or property, be sure you are ready to defend your actions—and possibly lose—before pressing the

Section 5: Considerations
Topic 24: Alternative Communication Methods

mic button.

Other services, such as GMRS, require a license that is relatively easy to obtain, although not free. If your group is planning to use licensed radios, obtain your license well before any emergency and keep it current. If you own a radio, but no license, a judge could claim premeditation if you use it and disturb licensed users.

Using Modified Ham Radios

While it is easy to modify many VHF and UHF Amateur radios for operation in nearby public service and business bands, it is not legal to do so for regular "emergency" use. Radios used in those bands must be "Type Accepted" by the FCC for the purpose, and Amateur radios are not. If you plan to use other radio frequencies discussed in this unit, it is better to purchase the proper radio. However, if the need arises and your ham radio is all you have, the FCC will probably not prosecute you for using it—if the use falls within their strict rules for emergencies (see above).

Permissible Modes on the Other Radio Services

In most of the radio services listed below only voice communication is permitted. Packet and other forms of data or image transmission are illegal.

Citizens' Band (CB) Radio

As a widespread system of casual communication for the public, CB radio is still quite popular among the public and truckers. Since the 1950s, CB has been available to anyone for the purpose of short-range business and personal/family communication. No licensing is required, and tactical or self-assigned identifiers are acceptable. **Do not use your amateur call!**

CB radios operate in the 11-meter band, on forty designated channels from 26.965 to 27.405 MHz, with a maximum output power of four watts. Most use amplitude modulation (AM) but a few also offer single side band (SSB). The effective range between two CB mobile stations averages between two and eight miles. Depending on antennas, terrain and propagation, base to mobile communication is possible up to 25 miles. The use of SSB can significantly increase range, but SSB use is not widespread due to the extra cost. FCC rules permit communication to a maximum of 75 miles.

In many remote areas with little or no telephone service, families rely on CB radios for basic day-to-day communications. Many rural police and sheriff's organizations still monitor CB traffic. In a number of states, highway patrol officers install CB units in their patrol cars with the blessing of their agencies. However, many departments that used to monitor channel 9 have given up the practice. REACT groups in the area may still be monitoring.

In disaster situations, great emphasis is placed on the timely movement and distribution of supplies by truck. By far, the largest group of CB users is the trucking community. Channel 19 has been the unofficial "trucker" channel since the late 1960s, and in some areas is as good as

Section 5: Considerations
Topic 24: Alternative Communication Methods

channel 9 when calling for assistance. Channel 9 is reserved for emergency and motorist assistance traffic only. Aside from REACT, organizations in many parts of the world monitor channel 9 and other designated distress channels. In some countries, Citizens Radio Emergency Service Teams (CREST) teams serve the same functions as REACT.

Multi-Use Radio Service (MURS)

With little fanfare, the FCC added a new, unlicensed "citizen's" radio service in 2000. Both personal and business operation is permitted, with a maximum power of two watts. The MURS frequencies are 151.820, 151.880, 151.940, 154.570 and 154.600. While base operation is not specifically prohibited, the service is primarily intended for mobile and portable operation.

For about 20 years, certain businesses have been able to obtain licenses for operation on what the FCC calls "itinerant" frequencies. These channels became commonly referred to as the "color dot" channels. (A color dot label on the packaging identifies the frequency of the walkie-talkie.) One of the former itinerant channels, 154.570 MHz, (blue dot), is now a MURS channel. This means that a number of these low-cost one or two-watt output "itinerant" radios (which are usually user programmable for itinerant channels only) could be utilized for MURS. This allows you to equip unlicensed volunteers with a VHF portable having much the same simplex capability as a 2-meter handheld.

Family Radio Service (FRS)

Almost anywhere, in most every situation, you can find FRS radios in use. Family Radio Service portables are useful, effective and inexpensive. Like CB, the Family Radio Service is designed for short-range personal communications. Campers, hikers, vacationers and families on weekend outings use FRS units to keep in touch.

There are 14 available UHF channels, and 38 different CTCSS codes to limit background chatter and noise. Output power is from 100 to 500 mw, depending on the model. In an effort to standardize the ability to call for help using FRS, REACT recommends the use of FRS channel 1 (462.5625 MHz) with no CTCSS tone as an emergency calling channel. REACT is also lobbying the manufacturers of FRS equipment to suggest this plan in the user's information packed with new radios. A petition to the FCC requesting that this be made official was denied in late 2001. Monitoring the channel is recommended to all persons in outdoor areas whenever possible.

The first seven FRS channels are shared with the General Mobile Radio Service (GMRS). Although the original rules seem to prohibit it, a later FCC Report and Order explicitly permit communication between the two services. The chance of a distress call being heard on either service is greatly increased on these seven common channels.

Most FRS radios are available with 2 or 14 channels, although single channel radios can be found. It is important to note that the channel numbers on each radio are not always interchangeable between these units. Single channel radios are usually on channel 1, which corresponds to channel 1 in the 14-channel units.

Section 5: Considerations
Topic 24: Alternative Communication Methods

General Mobile Radio Service (GMRS)

The GMRS consists of fifteen UHF frequencies between 462.5625 and 462.7250 MHz. Eight are paired with matching repeater inputs five MHz higher, as with Amateur and commercial systems. Seven "interstitial" channels are shared with FRS, and operation there is restricted to simplex with a maximum of 5 watts. Power on the other channels is limited to 50 watts. GMRS stations have the option of working only simplex modes if desired, even on paired channels. There is no frequency coordination, and users must cooperate locally to effectively use channels. CTCSS codes are the same as for FRS, and the first 7 channels are common to both services. FM voice operation is permitted, but digital modes and phone patches are not.

Operating a GMRS station will require a low- cost system license from the FCC. You can apply using FCC Form 574, or apply online. FCC online licensing information can be obtained at http://www.fcc.gov/. System licenses are currently granted only to individuals. A system includes any and all radios operated by family members, and may include fixed, mobile, and repeater equipment. Use under the license is restricted to members of the licensee's immediate family. Licenses to entities other than individuals are no longer issued, but non-individual entities licensed before July 31, 1987 may continue to renew their licenses, and may not increase or modify their use.

The frequency of 462.675 MHz is recognized for emergency and travel information use, and is monitored by many REACT teams nationwide. Many teams operate repeaters on this and other frequencies.

Current uses for GMRS involve mostly personal and family communications. Hiking, camping and convoy travel are all common GMRS applications. GMRS use for emergency services is limited by the licensing requirements, but could be pressed into service in a disaster situation. One or more members might wish to become licensed if use of GMRS is likely, especially for liaison with locally active REACT teams.

Public Safety Radio

There are instances where the use of police and fire radio frequencies is possible. The agency itself might allow and train you for such use, or an individual officer may ask you to use his radio to call for help when he cannot. Keep your transmissions short and to the point. Do not tie up the channel with long explanations, and cease transmitting if they tell you to.

Cellular and PCS Phones

In a widespread disaster situation, these phone systems can quickly become overloaded. In smaller emergencies, they may still be usable. If a message is too sensitive to send via any two-way radio, try your cell phone. Cellular and PCS phone transmissions, especially digital, are considerably more secure. In addition, it is possible to send low-speed data or fax transmissions over the cellular network. An important consideration is that most cellular phone systems can send text messages. These digital messages are "fit in between" the systems' voice communications. It has often been found that even when a cellular system is overloaded by people trying to make normal calls, the text messaging still can get through, although delivery

Section 5: Considerations
Topic 24: Alternative Communication Methods

can be delayed several hours or more when the voice channels are in heavy use.

Marine Radio

FM marine radios operate on internationally allocated channels in the 160 MHz band. HF SSB radios operate on a variety of channels between 2 and 30 MHz. Operation of FM stations for vessels in US waters does not require a license, but operation on the HF channels does. Particularly in coastal areas, along major rivers or the Great Lakes, it may be a good idea to have a FM marine radio in your group's inventory. During major storms, you can monitor channel 16, the distress channel. If you hear a vessel in distress whose calls are going unanswered by the Coast Guard, you may legally answer them from an unlicensed land-based station under the FCC's "emergency communications" rules. If the Coast Guard is in communication with the vessel, do not transmit. Most other land-based operation is illegal, except where authorized by a FCC coast station license.

Aviation Radio

AM radios operating in the 108-136 MHz band are used in aircraft and in certain limited vehicles and ground stations. FCC licenses are required for all stations. Emergency locator transmitters (ELTs) are automatic devices that transmit a distress signal on 121.5 and 406 MHz.

Marine Emergency Position Indicating Radio Beacons (EPIRB) transmit digital ID codes on 406 MHz and a low-powered homing signal on 121.5 MHz.

The new land-based Personal Radio Beacons (PRB) transmit on 121.5 MHz. While it is unlikely that you will ever need to use an aircraft band radio except where it is provided by the served agency, it is good to be familiar with the radio service. Monitoring these frequencies for ELT, EPIRB, and PRB signals and distress calls is always a good idea.

Non-Radio Communication

Do not forget the most obvious means of communication—the land-line telephones. If they are still functioning, use the telephone and fax whenever the message might be too sensitive for radio. Fax is also useful for sending long lists, and where accuracy is critical. Do not tie up a radio frequency sending a long list of supplies if a working fax or phone is available.

Couriers

Since pre-history, runners have carried messages from place to place. When we are asked to deliver a sensitive or very lengthy message, and fax and phone lines are out of service, hand delivery might be the best choice if travel is possible. Acting as a courier does not eliminate the use of radio, since couriers need to be dispatched from place to place. Courier service is actually an excellent marriage of old and new technologies.

Section 5: Considerations
Topic 24: Alternative Communication Methods

Reference Links

Amateur Radio FCC Rules: http://www.arrl.org/part-97-amateur-radio

Emergency Locators: http://www.sarsat.noaa.gov/emerbcns.html

Multiple Use Radio Service (MURS) Rules:
http://wireless.fcc.gov/services/index.htm?job=service_home&id=multi_use

Family Radio Service (FRS) Rules:
http://wireless.fcc.gov/services/index.htm?job=service_home&id=family

General Mobile Radio Service (GMRS) Rules:
http://wireless.fcc.gov/services/index.htm?job=service_home&id=general_mobile

Citizen's Band (CB) Rules:
http://wireless.fcc.gov/services/index.htm?job=service_home&id=cb

Section 5: Considerations
Topic 24: Alternative Communication Methods

Review

Flexibility is important in disaster situations. Use of other communication systems may improve the overall effectiveness of the emergency communication response. Depending on the situation, trained Amateur Radio operators may have a variety of options to choose from.

Activities

Develop a list of at least three potential uses for non-ham radios in public service or emergency communication efforts in your area. You may base this on past or potential events. Discuss with your mentor which alternate radio system(s) best meets the need of each situation on your list and explain why.

Section 5: Considerations
Topic 24: Alternative Communication Methods

Welcome to Topic 24 Knowledge Review

In order to demonstrate mastery of the information presented in the topic, you will be asked a series of un-graded questions. There are approximately 5 questions on the following pages in multiple-choice or true/false format. Feedback will be offered to you based on the answer you provide.

Question 1:

Which can you NOT use to identify your transmissions on Citizens' Band radio?

a) Your Amateur call.

b) Your "handle".

c) A self-assigned identifier.

d) A tactical callsign.

Question 2:

Which is the best course of action for summoning help via CB?

a) Use channel 1, since the lowest frequency has the longest ground-wave signal.

b) Call at regular intervals on Channels 9 and 19 for a response.

c) Call only on channel 9, since it is designated for assistance and emergencies.

d) Say "Break-Break" or "MAYDAY" on any channel.

Question 3:

Which is NOT an advantage of using Family Radio Service (FRS) systems?

a) They are readily available at low cost.

b) Operation of FRS radios is simple and requires little training.

c) There is no requirement for licensing to use FRS.

d) Low transmitter power.

Section 5: Considerations
Topic 24: Alternative Communication Methods

Question 4:

Who may currently license a GMRS system with the FCC?

a) A privately owned business, for routine communications.

b) An individual, for family and personal use.

c) A charitable institution, for benevolent purposes.

d) A local repeater club.

Question 5:

Which is *NOT true* of the MURS?

a) A station license is required.

b) Power output is limited to 2 watts.

c) Radios operate in the VHF band.

d) Data emissions are permitted.

Section 5: Considerations
Topic 25: What to Expect in Large Scale Disasters

TOPIC 25:

What to Expect in Large Scale Disasters

Objectives

Welcome to Topic 25.

This Learning Topic will introduce you to the enormity of challenges presented by a widespread disaster. After reading this material you will have an idea of what you might face in such a calamity and how it will be of benefit to you in your organizational and operational planning.

Student Preparation required:

None.

Introduction

Editor's note - This unit is based in part on observations by Bob Dyruff, W6POU, noted California authority on disaster communications. Dyruff assisted governmental and volunteer agencies in disaster planning for years and was the ARRL Assistant Director for Emergency Communications in the Southwestern Division among other posts in the ARRL Field Organization. It was written "Pre-Katrina." Obviously the events of Hurricane Katrina changed many things. It is interesting how accurately he predicted the coming events and how little needed to be edited here.

Onset: Critical Communication Requirements in a Disaster

What happens to critical communication assets during the onset of disaster conditions? First, there is a huge increase in the volume of traffic on public-safety radio channels, accompanied by prolonged waiting periods to gain access. As the disaster widens, equipment outages occur at key locations. Messages are not handled in order of priority, and urgent messages are often lost.

As agencies respond, the need arises for agencies to communicate with one another. Meeting that need is an up-hill battle as these agencies have incompatible radio systems, and use unfamiliar or unattainable frequencies, names, terms and procedures. Exacerbating the situation is the fact that most agencies are reluctant to use another agency's system, or to allow theirs to be used by others.

In a large-scale situation, a need arises to contact locations at distances beyond the range of a given radio or system (50 to 350 miles or more). Message reply delays are experienced, leading

Section 5: Considerations
Topic 25: What to Expect in Large Scale Disasters

to deferred decisions on crucial matters, message duplication and confusion. A need arises to generate and decipher handwritten messages sent through relaying stations.

Different modes of communication are required in addition to voice:

- Volume data in printed form—data modes, high-speed packet and facsimile.
- Morse code or PSK31 under difficult reception conditions.
- Encoded data for extreme privacy.
- Television—mobile, portable, aeronautical and marine.
- Telephone interconnections from/to radio systems.

Simultaneously with a high volume of message traffic, stations must cope with messages having widely differing priorities. Also, priority and precedence designations differ among agencies if any are used at all.

Operational problems arise such as:

- High-volume traffic circuits with no supply of message forms.
- Using the only printed forms available that were designed for a different, unrelated agency or function.
- Attempting to decipher scribbling from untrained message writers;
- Using scribes who cannot understand radio parlance or read through QRM.
- Becoming inundated with traffic volume so heavy it results in confusion over which messages are to be sent, which were sent, which have been received for delivery, and which have been received to be filed for ready reference.

What happens in the first 72 hours?

In the early hours of an emergency turning into a major disaster, it takes precious time to overcome the obstacles to placing fully activated mutual aid resources into operation. Communication is one of those vital resources.

The greatest concentration of relief efforts is generally found in the incorporated cities served by agencies with paid professionals— assuming their equipment, facilities and personnel remain operable. While urban areas experience more concentrated damage, suburbs and isolated areas of a county suffer from remoteness from fire departments, public works, law enforcement and the services of all other agencies. All organizations scramble to respond to an unprecedented demand for service within their authorized jurisdiction. There may be indecision and conflicts between community leaders.

Section 5: Considerations
Topic 25: What to Expect in Large Scale Disasters

In these circumstances the public is often isolated, unable to call for help or determine the nature and extent of the disaster so that they can make plans to:

- "Wait it out."
- Prepare to evacuate.
- Actually, evacuate with some possessions to a safe place.
- Obtain physical aid for an impending catastrophe.

Lack of information results in further attempted use of the telephone when the system is already saturated, if indeed it is still operating at all. An unexpected event in Katrina was that calls can often be received from out-of-town but not made across town.

The opportunity to even call for help is often unavailable to most citizens during the first 72 hours. Occasionally, a passing public safety vehicle or one equipped with an operational commercial, utility, amateur or CB radio can be "flagged down" to make a call—assuming it can contact a person who can help.

Too little information is gathered about the public's immediate needs, and ways to meet them. Distorted public perceptions develop through misinformation. At the same time, essential damage-assessment report data is needed by state and federal agencies to initiate relief aid from outside the disaster area.

Many broadcast stations (*those still on the air*) initially disseminate rumors and speculation in the absence of factual information. Those few people who possess an operating battery-powered broadcast band radio can tune until they find a local station that can provide helpful information. Others receive such information second hand, if at all.

Everywhere, people walk aimlessly seeking a route to family and friends. Many, fearful of looting, remain in hazardous buildings, or return, as do shopkeepers, to salvage valuables. As darkness falls, looting and rumors of looting are generated.

Word circulates about shelter locations. Some displaced persons stay at homes of friends, relatives or strangers. Others are housed at public shelters for days, still searching for family members elsewhere, and without communication. The opportunity to notify concerned distant relatives is rarely available except via the American Red Cross' "Safe and Well" program – but that is computer based, and the Internet may not exist.

Later, often too late, information trickles in about problem areas or cases that have been overlooked or mishandled due to the lack of communication. Some potential evacuees are overlooked. These may be individual families or even thousands trapped in a major sports stadium.

Once the immediate threat to life has passed, survival instincts prevail. People operate essentially on their own for an indefinite period while public agencies seek to organize and respond to the most urgent problems of which their communications make them aware.

After-shocks, flare-up of fires, weakening or breaking of dams and new flood crests, build-up of winds, broken levees, etc., result in some relief work being undone and the posing of new threats.

Section 5: Considerations
Topic 25: What to Expect in Large Scale Disasters

Following Katrina, there were great strides made to achieve inter-agency communications, but it still has a long way to go. Inter-agency communication capabilities remain poor. At the end of 72 hours, the disaster area remains in virtual isolation except for helicopter service for known critical cases and official use.

Little centralized information is available. Amateur Radio operators from neighboring counties and states offer to help but are often unable to cross the roadblocks established to limit access by sightseers and potential looters. Disorganized local volunteers often lack essential skills and orientation. Costly mistakes are made and systems bog down. The dead pose a serious health problem. Stress rises among the citizenry. Little overall assessment emerges in the first 72 hours about available emergency resources and relief supplies.

- Shortages are apparent and growing.
- Travel continues to be difficult and slow.
- Relief supplies trickle in to uncertain storage locations.
- Some supplies are useless.

Restaurants remaining open are unable to cook without gas or to serve the masses that flood them. Food and water shortages have become critical. Normal water sources may have been cut off or contaminated.

Gasoline is unavailable – the pumps need electricity to work, and there is no power.

Eventually, essential functional communication networks evolve as priorities are asserted and clusters of traffic emerge. Relief efforts are mounted when someone takes charge, makes a decision and directs the efforts of others.

The command and control process requires communication—the ingredient in short supply in all disasters.

At critiques following a disaster, amidst the finger pointing blame and chest thumping claims, the cry is heard: "Next time we must be better prepared!" – and a committee is formed.

Section 5: Considerations
Topic 25: What to Expect in Large Scale Disasters

Reference Links

FEMA planning:

http://www.fema.gov/news/newsrelease.fema?id=52006

FEMA – after the disaster:

http://www.fema.gov/rebuild/index.shtm

Section 5: Considerations
Topic 25: What to Expect in Large Scale Disasters

Review

In this Learning Topic, you have examined a realistic assessment of the conditions present in large-scale disaster situations.

Activities

You have examined a realistic assessment of the conditions present in large-scale disaster situations. Speak with another emcomm volunteer (or from your own personal experience) and compare the event described to an actual local disaster. Discuss the results with your mentor.

Section 5: Considerations
Topic 25: What to Expect in Large Scale Disasters

Welcome to Topic 25 Knowledge Review

In order to demonstrate mastery of the information presented in the topic, you will be asked a series of un-graded questions. There are approximately 5 questions on the following pages in multiple-choice or true/false format. Feedback will be offered to you based on the answer you provide.

Question 1:

What is the first thing that happens after a disaster has occurred?

a) The Federal Emergency Management Agency arrives on the scene.

b) The Red Cross and Salvation Army arrive with food and bedding for victims.

c) Massive increase in the volume of traffic on public-safety radio channels.

d) The press provides up to date and accurate information to the public.

Question 2:

Which of the following statements is NOT true of interagency communication?

a) Many agencies use incompatible radio systems.

b) Many agencies are reluctant to use each other's radio system.

c) Agencies all use the same radio systems and frequencies.

d) Amateur Radio can be used to link agencies.

Question 3:

In the first 72 hours of a disaster situation, where is the greatest concentration of relief effort to be found?

a) Urban areas.

b) Suburban areas.

c) Rural areas.

d) Outside the affected area.

Section 5: Considerations
Topic 25: What to Expect in Large Scale Disasters

Question 4:

Which organization handles health and welfare messages on behalf of the victims?

a) Department of Homeland Security.

b) Hurricane Watch Net.

c) National Weather Service.

d) American Red Cross.

Question 5:

What is the usual situation in a disaster after the initial 72 hours?

a) The disaster area remains in virtual isolation.

b) The disaster is over and everybody can go home.

c) A few victims still need assistance.

d) Communication systems are back to normal.

Section 5: Considerations
Topic 26: Hazardous Materials Awareness

TOPIC 26:

Hazardous Materials Awareness

Objectives

Welcome to Topic 26.

This Learning Topic introduces you to the reporting of hazardous materials (HazMat) incidents and stresses personal safety awareness for emcomm volunteers.

Student Preparation required:

None required for this Learning Topic.

Introduction

Amateur Radio operators may encounter HazMat incidents during their travels, or they may be asked to assist with emergency communications in such incidents. Proper training is required for your own safety. Moreover, a wrong move by you during a HazMat operation can endanger not only your own safety, but also the safety of other responders as well as the entire local community.

The term "hazardous materials" (HazMat) refers to any substances or materials, which if released in an uncontrolled manner (e.g., spilled), can be harmful to people, animals, crops, water systems, or other elements of the environment. The list is long and includes explosives, gases, flammable and combustible liquids, flammable solids or substances, poisonous and infectious substances, radioactive materials, and corrosives. One of the major problems faced by emergency responders is determining which chemicals are involved and determining the potential hazards.

Hazardous Chemicals On The Move

As the primary regulatory agency concerned with the safe transportation of such materials in interstate commerce, the US Department of Transportation (DOT) has established several systems to manage HazMat materials. These include definitions of various classes of hazardous materials, placards and other marking requirements for vehicles, containers and packages to aid in rapid identification of cargoes, and an international cargo commodity numbering system.

The DOT requires that all freight containers, trucks and rail cars transporting these materials display placards identifying the hazard class or classes of the materials they are carrying. The placards are diamond-shaped, 10 inches on a side, color-coded and show an icon or graphic symbol depicting the hazard class (flammable, caustic, acid, radioactive, etc). They are

Section 5: Considerations
Topic 26: Hazardous Materials Awareness

displayed on the ends and sides of transport vehicles. A four-digit identification number may also be displayed on some placards or on an adjacent rectangular orange panel. If you have spent any time on the roads, you have undoubtedly seen these placards or panels displayed on trucks and railroad tank cars. You may recognize some of the more common ones, such as 1993, which covers a multitude of chemicals including road tar, cosmetics, diesel fuel and home heating oil. You may have also seen placards with the number "1203" (gasoline) on tankers filling the underground tanks at the local gas station.

In addition to truck and rail car placards, warning labels must be displayed on most packages containing hazardous materials. The labels are smaller versions (4 inches on a side) of the same placards used on vehicles. In some cases, more than one label must be displayed, in which case the labels must be placed next to each other. In addition to labels for each DOT hazard class, other labels with specific warning messages may be required. Individual containers also have to be accompanied by shipping papers that contain the proper product name, the four-digit ID number and other important information about the hazards of the material.

Hazardous Chemicals in Buildings

The National Fire Protection Association (NFPA) has devised a marking system to alert firefighters to the characteristics of hazardous materials stored in stationary tanks and facilities. This system, known as NFPA 704M, can also assist citizens visiting a site in identifying the hazard presented by the stored substance. Use of the system is voluntary, unless specified by local codes.

The NFPA 704M label is diamond-shaped, and is divided into four parts, or quadrants. The left quadrant, colored blue, contains a numerical rating of the substance's health hazard. Ratings are made on a scale of 0 to 4, with a rating of 4 indicating a danger level so severe that a very short exposure could cause serious injury or death. A zero, or no code at all in this quarter, means that no unusual hazard would result from the exposure. The top quadrant of the NFPA symbol contains the substance's fire hazard rating. As you might expect, this quadrant is red. Again, number codes in this quadrant range from 0 to 4, with 4 representing the most serious hazard. The NFPA label's right quadrant, colored yellow, indicates the substance's likelihood to explode or react. As with the health and fire hazard quadrants, ratings from 0 to 4 are used to indicate the degree of danger. If a 4 appears in this section, the chemical is extremely unstable, and even under normal conditions may explode or react violently.

A zero in this quadrant indicates the material is considered stable even in the event of a fire. The bottom quadrant is white, and contains information about any special hazards that may apply. There are three possible codes for the bottom quarter of the NFPA symbol:

1. OXY means this material is an oxidizer. It can easily release oxygen to create or worsen a fire or explosion hazard.

2. The symbol W indicates a material that reacts with water to release a gas that is either flammable or hazardous to health.

3. If the material is radioactive, the usual tri-blade "propeller" symbol for radioactivity will appear.

Section 5: Considerations
Topic 26: Hazardous Materials Awareness

Guidelines for Handling HazMat Incidents

1. Once you are in a safe position up-hill and up-wind, try to identify the material. However, it cannot be over-emphasized that you MUST stay well away from the site. Do NOT be tempted to get just a little closer so that you can read placards or other items. If you cannot read these items using a spotting scope or binoculars, simply report what you can see from a safe position. If you are able to see from a safe position, look for:

    - The four-digit number on a placard or orange panel.

    - The four-digit number preceded by "UN/NA" on a shipping paper, package or drum.

    - The name of the material on the shipping papers, placard, or package.

2. Call for help immediately and let the experts handle the situation. Remember, even ordinary firefighters and police are prohibited by federal law from taking certain actions at some HazMat incidents. Do not attempt to personally take any action beyond your report and preventing others from approaching. This is an instance when it is vitally important to know your limitations, not just for your own safety, but also for the safety of others.

3. When reporting a HazMat incident, include the following information:

    a.) Identify yourself.

    b.) Give your current location and the location of the incident, i.e. street address or cross streets, road and mile marker, distance from nearest town, etc.

    c.) Briefly describe what you see (from a distance), i.e. liquid spill, gaseous cloud, etc, and any placard numbers or other information you can safely see.

    d.) If a gaseous cloud or liquid spill exists, give the direction the contaminant is flowing or moving. Give any pertinent weather or other information you can observe from a safe distance that might help the experts in responding to the incident. Be concise.

Section 5: Considerations
Topic 26: Hazardous Materials Awareness

Reference Links

Details of the placards and emergency response procedures can be found in the comprehensive DOT Emergency Response Guidebook, copies of which may be available for your review at your local Emergency Management, police, sheriff or fire department. A copy is also available online at:

http://phmsa.dot.gov/hazmat/library/erg

You may also consult your Local Emergency Planning Committee (LEPC) or State Emergency Response Commission (SERC) concerning what role Amateur Radio might have in your local plan.

For more information about hazardous materials in general, contact:

FEMA, Technological Hazards Division
Federal Center Plaza, 500 C St., SW,
Washington, DC, 20472
(202) 646-2861

Section 5: Considerations
Topic 26: Hazardous Materials Awareness

Review

If you happen upon a hazardous materials incident, first take precautions to protect yourself and others with you by remaining at a safe distance, upwind and uphill. Next, report any basic information you can safely gather, including placard legends and numbers, wind conditions, scene conditions, and other information to the appropriate public safety agency. Take no direct action except to report, and to protect yourself and others.

Activities

Describe to your mentor how you would handle the following situation:

You are traveling through a rural area right behind a tornado, reporting damage and casualties to the local fire and police agencies as you go. Cresting a hill, you see a tank trailer overturned on the road ahead. No one else is around. A variable wind is blowing the leaking fumes in several directions unpredictably. You cannot see the placards on the truck from where you are.

Section 5: Considerations
Topic 26: Hazardous Materials Awareness

Welcome to Topic 26 Knowledge Review

In order to demonstrate mastery of the information presented in the topic, you will be asked a series of un-graded questions. There are approximately 5 questions on the following pages in multiple-choice or true/false format. Feedback will be offered to you based on the answer you provide.

Question 1:

Which of the following BEST describes where you should be located when in the vicinity of a HazMat incident?

a) Far away enough to ensure your safety.

b) Downhill and downwind.

c) Close enough to read the numbers on any placards with your naked eyes.

d) Alongside emergency responders wearing exposure suits.

Question 2:

Which federal agency is responsible for warning the public about hazardous materials containers and shippers?

a) Federal Emergency Management Agency.

b) Federal Response Plan.

c) National Communications System.

d) Department of Transportation.

Question 3:

Before transmitting in the area of a HazMat incident what should you always do?

a) First identify the agents by reading the placard or container labels.

b) Be far enough away so that no vapors or fumes are present.

c) Wait to report the incident until police or fire officials have arrived.

d) Take action to stop or contain any agents that might be leaking.

Section 5: Considerations
Topic 26: Hazardous Materials Awareness

Question 4:

On the sides of transporting vehicles how are different classes of hazardous materials identified?

a) Placards.

b) Four-digit numbers.

c) Warning labels and/or icons.

d) All of the answers are correct.

Question 5:

Gasoline tankers filling the neighborhood gas station's underground tanks are identified with a placard bearing which of the following?

a) 1203.

b) 1993.

c) 2003.

d) 2706.

Section 5: Considerations
Topic 27: Marine Communications

TOPIC 27:

Marine Communications

Objectives

Welcome to Topic 27.

Reading this Learning Topic is intended to give you, the emergency communicator a basic knowledge of marine communications and the proper procedures to follow in the event of a maritime emergency.

Student Preparation required:

Understand the following definitions:

    Vessel: A general term for all craft capable of floating on water and larger than a rowboat.

    Ship: A general term for larger seagoing vessels of every kind.

    Boat: A term applied to smaller craft propelled by oars, sails or engines.

    Marine: An adjective meaning related to or connected with the sea.

Introduction

The most common marine radio mode is VHF- FM, (156 to 162 MHz), with an effective range from ship to ship of 10 to 15 miles, and ship to shore of 20-30 miles. Vessels that routinely travel outside this distance generally have MF/HF-SSB, satellite communications or both. CW communication on MF/HF is no longer used.

No license is currently required for pleasure boats operating on the FM channels in US territorial waters. The FCC limits VHF-FM marine radios to a maximum of 25 watts. Radios are also required to be capable of 1-watt operation for short range and in-harbor use. For more regulatory information visit: http://wireless.fcc.gov/.

The use of VHF and MF/HF marine radios is restricted to vessels on the water. The use of portables or mobiles to communicate with crew on shore is not allowed. Certain commercial users, such as marinas, marine towing services and fish canneries may be licensed for limited base operations on certain channels. In an emergency, however, the FCC rules are suspended, and you may use whatever means of communication are necessary to protect life and property.

Section 5: Considerations
Topic 27: Marine Communications

Channel Selection

Marine FM frequencies have been assigned channel numbers, and all are designated for specific uses. Channel 16 has been designated worldwide as a distress and calling frequency. All vessels are required to maintain a listening "watch" on FM 16 while underway. With the growth of boating and the elimination of mandatory radio licenses for certain vessels operating in domestic waters, FM 16 has suffered from abuse and overuse. To maintain the integrity of FM 16 as a distress frequency, FM 9 has been designated as an alternate calling frequency. While FM 16 can be used for routine calling, most calls should be made on FM 9. This would apply to owners of newer marine radios, which are capable of simultaneously monitoring both FM9 and FM16 using either a "scan" or "dual watch" function.

The designated use for every marine channel is contained in the manual that comes with all VHF-FM radios. For example, FM 13 is designated for navigational purposes, and a number of channels are used for inter-ship communication. Others are not for public use. FM 83 is reserved for use by the Coast Guard Auxiliary. FM 22 is for public communication with the Coast Guard, but may not be used by boaters unless specifically instructed to do so by the Coast Guard radio operator on FM 16. FM 22 is also used by the Coast Guard to broadcast "Notice To Mariners" messages (NOTAMS), after announcing them on FM 16. FM 6 is an Inter-Ship Safety channel, and is often used for search and rescue operations.

A list of all marine channels and their assigned uses can be seen at
http://wireless.fcc.gov/services/index.htm?job=service_bandplan&id=ship_stations

Frequencies for key marine VHF channels

Channel	Frequency	Use
FM 9	156.45	Calling
FM 22	157.1	Coast Guard—NOTAMS
FM 16	156.8	Calling/Distress
FM 23	157.15	Coast Guard
FM 17	156.85	State/local gov't. shore sta.
FM 68	156.425	Intership
FM 18	156.9	Commercial Intership
FM 69	156.475	Intership
FM 21	157.05	Coast Guard
FM 83	157.175	Coast Guard Auxiliary

Section 5: Considerations
Topic 27: Marine Communications

Spoken Emergency Signals

To simplify identification of marine radio traffic, certain pro-words are used. When you hear one of these, you should listen carefully, write down any information and refrain from transmitting on the frequency until necessary. The pro-words are listed below with an explanation of each.

"MAYDAY MAYDAY"—the highest priority urgency call. The vessel calling is threatened by grave or immediate danger and requires immediate assistance. If you hear this call, copy the information on paper, resist the urge to contact the party calling and listen first for a reply from a Coast Guard unit. Only if no response is heard should you attempt communication with the vessel in distress.

"PAN PAN" (pronounced "pawn-pawn")— known as an "urgency" call—the vessel calling has an urgent message concerning the safety of a vessel or person. Again, copy the message, but respond only if no answer is heard. This signal may also be used by the Coast Guard for certain urgent messages to all vessels on the channel.

"SECURITE" (pronounced "securitay")—the safety signal SECURITE is used for official messages about the safety of navigation or important weather warnings. The Coast Guard can be heard using this pro-word in regular "notice to mariners" transmissions.

"SILENCE"—the Coast Guard may declare SILENCE on a specific channel. Only those units actively involved in the incident may transmit on that frequency until the Coast Guard lifts the "silence" order.

Incident Reporting

There are two types of incidents that hams should report directly to the Coast Guard: vessels in distress, and oil or chemical spills into public waters. The first should be reported directly to the nearest Coast Guard station. Oil and chemical spills should be reported to the Coast Guard's National Response Center at 1-800-424-8802.

The secondary reporting method is via the NRC Internet Web site http://www.nrc.uscg.mil/. If neither is available, try contacting the nearest Coast Guard facility.

Distress Information

If you hear a distress call, listen first to see if the Coast Guard responds within a minute or two. If not, attempt to gather the following information:

- Position of the vessel involved, number of persons on board, nature of the distress.
- Name of the vessel.
- Call sign (if any).
- Length and type of vessel.
- Color.
- Any descriptive features—number of masts, flying bridge, etc.
- Weather conditions on scene.

Section 5: Considerations
Topic 27: Marine Communications

- Frequency being used to communicate with the vessel.
- On board emergency equipment: Life raft, Emergency Position Indicating Radio. Beacon (EPIRB) and class of EPIRB if possible.

Once you have the information, advise all persons on board to don life jackets, and contact either 911 dispatch or the closest Coast Guard facility by phone. In some cases, a local fire or police boat may be able to respond more quickly than the Coast Guard, who may be some distance away. Identify yourself as an Amateur Radio operator relaying an emergency message. Pass on all the information that you have gathered and assist as requested. Provide your name and phone number or other means of contact so that responding local public safety agencies or the Coast Guard may reach you if needed. It is possible that you are the only station that can communicate with the distressed vessel.

Routine Communication

Calling a vessel on a marine channel is very similar to 2 meters. If using channel 9, transmit the name of the vessel you want to talk with twice, followed by your station's name twice, and the channel designation. For example: "Fishy Business, Fishy Business, this is Dream Boat, Dream Boat, Channel 9."

Listen for at least 30 seconds before repeating the call. Once you get an answer, direct the station to shift to a "working" channel: "Fishy Business this is Dream Boat; shift to channel 69."

In order to avoid confusion on congested channels, FCC rules require you to identify your vessel on each transmission, although some stations shift to a shortened call after the initial contact is established. **The use of 10 codes and "Q" signals is not permitted on marine VHF-FM.**

MF/HF SSB Communications

Vessels that operate further offshore may operate a MF/HF-SSB unit on designated channelized international frequencies. Vessels using a MF/HF radio must also have a VHF-FM radio aboard. The US Coast Guard maintains "guard" on (they monitor) 2182 kHz, the calling and distress frequency, as well as other designated frequencies in this band. A complete list of MF and HF maritime frequencies and assignments can be seen at

http://www.navcen.uscg.gov/?pageName=mtHighFrequency

Many boaters traveling on the high seas carry HF Amateur Radio aboard. A listing of Amateur Radio Maritime Nets is contained on the ARRL Web site http://www.arrl.org/arrl-net-directory. These nets may also be used to pass emergency traffic. Distress traffic received over MF/HF-SSB should be handled in the same way as on VHF- FM.

Section 5: Considerations
Topic 27: Marine Communications

Reference Links

FCC regulatory information:

http://wireless.fcc.gov/services/index.htm?job=service_home&id=maritime

US Coast Guard:

http://www.uscg.mil/

Section 5: Considerations
Topic 27: Marine Communications

Review

Marine radio uses both VHF-FM and MF/HF- SSB. Coastal operations are on VHF-FM, and channel 16 is the international emergency channel. If you hear an unanswered distress call, you may assist by answering the call and relaying the information to the nearest Coast Guard or local marine patrol office.

Activities

If you live within fifty miles of a seacoast, a major navigable river, or any of the Great Lakes, identify the US Coast Guard station nearest to your community and its telephone number and share this information with your mentor.

Section 5: Considerations
Topic 27: Marine Communications

Welcome to Topic 27 Knowledge Review

In order to demonstrate mastery of the information presented in the topic, you will be asked a series of un-graded questions. There are approximately 5 questions on the following pages in multiple-choice or true/false format. Feedback will be offered to you based on the answer you provide.

Question 1:

When is it permissible to utilize channel FM 22?

a) At any time after making an initial call on FM 16.

b) Whenever channel FM 9 or FM 16 are busy.

c) Only when directed by the Coast Guard.

d) At no time, it is for Coast Guard use only.

Question 2:

What should you do if you hear an unanswered marine distress call?

a) Contact the nearest Coast Guard facility and advise them of the call.

b) Answer the caller immediately and ask what the emergency is.

c) Get in your own boat and attempt a rescue.

d) Listen for a response. If none, respond and gather all information possible and then contact the nearest Coast Guard facility.

Question 3:

When must you identify yourself on VHF-FM marine radio?

a) Only on the initial call.

b) Only on the initial call and the final call.

c) Only on the original call and then every ten minutes.

d) On all transmissions.

Section 5: Considerations
Topic 27: Marine Communications

Question 4:

Which vessels operate MF/HF SSB radios?

a) Any vessel that wants to.

b) Only sea-going vessels that operate outside the range of VHF-FM radios.

c) Only those vessels that operate offshore and have a VHF-FM marine radio.

d) Only those vessels that have an Amateur Radio operator aboard.

Question 5:

Which channel(s) may be used for calling another vessel?

a) FM 83.

b) FM 9.

c) FM 16.

d) Both FM9 and FM 16.

Section 6: Alternatives and Opportunities
Topic 28: Modes, Methods and Applications

TOPIC 28:

Modes, Methods and Applications

Objectives

Welcome to Topic 28.

Reading this Learning Topic will help you chose the correct operating mode for each situation in an emcomm environment.

Student Preparation required:

You should be generally familiar with phone (voice), CW, packet, and other digital modes.

Introduction

Your purpose as emergency communicators is to provide accurate and rapid transfer of information from one place to another. To do that job well, you must understand the strengths and weaknesses of each mode of communication. In addition, you must be thoroughly familiar with the needs and priorities of the agencies you are serving. Some messages must be delivered quickly, and others are less urgent. Some are detailed, and some are simple. Sometimes you should not even use radio.

Some Concepts to Consider

Communication modes fall into several categories:

    Point to point – Telephone, fax, some digital radio modes
    Multi-point – Voice and CW radio, some digital modes
    High precision – Fax, e-mail, digital modes
    Low precision – Voice, CW, telephone
    High priority – Voice, telephone
    Low priority – Fax, e-mail, digital modes, CW

Messages fall into similar categories:

    Point to point – Messages intended for one party
    Point to multi-point – Messages intended for a group
    Multi-point to point – Messages from members of a group directed to one station
    High precision – Lists of items, medical or technical terminology, specialized or detailed information

Section 6: Alternatives and Opportunities
Topic 28: Modes, Methods and Applications

    Low precision – Traffic reports, damage estimates, simple situation reports
    High priority – Fast delivery is critical
    Low priority – Messages can be delivered in a more relaxed time frame

Each type of message should be sent using the most appropriate mode, taking into consideration the message's contents, and its destination(s). An example might serve to illustrate these concepts.

Mode Example: A localized flash flood hit a north Florida county a few years ago, prompting the evacuation of a low-lying neighborhood. The Red Cross opened a shelter in a church several miles away from the affected area. ARES was mobilized to provide communication support. In spite of the weather, the shelter still had electricity and phone service.

When the county Emergency Coordinator (EC) stopped by the site, the ARES operator on duty was using his battery- operated 2-meter hand-held radio and the wide-area repeater to talk to Red Cross HQ across town. The ham was reading a three-page list of names and addresses of evacuees who had checked into the shelter. To ensure proper transcription, he was spelling each name phonetically, pausing after each name to see if the headquarters station needed fills. Needless to say, this was a time-consuming process. The operator had been reading for almost 15 minutes and was still on the second page of the list.

Less than 10 feet away from his operating position sat a fax machine. The EC turned on the machine, dialed the Red Cross fax number, and fed in the remaining page of the list. The ham on duty had used over 15 minutes of air time and precious battery capacity to read two pages. The third page was faxed in less than 20 seconds.

Neither the operator at the shelter nor the one at headquarters had considered using the telephone or fax machine, even though these communication options were available and functioning. In all fairness to the hams in this situation, their training and practice had led them to concentrate on 2-meter voice to the exclusion of other modes of communication. So, instead of an efficient, point-to-point communication channel (telephone line), they had used a busy multi-point channel (the wide-area repeater). Instead of using a mode that generated automatic hard copy, they used one that required handwritten transcription. Instead of a high- precision transfer (fax), they had used a low- precision one (voice) requiring spelling and phonetics. The situation was especially poignant because the repeater had been needed at the time for a different type of communication – the transfer of mobile operator's reports, which could not be done over the telephone. Further, it was later discovered that the "broadcast" of evacuee's names and addresses over non-secure communication channels was a violation of Red Cross policy.

Of course, telephones and fax machines will not be available in every emergency. Sometimes only one mode will be available, especially when the emergency is totally unanticipated, utility service is interrupted over a wide area and the communicators are caught unprepared. But, with proper planning you can increase the likelihood that more than one option will be available. After all, we go to great lengths to make sure that 2 meter radios are readily available, so why not other communication options as well?

Tactical Messages: Tactical messages are usually low-precision and time-critical, and can be passed most efficiently using voice. Depending on the nature of the message, it may take the

Section 6: Alternatives and Opportunities
Topic 28: Modes, Methods and Applications

form of formal written traffic, or at the other extreme, it may mean that the microphone is handed to a person from the served agency. This is frequently the quickest way to get the job done.

Lists and Detailed Messages: Some messages contain long lists of supplies, or details where accuracy is important. Voice transmission can introduce errors, and long messages can waste valuable net resources. The various digital modes (including land-line fax and email) offer the best means of handling these messages, since they are both fast and accurate. Digital messages also have the benefit of repeatable accuracy. When a message is passed through several stations, it remains unchanged since no operator intervention occurs.

Sensitive Information: Some messages contain information that should be kept private. Reporters and the general public commonly use scanning receivers to monitor public safety and Amateur Radio communications. Names and addresses of evacuees should never be transmitted over voice channels, since thieves with scanners can use this information to loot unattended homes.

Learn in advance your served agency's privacy policy regarding certain types of information. Some groups have switched to digital modes, such as packet, in an attempt to offer more privacy. Although digital transmissions require more than a simple scanner to intercept, they cannot be relied upon for absolute privacy. The equipment needed to receive most digital modes is available, and is even built into some newer receivers. Anyone wishing to monitor digital transmissions can certainly do so. Discuss this issue with your served agency before using any Amateur Radio mode to handle sensitive messages. Remember - any means of assuring meaningful message security on Amateur Radio would be in violation of the Part 97 prohibition against the use of codes and ciphers. If absolute privacy is required, the message should not be transmitted by Amateur Radio. In some cases, the most appropriate method might be hand delivery by a radio-dispatched courier.

Digital Modes

Traffic nets handling large volumes of written or high precision traffic should consider using one of the digital modes. Digital modes can be used to transmit long lists such as health and welfare traffic, and logistics messages involving lists of people or supplies. Some digital modes provide virtually error-free transmission and relays can be accomplished by retransmitting the received digital message without having to retype it. Packet systems can provide automatic relays. Digital modes that do not provide automatic error correction should only be used when clean and interference-free signals can be guaranteed. These modes include RTTY, AMTOR mode A, and PSK31 in BPSK mode.

HF: While there are many "favorites" with promoters for specific modes, over the years it appears that the most commonly used digital modes for emergency HF operation are packet, AMTOR mode B, and PSK31 in QPSK mode. But this is changing with new options to interface with the Internet. In general, antenna and radio considerations are similar to voice or CW operation, although certain digital signals require less power than voice modes to achieve the same effect.

VHF/UHF: The TNC2 (Terminal Node Controller, Version 2) FM packet is the most common mode used on VHF and UHF frequencies. The antenna and coverage considerations are the same as for FM voice.

Section 6: Alternatives and Opportunities
Topic 28: Modes, Methods and Applications

Packet: Packet communication is error-free in point to point "automated repeat request" (ARQ) or "forward error correction" (FEC) broadcast modes. The most effective way to send messages via packet radio is to use a "bulletin board". The sending station "posts" his messages on the bulletin board and other stations can then retrieve their messages at will. Urgent messages can also be sent directly to the receiving station if needed.

Bulletin-board stations are also useful when a number of stations are sending messages to a single point, such as a command post, weather service office, or emergency operations center. Similarly, bulletin-boards can be useful in handling outgoing traffic. Stations with traffic can post messages to the bulletin-board. The traffic handlers can periodically pick up the traffic and send it to the outbound NTS nets.

If your group is using FM packet, ask if transmissions are simplex point to point, or if nodes, digipeaters, or bulletin-board forwarding systems are being used. You will need to know which frequencies and modes are used and for what purpose, what their call signs or aliases are, and how various parts of the system interconnect. A consideration is that multipath propagation may distort digital signals enough to cause failure when a voice might still be understandable. The solution is the same as in voice mode – move the antenna a few inches or feet until you get a clear signal.

AMTOR Mode B: AMTOR mode B (also known as "FEC" mode) is an advanced teletype mode with forward error correction, making it ideal for high precision messages over long distances.

PSK31: The ability of PSK31 to be usable in very poor conditions makes it ideal for HF emergency communication. In addition, the efficiency resulting from the very narrow bandwidth of the PSK31 signal means that even a low power transmitter will work quite well. There are two PSK31 modes: BPSK, which has no error correction, and QPSK, which has forward error-correction. BPSK should be used unless the received copy is poor, since QPSK is 3dB less efficient and requires more careful tuning. Under all but the worst conditions, BPSK will provide perfect transmissions.

Packet Teleprinting Over Radio (PACTOR): This is a combination of packet and AMTOR. It is designed for HF use only, and combines the best features of both. PACTOR uses FEC and ARQ modes, and a standard keyboard. PACTOR is quite robust (more so than AMTOR and RTTY), but can be slowed by poor band conditions.

TCP/IP Packet: TCP/IP Internet protocols and network services are useable on packet radio. TCP/IP systems have advantages over conventional packet protocols that could be important in amateur emcomm operations. One IP system is JNOS, which has extensions written by Johannes Reinalda, WG7J, to the original NOS (Network Operating System) written by Phil Karn, KA9Q.

JNOS is a TCP/IP oriented e-mail system. If you're familiar with Internet e-mail, you're familiar with typing e-mail into JNOS. It sends e-mail via SMTP mail protocol and can interface to Internet. A JNOS station can relay packet radio messages to the Internet and vice versa, unattended. It will print incoming messages automatically onto a printer, unattended. If the printer is a cut-sheet printer such as an inkjet or laser printer, individual messages will automatically appear on separate sheets.

The operator can open up to eight windows for multiple sessions for messaging. It has a ninth

Section 6: Alternatives and Opportunities
Topic 28: Modes, Methods and Applications

window for command mode for controlling the system, and a tenth window for debugging. It can multi-task efficiently on a 386 computer with 1megabyte of memory. In a minimal configuration, it can run on a PC/XT (640KB 8086) as an end-node station. It supports multiple communications ports and multiple radio/TNC combinations. It is shareware, and is available on the internet.

APRS: While not a message handling mode, APRS is a digital information mode with applications in emcomm. Originally called "Automatic Position Reporting System", this mode is now sometimes called "Automatic Packet Reporting System", owing to new applications of the technology. The newest application of APRS is the automated reporting of data from digital weather stations. The original application for APRS, developed by Bob Bruninga, WB4APR, is to track a station's location. A GPS receiver is connected to a computer, and its position information is transmitted to other stations using APRS packet software, displaying the location of the sending station on a map. APRS also has a messaging mode similar to Internet "Instant Messaging" where quick one-line messages can be exchanged.

APRS has two obvious applications for emcomm - First, the locations of various emergency vehicles can be tracked visually in real time in an automated and unattended fashion. Second, weather and other environmental data can be reported automatically in near real-time. Both applications can both speed data acquisition and reduce the work load on critical emergency nets.

D-Star and Winlink 2000

These two systems are rapidly growing in popularity and have already served well in emergency situations.

Winlink 2000 is another digital, error-free mode that transmits conventional email messages over the Internet when it is available. If the Internet is down locally, the emails can be sent by radio to another Winlink station that has Internet service and enter the Internet there. Like normal email, the messages can be sent anywhere that has a functioning email address. Also like normal email, there can be a delay in their reception at times. Because it uses ordinary email forms, it is familiar to served agency personnel. Winlink operators mostly use VHF or UHF, but it can use HF too.

D-Star is also a digital system -but there are significant differences. D-Star allows for both voice and data communications. Even small hand-held radios can send and receive short digital messages. D-Star uses VHF which allows for a slow bit-rate, or UHF which is much faster. It does not currently have HF options. D-Star also uses the Internet for long-distance messaging. For example, a short digital message may be composed on a hand-held portable radio, be sent over the air to a D-Star repeater, enter the Internet, be received by another D-Star repeater in another state and then sent out over the air to the addressee.

Both of these systems have their advantages and their devotees

Related Considerations

Become familiar with, and practice using, any digital mode or system well in advance of an

Section 6: Alternatives and Opportunities
Topic 28: Modes, Methods and Applications

emergency. Most are complex enough that some experience is required to use them efficiently and effectively.

Digital communications can be enhanced by composing the message off-line in a text editor. With a little ingenuity, "fill in the blank" forms can be created in most word processors to reduce the amount of typing required and help standardize message formats. For packet communication, consider an emcomm-specific program like ARESPACK (see Reference Links below).

The high duty-cycle of many digital modes requires a rugged radio and power supply with adequate cooling. Test your equipment under field conditions for an extended period of time to identify any possible problems.

Amateur Television (ATV)

There are two forms of ATV – slow-scan and fast-scan. Fast-scan ATV is live, full motion TV similar to what you see on commercial TV, but usually at reduced quality. Slow-scan ATV uses a voice-grade channel to send a still picture line by line. It can take more than a minute for a color picture to be transmitted.

ATV has a number of emcomm applications, but all involve letting emergency managers see what is going on in the field without ever leaving their offices. ATV crews usually take a passive "observer" approach, and avoid interaction with bystanders to ensure that a situation is accurately represented. No emcomm ATV transmission should ever be "staged" for the camera.

Section 6: Alternatives and Opportunities
Topic 28: Modes, Methods and Applications

Reference Links

ARRL has a wealth of information on various digital modes at:

http://www.arrl.org/digital-modes

ARRL also has a course on "Digital Emergency Communications":

http://www.arrl.org/shop/ARRL-Digital-Technology-for-Emergency-Communications-Course

Section 6: Alternatives and Opportunities
Topic 28: Modes, Methods and Applications

Review

Choosing the correct mode and frequency for each type of message will make your nets more efficient and improve service to your agency. Voice modes are low precision, multi-point modes, and many digital modes are high precision point to point modes. Sometimes, Amateur Radio is not the best way to send a message. Confidential messages are best sent via telephone, fax or courier.

Activities

Choose and complete two of the following:

1. Consider your own personal radio resources. Of the modes mentioned within this lesson, discuss with your mentor which you would consider acquiring for your own use? Why? Which would you not consider acquiring? Why not?

2. Select three of the digital modes. Identify the positive and negative aspects of using each of the three in an emcomm situation and discuss with your mentor.

3. Based on the considerations you have identified above, develop a simple communication equipment plan for a small emcomm unit based in a small community. Within your plan, be sure to identify and discuss with your mentor the equipment and modes you would employ.

4. Discuss with your mentor how the plan you developed above would be different if your emcomm group were quite large and located in a large community.

Section 6: Alternatives and Opportunities
Topic 28: Modes, Methods and Applications

Welcome to Topic 28 Knowledge Review

In order to demonstrate mastery of the information presented in the topic, you will be asked a series of un-graded questions. There are approximately 5 questions on the following pages in multiple-choice or true/false format. Feedback will be offered to you based on the answer you provide.

Question 1:

Which of the following best describes your purpose as an emergency communicator?

a) To operate the radio.

b) To coordinate communications for the EOC.

c) To provide accurate and rapid transfer of information from one place to another.

d) To provide internal communication support to one (and only one) responding agency.

Question 2:

Which of the following best describes tactical messages?

a) They are high precision and time critical.

b) They are low precision and time critical.

c) They are point-to-point and NOT time critical.

d) They are point-to-multipoint and low precision.

Question 3:

Long lists and detailed messages are best handled by which of the following modes?

a) Voice or CW.

b) Fax or digital.

c) CW or digital.

d) Phone or fax.

Section 6: Alternatives and Opportunities
Topic 28: Modes, Methods and Applications

Question 4:

During an emergency, you are using voice transmissions to pass messages. Which of the following "guidelines" should govern your action if you were asked to transmit the names and addresses of victims?

a) Transmit the information exactly as presented to you.

b) Use a pre-established code to transmit the information.

c) If absolute privacy is required; do not transmit the information by Amateur Radio.

d) Switch to a digital mode and be assured of complete privacy.

Question 5:

Which of the following PSK31 modes has an error correction feature?

a) BPSK.

b) QPSK.

c) RPSK.

d) SPSK.

Section 6: Alternatives and Opportunities
Topic 29: Other Learning Opportunities

TOPIC 29:

Other Learning Opportunities

Objectives

Welcome to Topic 29.

This Learning Topic offers ways to develop and perfect the skills you have learned in this course.

Student Preparation required:
None

Introduction

Someone once asked a famous violinist how to get to Carnegie Hall in New York City. His answer was "practice, practice, practice."

So it is with emergency communication skills. If you want your performance in the next big disaster to be flawless, practice is essential. Fortunately, there are plenty of opportunities to do so if you take the time to seek them out.

Regularly Scheduled Nets

Many local ARES and RACES groups hold regularly scheduled training nets. Well-designed nets will vary the format and goals frequently in order to keep them interesting. One month may be devoted to learning about the county's new damage report form, and another with moving welfare messages to and from the National Traffic System (NTS).

Local Classroom and On-Air Training Sessions

Your emcomm organization and/or served agency may offer a variety of educational opportunities. Agencies may offer job specific training, such as the American Red Cross' Introduction to Disasters, Mass Care Overview, Shelter Operations and Disaster Damage Assessment courses. Smaller training sessions may deal with the use of certain forms or procedures. In addition to regular nets, special on-air training sessions may be held on a repeater or simplex frequency as an alternative to classroom sessions when the subject is simple or utilizes a net environment.

Section 6: Alternatives and Opportunities
Topic 29: Other Learning Opportunities

Public Service Events

Some of the best practice for tactical disaster communication is your local "athon". It does not matter if it is a bike-athon, walk-athon or crawl-athon, but the larger the event, the better the experience. A large, fast moving event closely simulates the conditions experienced in disaster communication situations. Even a smaller or slower event will allow you to practice tactical net operating skills or experiment with various modes under field conditions.

Learning Resources on the Internet

We strongly recommend downloading and printing copies of the ARRL Public Service Manual and ARES Field Resources Manual. Put them in a three ring binder and make them part of your jump kit for easy reference at home or in the field. In addition, you may want to check with your Section Manager to see if there are additional documents you should keep in your jump kit for your local area.

- ARRL Section Manager List: http://www.arrl.org/sections
- ARRL Net Directory: http://www.arrl.org/arrl-net-directory
- ARRL Public Service Manual: http://www.arrl.org/public-service-communications-manual
- ARRL Digital Mode Information: http://www.arrl.org/digital-modes
- FEMA Emergency Management Institute: http://training.fema.gov/is/crslist.asp - see "ISP Course List" and "NIMS" Courses"
- FEMA Virtual Library http://www.fema.gov/library/index.jsp
- FCC Rules and Regulations http://www.arrl.org/part-97-amateur-radio
- National SKYWARN: http://skywarn.org/
- NOAA Watch – NOAA's All Hazard Monitor: http://www.noaawatch.gov/
- Ham Radio at the NWS Hurricane Center: http://www2.fiu.edu/orgs/w4ehw/
- NWS Doppler Radar Sites: http://www.weather.gov/radar_tab.php
- FEMA Community Emergency Response Teams (CERT): http://www.citizencorps.gov/cert/

Other ARRL Courses

- PR-101: The ARRL course for dealing with media and public relations. Available on CD. http://www.arrl.org/shop/PR-101-Course-on-CD-ROM

- Public Service and Emergency Communications Management for Radio Amateurs (EC-016): This new AREC course is designed for those in leadership positions who wish to further develop management skills. If you are an AEC, EC, DEC, or SEC, or are serving in another leadership or training capacity this is the course for you. Available online. http://www.arrl.org/ec-016-course

Section 6: Alternatives and Opportunities
Topic 29: Other Learning Opportunities

- The ARRL Digital Technology for Emergency Communications Course will introduce you to all the ways Amateur Radio operators are using digital technology as a valuable emergency communications tool. Available on CD. http://www.arrl.org/shop/ARRL-Digital-Technology-for-Emergency-Communications-Course/

Books

- *The ARES Field Resources Manual* (ARRL) is a handy and rugged spiral bound field guide packed with essential emcomm information. It should be in the ready kit of every emcomm volunteer.
- The ARRL *Operating Manual* covers all the basics of Amateur Radio operation & more.
- The ARRL *FCC Rules and Regulations for the Amateur Radio Service* includes the complete Part 97 rules from Title 47 of the Code of Federal Regulations.
- ARRL's *HF Digital Handbook* covers PSK31, MFSK16 and other popular digital modes.
- *VHF Digital Handbook by Steve Ford WB8IMY* includes discussion of digital applications of packet radio, APRS and Winlink 2000 in public service and emergency communications.
- *Transmitter Hunting: Radio Direction Simplified* by Joseph Moell, K0OV, and Thomas Curlee, WB6UZZ (ARRL) is the "bible" of radio direction finding.
- *The ARRL RFI Handbook* will help you locate and resolve all sorts of radio interference.
- *The ARRL Antenna Book* covers portable & emergency antennas for 40 and 80 meters.
- *The ARRL Repeater Directory* lists all VHF and UHF repeaters in the USA, Canada and many other countries. This directory is updated annually.
- *Storm Spotting and Amateur Radio* by Michael Corey W5MPC and Victor Morris AH6WX is a resource for the Amateur Radio operator who volunteers as a storm spotter.
- *Emergency Power for Radio Communications* discusses methods of alternative power generation for a variety of situations.
- *The ARRL Emergency Communication Library v. 1.0* provides informative documents and presentations on many aspects of emergency communication operating.

All of the above are available from ARRL at: http://www.arrl.org/arrl-store

Software

- **Tucson Amateur Packet Radio:** (TAPR) has a variety of packet software available. http://www.tapr.org/

- **FNpack:** A free Windows ® based packet messaging software package from Ken AC1H and the Twin State Radio Club, Inc. FNpack lets you automate much of the process of handling ARRL format messages, as well as to create your own forms. FNpack also has a novel unproto "net" mode. It can be downloaded at http://www.w1fn.org/. Also available on the same site is FNpsk, which offers much of the same functionality for PSK31 users.

- **Narrow Band Emergency Messaging System (NBEMS):** A suite of programs for emergency applications. See http://www.w1hkj.com/download.html for software download.

Section 6: Alternatives and Opportunities
Topic 29: Other Learning Opportunities

- **PSKMail:** A bare bones program that uses very limited bandwidth for passing messages. For Linux operating systems. http://pskmail.wikispaces.com/

- **WXSpots Network A:** useful tool on the Internet devoted to severe weather spotting as a means to enhance SKYWARN and similar operations. http://www.wxspots.com/

- **Winlink 2000**: http://www.winlink.org/

Section 6: Alternatives and Opportunities
Topic 29: Other Learning Opportunities

Review

Emcomm education is an ongoing process. To be an asset to your emcomm organization and its served agencies, you should take advantage of every possible learning opportunity.

Activities

1. Choose the next step you will take to either become involved with a local emcomm group, and/or the next step in your emcomm education. Share your choices with your mentor.

2. Interview three Amateur Radio operators who have actually been on an emergency deployment. Ask them to evaluate their preparedness for the experience, the degree they successfully supported emergency communications and how they evaluate their overall response. Share these experiences with your mentor

3. If you were placed in charge of training a new group of emcomm team members, what five topics would you give the highest priority? Share your answers with your mentor.

Section 6: Alternatives and Opportunities
Topic 29: Other Learning Opportunities

Welcome to Topic 29 Knowledge Review

In order to demonstrate mastery of the information presented in the topic, you will be asked a series of un-graded questions. There are approximately 5 questions on the following pages in multiple-choice or true/false format. Feedback will be offered to you based on the answer you provide.

Question 1:

Which of the following was NOT recommended as a means of practicing actual emcomm skills?

a) Regularly scheduled nets.

b) On-air training sessions.

c) Discussion groups.

d) Public service events.

Question 2:

What is the purpose of ARRL's *Public Service and Emergency Communications Management for Radio Amateurs* course?

a) To review the skills and knowledge presented in this course.

b) To provide training for prospective Emergency Operation Center Managers.

c) To prepare individuals for the jobs of NCS and Net Manager.

d) To prepare individuals for management level jobs such as EC, DEC or SEC or other leadership or training roles.

ARRL: Introduction to Emergency Communication Course
Answers to Topic Review Questions

Topic 1	Topic 2	Topic 3	Topic 4	Topic 5a
1 D	1 C	1 B	1 B	1 D
2 A	2 B	2 A	2 C	2 D
3 A	3 D	3 C	3 C	3 A
4 B	4 C	4 D	4 C	4 C
5 C	5 C	5 D	5 D	5 C

Topic 5b	Topic 6	Topic 7a	Topic 7b	Topic 7c
1 D	1 A	1 A	1 B	1 C
2 D	2 B	2 D	2 A	2 D
3 B	3 A	3 B	3 C	3 D
	4 D	4 B	4 C	4 A
	5 C	5 A	5 A	5 C

Topic 7d	Topic 8	Topic 9	Topic 10	Topic 11
1 C	1 C	1 C	1 B	1 D
2 A	2 B	2 B	2 D	2 D
3 B	3 A	3 D	3 D	3 C
	4 C	4 B	4 A	4 D
	5 C	5 C	5 C	

Topic 12	Topic 13	Topic 14	Topic 15	Topic 16
1 C	1 B	1 C	1 B	1 B
2 A	2 D	2 A	2 D	2 A
3 D	3 D	3 C	3 C	3 B
4 A	4 B	4 D	4 C	4 C
	5 A	5 B	5 D	5 A

Topic 17	Topic 18	Topic 19	Topic 20	Topic 21
1 A	1 D	1 A	1 D	1 D
2 D	2 C	2 D	2 D	2 B
3 A	3 D	3 D	3 C	3 A
4 D	4 D	4 C	4 B	4 D
5 B	5 D	5 C	5 C	

Topic 22	Topic 23	Topic 24	Topic 25	Topic 26
1 D	1 D	1 A	1 C	1 A
2 D	2 B	2 B	2 C	2 D
3 C	3 A	3 D	3 A	3 B
4 B	4 D	4 B	4 D	4 D
5 D		5 A	5 A	5 A

Topic 27	Topic 28	Topic 29
1 C	1 C	1 C
2 D	2 B	2 D
3 D	3 B	
4 C	4 C	
5 D	5 B	

Federal Communications Commission　　　　　　　　　　　FCC 10-124

**Before the
Federal Communications Commission
Washington, D.C. 20554**

In the Matter of	)	
	)	
Amendment of Part 97 of the Commission's Rules	)	WP Docket No. 10-72
Regarding Amateur Radio Service	)	
Communications During Government Disaster	)	
Drills	)	
	)	
Amateur Radio Policy Committee Petition for	)	
Rulemaking	)	
	)	
Request by American	)	WP Docket No. 10-54
Hospital Association for Blanket Waiver to	)	
Permit Hospitals to Use Amateur Radio as Part of	)	
Emergency Preparedness Drills	)	

REPORT AND ORDER

Adopted: July 14, 2010　　　　　　　　　　　　　　　　　　　　　**Released: July 14, 2010**

By the Commission:

TABLE OF CONTENTS

　　　　　　　　　　　　　　　　　　　　　　　　　　　　　　　　　　　　　　Paragraph
I.　INTRODUCTION 1
II.　BACKGROUND 3
III.　DISCUSSION 8
IV.　PROCEDURAL MATTERS 22
　　A.　Final Regulatory Flexibility Certification. 22
　　B.　Paperwork Reduction Act Analysis 24
　　C.　Congressional Review Act. 25
V.　ORDERING CLAUSES 26
APPENDIX A – List of Commenters
APPENDIX B – Final Rules

I.　INTRODUCTION

　　1.　In this *Report and Order*, we amend the Commission's amateur radio service rules.[1] Specifically, we amend the rules to permit amateur radio operators to transmit messages, under certain limited circumstances, during either government-sponsored or non-government sponsored emergency and disaster preparedness drills, regardless of whether the operators are employees of entities participating in

---
[1] *See* 47 C.F.R. Part 97.

the drill. Although public safety land mobile radio systems are the primary means of radio-based communications for emergency responders, experience has shown that amateur radio has played an important role in preparation for, during, and in the aftermath of, natural and man-made emergencies and disasters.

2. Current rules provide for amateur radio use during emergencies.[2] At the same time, the rules prohibit communications in which the station licensee or control operator has a pecuniary interest, including communications on behalf of an employer.[3] While there are some exceptions to this prohibition, there is none that would permit amateur station control operators who are employees of public safety agencies and other entities, such as hospitals, to participate in drills, tests and exercises in preparation for such emergency situations and transmit messages on behalf of their employers during such drills and tests.[4] Accordingly, we amend our rules to provide that, under certain limited conditions, amateur radio operators may transmit messages during emergency and disaster preparedness drills and exercises, limited to the duration of such drills and exercises, regardless of whether the operators are employees of entities participating in the drills or exercises.

II. BACKGROUND

3. One of the fundamental principles underlying the amateur radio service is the "[r]ecognition and enhancement of the value of the amateur service to the public as a voluntary noncommercial communication service, particularly with respect to providing emergency communications."[5] Further, the rules state that "[n]o provision of these rules prevents the use by an amateur station of any means of radio communication at its disposal to provide essential communication needs in connection with the immediate safety of human life and immediate protection of property when normal communication systems are not available."[6] Indeed, amateur radio operators provide essential communications links and facilitate relief actions in disaster situations. While land mobile radio services are the primary means of conducting emergency communications, amateur radio plays a unique and critical role when these primary facilities are damaged, overloaded, or destroyed.[7] For example, during Hurricane Katrina, amateur radio operators volunteered to support many agencies, such as the Federal Emergency Management Agency, the National Weather Service, and the American Red Cross. Amateur radio stations provided urgently needed wireless communications in many locations where there were no

---

[2] *See* 47 C.F.R. §§ 97.401, *et seq*.

[3] 47 C.F.R. § 97.113(a)(3).

[4] In this regard, Bureau staff recently issued a Public Notice providing guidance for requesting waiver relief to facilitate government-sponsored emergency preparedness and disaster drills. *See* Amateur Service Communications During Government Disaster Drills, *Public Notice,* 24 FCC Rcd 12872 (WTB, PSHSB, EB 2009) (*Disaster Drills Public Notice*). The waiver process outlined in this Public Notice remained available throughout this rulemaking proceeding.

[5] 47 C.F.R. § 97.1(a).

[6] 47 C.F.R. § 97.403.

[7] *See* Recommendations of the Independent Panel Reviewing the Impact of Hurricane Katrina on Communications Networks, *Order*, EB Docket No. 06-119; WC Docket No. 06-63, 22 FCC Rcd 10541, 10576 ¶ 111 (2007) (noting that the amateur radio community played an important role in the aftermath of Hurricane Katrina and other disasters).

other means of communicating and also provided other technical aid to the communities affected by Hurricane Katrina.[8]

4. Since amateur radio is often an essential element of emergency preparedness and response, many state and local governments, public safety agencies, and hospitals incorporate amateur radio operators and the communication capabilities of the amateur service into their emergency planning. In this regard, some entities, such as hospitals, emergency operations centers, and police, fire, and emergency medical service stations, have emphasized the participation of their employees who are amateur station operators in emergency and disaster drills and tests. For example, a representative of the New Orleans Urban Area Security Initiative recently emphasized the importance of conducting emergency drills and the need for amateur participation.[9]

5. The Commission's rules expressly permit operation of amateur stations for public service communications during emergencies, and on a voluntary basis during drills and exercises in preparation for such emergencies. Given, however, that the Amateur Radio Service is primarily designated for "amateurs, that is, duly authorized persons interested in radio technique solely with a personal aim and without pecuniary interest,"[10] the rules expressly prohibit amateur stations from transmitting communications "in which the station licensee or control operator has a pecuniary interest, including communications on behalf of an employer."[11] Accordingly, public safety and public health entities seeking to have employees operate amateur stations during government-sponsored emergency preparedness and disaster drills presently must request a waiver.[12] In this connection, Commission staff has granted several waivers on a case-by case basis.[13]

---

[8] *See* Letter from Kenneth Hughes, Communications Planner, New Orleans Region Urban Area Security Initiative, to Jamie A. Barnett, Chief, Public Safety and Homeland Security Bureau, Federal Communications Commission, dated November 13, 2009, WP Docket No. 10-72 (*Hughes Letter*) (noting that although Hurricane Katrina rendered local land mobile radio systems inoperative, amateur radios became the "only functioning life-line within the greater New Orleans area," for example by use at hospitals to "arrange for emergency airlifts for critical patients").

[9] *See Hughes Letter* at 1 (citing to the "importance of having amateur radio operators not only available during emergencies, but intimately engaged in establishing governance and other standard operating procedures, and, most importantly, in training and exercises, all in accordance with the National Emergency Communications Plan"). We are also in receipt of a related Petition for Rulemaking submitted by the Amateur Radio Policy Committee (ARPC). *See* Petition for Rule Making, WP Docket No. 10-72 (filed Oct. 15, 2009) (seeking to amend the rules to permit amateur transmissions "necessary for disaster relief or emergency response, including training exercises, planning, drills or tests, without regard to whether the amateur operator has related employment, where the transmissions are for the exclusive use of amateur radio operators for noncommercial purposes"). We have incorporated the ARPC Petition into the docket of this proceeding.

[10] *See* 47 C.F.R. § 97.3(a)(4).

[11] *See* 47 C.F.R. § 97.113(a)(3). The prohibition was adopted in its current form in 1993. *See* Amendment of Part 97 of the Commission's Rules to Relax Restrictions on the Scope of Permissible Communications in the Amateur Service, *Report and Order*, PR Docket No. 92-136, 8 FCC Rcd 5072 (1993).

[12] *See Disaster Drills Public Notice*.

[13] *See, e.g.,* Letters from Deputy Chief, Mobility Division, Wireless Telecommunications Bureau granting waiver requests: Letter to Annie Robinson, Mendocino County HHSA/CHS, DA 10-1004 (June 2, 2010); Letter to Gregory Williams, Director, Monroe County Office of Emergency Management, DA 10-1003 (June 2, 2010); Letter to Frederick A. Zacher, DeWitt County Emergency Services and Disaster Agency, DA 09-2420 (Nov. 16, 2009); Letter to Matt May, Assistant Director, Johnson County Emergency Management Agency, DA 09-2332 (Oct. 28, 2009); Letter to Robert L. Stephens, Kentucky Department of Military Affairs, DA 09-2302 (Oct. 27, 2009).

6. On February 17, 2010, the American Hospital Association (AHA) filed a request for a blanket waiver of Section 97.113(a)(3) of the Commission's rules to permit hospitals seeking accreditation to use amateur radio operators who are hospital employees to transmit communications on behalf of the hospital as part of emergency preparedness drills.[14] On March 3, 2010, the Wireless Telecommunications and Public Safety and Homeland Security Bureaus jointly issued a Public Notice seeking comment on the foregoing request.[15]

7. On March 18, 2010, we adopted a *Notice of Proposed Rulemaking* (*NPRM*) seeking comment on whether to amend the rules to permit amateur radio operators to participate in government-sponsored emergency and disaster preparedness drills and tests, regardless of whether the operators are employees of the entities participating in the drill or test.[16] We also invited comment on whether there were circumstances in which amateur operators should be allowed to participate on their employer's behalf in non-government-sponsored tests or drills.[17] Comments were due May 24, 2010, and reply comments were due June 7, 2010.

III. DISCUSSION

8. *Government-sponsored Emergency Drills.* In the *NPRM*, we tentatively concluded to permit amateur radio operators to participate in government-sponsored emergency and disaster preparedness drills and tests, regardless of whether the operators are employees of the entities participating in the drill or test.[18] In reaching this tentative conclusion, we stated that employee status should not preclude or prevent participation in government-sponsored emergency and disaster tests and drills.[19] We also tentatively concluded that extending authority to operate amateur stations during such drills will enhance emergency preparedness and thus serve the public interest.[20]

9. In response to the *NPRM,* public safety agencies and other emergency first responder entities voiced general support for the proposal.[21] These commenters note that public safety agencies frequently incorporate amateur radio and indeed are encouraged to do so as a part of Commission

---

[14] Letter dated Feb. 17, 2010 from Kristin L. Welsh, Vice President for Strategic Initiatives and Business Community Liaison, AHA, to Scot Stone, Deputy Chief, Mobility Division, Wireless Telecommunications Bureau, FCC (*AHA Petition*).

[15] Wireless Telecommunications Bureau and Public Safety and Homeland Security Bureau Seek Comment on Request by American Hospital Association for Blanket Waiver to Permit Hospitals to Use Amateur Radio as Part of Emergency Preparedness Drills, WP Docket No. 10-54, *Public Notice,* 25 FCC Rcd 3441 (WTB, PSHSB 2010).

[16] Amendment of Part 97 of the Commission's Rules Regarding Amateur Radio Service Communications During Government Disaster Drills, WP Docket No. 10-72, *Notice of Proposed Rulemaking*, 25 FCC Rcd 3441 (2010) (*NPRM*).

[17] *NPRM* at ¶ 7.

[18] *Id.* at ¶ 5.

[19] *Id.*

[20] *Id.*

[21] CPSRA Comments at 2, CEMA Comments at 1, MEMA Comments at 1-4, Los Angeles Comments at 1-2, Arlington County, Virginia Comments at 5, SVRIP Comments at 1, Daytona Comments at 2, HAP Comments at 5-7, Seattle Reply Comments at 2-4, NPSTCl Comments at 6.

policy.[22] Several amateur groups and clubs also support the rule amendment, because it will improve the skills of employees who may be called upon to use their expertise in times of emergency or disaster.[23] Other commenters suggest that the rule amendment would likely increase the usefulness of existing national-level programs such as the Radio Amateur Civil Emergency Service (RACES),[24] the Amateur Radio Relay League's Amateur Radio Emergency Service (ARES©), or the US Department of Defense's Military Auxiliary Radio System (MARS).[25]

10. On the other hand, several commenters state that the proposal would erode the amateur status of the service, which is an essential characteristic of amateur radio.[26] Nickolaus E. Legget argues that this "would lead to a 'backdoor' de facto reallocation of some frequencies to hospitals and related operations."[27] Other commenters maintain that this proposal would exacerbate the tendency of some hospitals or other public safety agencies to replace commercially available CMRS equipment with less expensive amateur radio equipment, intending to rely on amateur radio and employee licensees for communications.[28] One commenter, James T. Philopen, states that the Commission lacks authority to amend the existing rule under Article 1, Section II Radio Service, subpart 56 of the International Telecommunications Treaty, which defines the Amateur Radio service as one "without pecuniary

---

[22] *See, e.g.,* HAP Comments at 1-2 (citing to http://www.fcc.gov/pshs/emergency-information/guidelines/health-care.html [PSHSB Emergency Information Guidelines, Healthcare Sector] and http://www.fcc.gov/pshs/clearinghouse/best-practices.html [PSHSB Clearinghouse Best Practices]).

[23] *See, e.g.,* ARRL Reply Comments at 1, West Comments at 2, Duckworth Comments at 1, Husher Comments at 1, Simpson Comments at 1, Daniel Comments at 1, Knight Comments at 1, Myers Comments, Holmes Comments at 1. Squire Comments at 1, Brown Comment a t 1, Forbes Comments at 1, Jarvi Comments at 1, Burbridge Comments at 1, Williamson Comments at 1, Gori Comments at 1, Griffin Comments at 1, Williamson Comments at 1, Hanser Comments at 1, Clifton, Van Wanbeck Comments at 1, Mackay Comments at 1, Williamson Comments at 1, Johnson Comments at 1, Wathen Comments at 1, Oakley Comments at 1, Ives Comments at 1, Guice Comments at 1, Jung Comments at 1, Woodword Comments at 2. *See also* Young Comments (urging the Commission to state that amendment will not be used "as a way to circumvent the purpose of amateur radio").

[24] *See* 47 C.F.R. § 97.407.

[25] *See* Russel Comments at 1, SVRIP Comments at 1, Carr Comments at 1, Freitag Comments at 1.

[26] *See, e.g.,* Wintersole Comments at 1, Swift Comments at 1 (arguing that the rule will undermine the "'Volunteer Spirit'" of amateur radio) Gary Sawyer Comments at 1 (arguing that "amateur radio is not the only or the last solution" and that volunteer amateurs can serve this function), Courson Comments at 1 (arguing that the proposed language is too vague and would lead a "hospital class" of licensees), Anders Comments at 2-3 (arguing that agencies will be encouraged to require employees to seek licenses and will ultimately result in the loss of amateur frequencies to government agencies), Johnston Comments at 2-3 (stating that it would be a "massive breach" of the fundamental core of the Amateur service), Rinaca Comments at 1 (arguing RACES could cover needs of emergency communications), Houlne Comments at 2-5, Wisehart Comments at 1-2, Connell Comments at 4, Jackson Comments at 1, Keith Comments at 1, Tureny Comments at 1, Sawyer Comments at 1, Hirsh Comments at 1, McDowell Comments at 1, George Comments at 1.

[27] *See* Legget Comments at 3. *See also* Jackson Comments at 1 (arguing that the rule will result in government and non-government organizations relying more heavily on amateur radio for disaster communications rather than investing in more robust communications systems), Houlne Comments at 3 (arguing that employers see the lower cost of amateur radio equipment as relief for strained budgets). Even supporters of the amendment express concern that governmental bodies will be tempted to use amateur radio frequencies and equipment to conduct routine business. *See, e.g.,* McVey Comments at 2-4 (arguing that the rule should emphasize that is not to routine business is not to be conducted using amateur radio), ARRL Reply at 5-6 (cautioning that the Commission should not permit the substitution of amateur radio for appropriate land mobile, commercial mobile or personal radio services).

[28] *See, e.g.,* Stanley Comments at 1, Johnston Comments at 8.

interest."[29] Another commenter objects to the proposed amendment, stating that such a rule would lead to employees being coerced into using their amateur privileges, including using their amateur privileges in ways prohibited by our rules.[30] Finally, a handful of commenters suggest alternative language or request additional definitions to the proposed rule,[31] or recommend alternative regulatory treatment.[32]

11. As we noted in the *NPRM*, experience has shown that amateur operations can and have played an essential role in protecting the safety of life and property during emergency situations and disaster situations.[33] Moreover, the current amateur radio service rules, which permit participation in such drills and tests by volunteers (*i.e.*, non-employees of participating entities), reflect the critical role amateur radio serves in such situations.[34] However, as evidenced by recent waiver requests, state and local government public safety agencies, hospitals, and other entities concerned with the health and safety of citizens appear to be limited in their ability to conduct disaster and emergency preparedness drills, because of the employee status of amateur radio licensees involved in the training exercises.[35] We therefore amend our rules to permit amateur radio operators to participate in government-sponsored emergency and disaster preparedness drills and tests, regardless of whether the operators are employees of the entities participating in the drill or test. We find that extending authority to operate amateur stations during such drills will enhance emergency preparedness and response and thus serve the public interest.

12. In reaching this decision, we do not find persuasive those comments stating that this decision will erode the amateur radio service. The exception we provide today is limited to the duration and scope of the drill, test or exercise being conducted, and operational testing immediately prior to the drill, test or exercise. Further, when such operations are conducted in these limited circumstances, the amateur communications are only one component of the overall and more extensive communications activities that are involved with emergency drills and tests. Thus, we do not foresee the use authorized herein to be extensive enough to amount to an erosion of the amateur radio service. Moreover, under

---

[29] Philopen Comments at 1.

[30] *See* Casselberry Comments at 1. *See also* Johnston Comments at 2 (stating that government entities would encourage their employees to misuse the service), Hamel Comments at 1 (recommending the addition of the word "voluntarily" to ensure participation is not part of the employee's paid duties), Houlne Comments at 3 (asserting that employers are beginning to require their employees to seek amateur radio licensees so they do not have to rely on volunteers).

[31] *See* Montierth Comments at 2, King Comments at 1-2, Bourne Comments at 2, Anders Comments (recommending definitions of "government sponsored" and "emergency" or "disaster relief").

[32] *See* Montierth Comments at 2. One commenter, Johnston, filed a petition for rulemaking, seeking the reestablishment of the Commission's former Part 99 Disaster Radio Service. *See* Johnston, Petition for Rulemaking (filed June 9, 2010). This petition was not filed as part of the instant docket. Because the petition raises issues beyond the scope of the instant proceeding, we will act on it separately.

[33] *NPRM* at ¶ 1.

[34] *Id.* at ¶ 5. *See also* 47 C.F.R. §§ 97.1, 97.111(a)(2), 97.401-407.

[35] *See, e.g.,* the following letters from the Deputy Chief, Mobility Division, Wireless Telecommunications Bureau, granting waiver requests: Letter to Frederick A. Zacher, DeWitt County Emergency Services and Disaster Agency, DA 09-2420 (Nov. 16, 2009); Letter to Matt May, Assistant Director, Johnson County Emergency Management and Homeland Security, DA 09-2377 (Nov. 4, 2009); Letter to Dale D. Rowley, Director, Waldo County Emergency Management Agency, DA 09-2332 (Oct. 28, 2009); Letter to Robert L. Stephens, Emergency Communications Supervisor, Kentucky Department of Military Affairs, DA 09-2302 (Oct. 27, 2009); Letter to Annie Robinson, Senior Program Specialist, Hospital Preparedness Program, Mendocino County HHSA/CHS, DA 10-1004 (Jun. 4, 2010); Gregory L. Boswell, R.N., Program Manager, County of Orange Health Care Agency, DA 10-797 (May 10, 2010).

existing rules, licensed employees may use amateur radio privileges when an emergency has rendered other communications unavailable.[36] Our decision reflects the practical reality that a large number of agencies and organizations at the state and local levels coordinate with their local volunteer amateur radio operators to conduct emergency drills and exercises in concert with other modes of communication, such as land mobile radio. This integrative activity is essential to allow for a practiced response on the part of the first responder community in the event of an emergency. Because some of those drills and exercises include transmission of amateur communications by employees of participating entities, this rule amendment will support our ongoing emergency preparedness and response priorities and is therefore consistent with the public interest.

13. We also reject the comments claiming that we lack the authority to amend our amateur rules because it conflicts with the Communications Act and the prohibition on "pecuniary interest" in the ITU treaty. The Commission's authority under the Communications Act to propose, promulgate and amend rules for the purpose of promoting safety of life and property through the use of wire and radio communication is well-established.[37] Moreover, the limited action we are taking here does not violate the ITU treaty. The ITU Radio Regulations specifically state that "[a]dministrations are encouraged to take the necessary steps to allow amateur stations to prepare for and meet communication needs in support of disaster relief."[38] The rule amendments we adopt today do not undermine the "pecuniary interest" limitation. Rather, the amended rules provide a discrete exception to the existing rule that prohibits any pecuniary interest attributable to the operator including communications on behalf of an employer. We also find unpersuasive comments that suggest that the amended rules either will cause employees to be coerced to transmit amateur radio messages or would cause entities to use amateur radio privileges in any way that would violate the Commission's rules.[39] The flexibility of amateur operators will remain limited by the requirements of the Communications Act and the Commission's rules, including the rule amendments we adopt herein. Our action today does not alter the responsibilities of these operators, and, as was the case under the prior rules, amateur licensees are obliged to operate their radio stations in compliance with the terms of their licenses, notwithstanding any conflicting instruction from their employers. In any event, we do not expect that employer overreaching is likely to be a problem, given that the amended rules reflect a spirit of cooperation recognized by both the public safety community and the amateur radio community as necessary for preparing for times of emergency or disaster.

14. We also find it unnecessary to adopt alternative language or specify additional definitions.[40] We find our proposed language is sufficiently clear. The purpose of the rule amendment is to promote the effectiveness and usefulness of emergency operations by permitting licensed employees to practice the skills they would use in an actual emergency as a last resort, *i.e.*, should other means of communications fail or be unavailable. We find that the amended language is narrowly tailored to achieve these ends.

---

[36] 47 C.F.R. § 97.403.

[37] *See* 47 U.S.C. § 151 (establishing the Commission for "purpose of promoting safety of life and property through the use of wire and radio communication").

[38] Article 25.9A, Section 5A, International Telecommunications Union Radio Regulations.

[39] *See, e.g.,* Casselberry Comments at 1, Jackson Comments at 1 (arguing that the rule will result in government and non-government organizations relying more heavily on amateur radio for disaster communications rather than investing in more robust communications systems), Houlne Comments at 3 (arguing that employers see the lower cost of amateur radio equipment as relief for strained budgets).

[40] *See* Montierth Comments at 2, King Comments at 1-2, Bourne Comments at 2, Anders Comments (recommending definitions of "government sponsored" and "emergency" or "disaster relief").

15.   In amending the amateur radio rules, we reiterate that we do not intend to disturb the core principle of the amateur radio service as a voluntary, non-commercial communication service carried out by duly authorized persons interested in radio technique with a personal aim and without pecuniary interest.[41] Rather, we believe that the public interest will be served by establishing a narrow exception to the prohibition on transmitting amateur communications in which the station control operator has a pecuniary interest or employment relationship, and that such an exception is consistent with the intent of the amateur radio service rules.[42] Accordingly, we limit the amateur operations in connection with emergency drills to the duration and scope of the drill, test or exercise being conducted, and to operational testing immediately prior to the drill, test or exercise.[43]

16.   Some commenters request more specific limits on the duration of the use of amateur radio services to prevent continuous drills and the bandwidth from becoming *de facto* emergency service spectrum.[44] We decline to adopt specific time restrictions other than a limit tied to the duration of the exercise. We find that such matters should be left to the discretion of the sponsoring agencies. We emphasize, however, that the amendment does not permit communications unrelated to the drill or exercise being conducted. Other commenters suggest that the rules should specifically provide for more expansive operational testing.[45] Boeing suggests that testing be permitted thirty days prior to a scheduled government sponsored drill.[46] We decline to specify the timing or duration of emergency drills. As evidenced by the waiver requests that have been submitted, we expect that agencies will schedule emergency drills or exercises at appropriate times and for appropriate durations.

17.   *Non–Government-sponsored Emergency Drills.* In the *NPRM*, we proposed that the emergency tests and drills must be sponsored by Federal, state, or local governments or agencies, in order to limit the narrow exception to ensure that drills further public safety.[47] We noted, however, that there may be circumstances where conducting emergency drills for disaster planning purposes, even if not government-sponsored, would serve the public interest.[48] Accordingly, we sought comment on whether

---

[41] *See* 47 C.F.R. §§ 97.1, 97.3(a)(4).

[42] We note that the Commission has carved out other narrow exceptions to the prohibition on transmission of amateur communications in which the station control operator has a pecuniary interest. *See* 47 C.F.R. § 97.113(c) (permitting control operators who are employed in teaching positions to transmit amateur communications as part of classroom instruction at an educational institution) & (d) (permitting the control operator of a club station to accept compensation for transmitting telegraphy practice or informational bulletins under certain conditions).

[43] *NPRM* at ¶ 6.

[44] *See, e.g.,* Kimtantas Comments at 1, Platt Comments at 1, Saverango Comments at 1, Harrison Comments at 1, Slye Comments at 1, McVey Comments at 3, Anders Comments at 4.

[45] Hoffman Comments at 1, Harrington Comments at 1, Boeing Comments at 6-7, Abbey Comments at 1, Welton Comments at 1, Gosnell Comments at 1, Siddon Comments at 1.

[46] Boeing Comments at 6-7. Boeing also recommends that the rule should be amended to "permit amateur radio station operators to operate digital messaging stations on a continuous basis for emergency and disaster preparedness on behalf of their employers." *Id. But see* Boeing Reply at 5 (stating that if the Commission permits participation in non-governmental drills these recommendations would be unnecessary).

[47] *NPRM* at ¶ 7.

[48] *Id.* For example, we noted that the accrediting standards for health care organizations require hospitals and organizations that offer emergency services (or are community-designated disaster receiving stations) to annually conduct emergency preparedness drills for mass casualty scenarios. While such drills may be conducted for accreditation purposes rather than as part of a government-sponsored activity, they arguably serve similar purposes in terms of enhancing emergency preparedness and response. *Id.*

we should permit employee operation of amateur stations during non-government-sponsored emergency drills, if the purpose of the drill is to assess communications capabilities, including amateur radio, in order to improve emergency preparedness and response.[49]

18. Most of the commenters who support permitting employee operation of amateur stations during government sponsored drills also support such operation during non-government-sponsored emergency drills, if the purpose of the drill is to assess communications capabilities to further public safety.[50] However, a few commenters opposed expansion of the rule to include non-government sponsored emergency drills.[51] For example, Holtz states that this would "open the door for significant commercial abuse and exploitation of the amateur service;" that in the "absence of government sponsorship, there is ambiguity about whether any particular drill by a commercial entity is primarily for its own benefit, or for the public benefit;" and that this would create "an incentive for employers to pressure employees to get amateur licenses, and to pressure licensed amateurs to engage in questionable or prohibited practices," *i.e.*, to use "amateur radio as a lower-cost substitute for Part 90 systems."[52] In relation to such concerns, Sheppard suggests limiting this expansion to those operations "when the emergency drill or test is sponsored by an agency or organization which supports public safety or public health."[53] And Traynor suggests limiting such expansion to "organizations defined by FEMA as providing the nation with Critical Infrastructure and Key Resources (CIKR) as described in the National Infrastructure Protection Plan (NIPP)."[54] Earlier, in response to the AHA Petition, ARRL asked that AHA's requested waiver be limited to radio transmissions made by hospital employees that are "necessary to participation in emergency preparedness and disaster drills that include Amateur operations for the purpose of emergency response, disaster relief or the testing and maintenance of equipment used for that purpose."[55]

19. In addition to Federal, state and local authorities, other non-government entities, such as private hospitals, have a direct interest in the health and welfare of citizens, especially during times of emergency or disaster. During those times, emergency communications serve a critical purpose to both governmental and non-governmental entities as well as to the constituencies they serve. As we determined above, familiarization, planning, and training are required for effective use of amateur radio in an emergency. We therefore find that the public interest would be served by permitting amateur radio

---

[49] *NPRM* at ¶ 7.

[50] *See, e.g.,* ARRL Comments at 9-10; Intermountain Comments at 1; Baumgurte Comments at 1-2; Bellar Comments 1-2; Bennington Comments at 1; Blowsky Comments at 1; Bourne Comments at 1; CPRA Comments at 2; Crocket Comments at 2; Dancey Comments at 1; Gourley Comments at 1; Josephson Comments at 1; Kirk Comments at 1; HAP Comments at 5-7; Lothrop Comments Lothrop; Jacquelyn May Comments at 1; James May Comments at 1; MCHC Comments at 9-12; Moell Comments at 2; Newell Comments at 1; Newton Comments at 1; Richmond Comments at 1; Sheppard Comments at 6-7; Siddon Comments at 1; Stewart Comments at 1; Traynor Comments at 1; Vordenbaum Comments at 2; Bradford Wagoner Comments at 1; Whedbee Comments at 3; WADH Comments at 1; White Comments at 1; Witte Comments at 1, ARRL Reply Comments at 3-5, Boeing Reply at 2-5. *See also AHA Petition.*

[51] *See e.g.,* Holtz Comments at 1-2; McVey Comments at 4.

[52] Holtz Comments at 1-2, Johnston Comments at 8. *See* ARRL Reply at 5-6 (cautioning that the Commission should not permit the substitution of Amateur Radio for appropriate land mobile, commercial mobile or personal radio services).

[53] Sheppard Comments at 7.

[54] Traynor Comments at 1.

[55] *See* ARRL Comments to AHA Petition at 9.

operators to participate in non-government sponsored emergency and disaster preparedness drills and tests, regardless of whether the operators are employees of the entities participating in the drill or test.

20. While we recognize commenters' concerns regarding the potential for improper use of amateur radio in conducting emergency drills and tests, we find that the public interest in permitting non-government-sponsored entities to utilize, on a limited basis, amateur radio as part of emergency preparedness and response drills outweighs such concerns. As with government-sponsored emergency drills, we limit the amateur operations in connection with non-government sponsored emergency drills to the duration and scope of the drill, test or exercise being conducted, and operational testing immediately prior to the drill, test or exercise. Moreover, in light of the concerns raised by some commenters, we require that non-government sponsored drills and tests be limited to no more than one hour per week; except that no more than twice in any calendar year, they may be conducted for a period not to exceed 72 hours. This time limitation, which is consistent with the timeframes contained in the waiver requests filed with the Commission, should serve to further ensure the use of amateur radio for bona fide emergency testing.[56] We emphasize that the purpose for any drills we authorize herein must be related to emergency and disaster preparedness. By limiting the purpose in this manner, we further ensure that such drills will be appropriately limited.

21. *ARPC Petition and AHA Petition.* ARPC requested we amend Section 97.113(a)(3) in order to permit amateur radio licensees employed by public safety agencies to participate in drills conducted by their employer. Similarly in its request, AHA emphasized the need to allow hospital employees with amateur radio licenses to participate in emergency preparedness and disaster readiness tests and drills. We appreciate both of these filings, and, as discussed herein, support the requested rule changes. Because we amend the rules in a manner that addresses the concerns raised by both petitioners, we dismiss both petitions as moot.

IV. PROCEDURAL MATTERS

A. Final Regulatory Flexibility Certification.

22. The Regulatory Flexibility Act (RFA)[57] requires an initial regulatory flexibility analysis to be prepared for notice and comment rulemaking proceedings, unless the agency certifies that "the rule will not, if promulgated, have a significant economic impact on a substantial number of small entities."[58] The RFA generally defines the term "small entity" as having the same meaning as the terms "small business," "small organization," and "small governmental jurisdiction."[59] In addition, the term "small business" has the same meaning as the term "small business concern" under the Small Business Act.[60] A "small business concern" is one which: (1) is independently owned and operated; (2) is not dominant in

---

[56] These further limitations on non-government sponsored emergency drills also correspond to those applied to the Radio Amateur Civil Emergency Service (RACES). *See* 47 C.F.R. § 97.407(e)(4).

[57] *See* 5 U.S.C. § 603. The RFA, *see* 5 U.S.C. § 601– 612, has been amended by the Small Business Regulatory Enforcement Fairness Act of 1996 (SBREFA), Pub. L. No. 104-121, Title II, 110 Stat. 857 (1996).

[58] *See* 5 U.S.C. § 605(b).

[59] *See* 5 U.S.C. § 601(6).

[60] *See* 5 U.S.C. § 601(3) (incorporating by reference the definition of "small business concern" in the Small Business Act, 15 U.S.C. § 632). Pursuant to 5 U.S.C. § 601(3), the statutory definition of a small business applies "unless an agency, after consultation with the Office of Advocacy of the Small Business Administration and after opportunity for public comment, establishes one or more definitions of such term which are appropriate to the activities of the agency and publishes such definition(s) in the Federal Register."

its field of operation; and (3) satisfies any additional criteria established by the Small Business Administration (SBA).[61]

23. Because "small entities," as defined in the RFA, are not persons eligible for licensing in the amateur service, this proposed rule does not apply to "small entities."[62] Rather, it applies exclusively to individuals who are the control operators of amateur radio stations. Moreover, the rule being adopted is so narrow that no nexus exists between the regulated amateur licensees who may be employed, and costs to be born by employers (*e.g.* overtime pay). Therefore, if there were any costs imposed on employers, that is a matter outside the scope of the rule and thus the impact of the rule cannot be said to involve the imposition of any economic burden on those individual persons who are the only entities regulated and impacted by the rule adopted in this *Report and Order*. Finally, no commenters addressed our conclusion in the NPRM and small entities which filed comments uniformly supported the proposed rule changes. Therefore, we certify that the proposals in this *Report and Order* will not have a significant economic impact on a substantial number of small entities. The Commission will send a copy of the *Report and Order*, including a copy of this Final Regulatory Flexibility Certification, to the Chief Counsel for Advocacy of the SBA.[63] This final certification will also be published in the Federal Register.[64]

B. Paperwork Reduction Act Analysis.

24. This *Report and Order* does not contain proposed information collection(s), subject to the Paperwork Reduction Act of 1995, Public Law 104-13. In addition, therefore, the *Report and Order* does not contain any proposed new or modified "information collection burden for small business concerns with fewer than 25 employees," pursuant to the Small Business Paperwork Relief Act of 2002, Public Law 107-198, *see* 44 U.S.C. § 3506(c)(4).

C. Congressional Review Act.

25. The Commission will send a copy of this *Report and Order* to Congress and the Government Accountability Office pursuant to the Congressional Review Act, *see* 5 U.S.C. § 801(a)(1)(4).

V. ORDERING CLAUSES

26. Accordingly, IT IS ORDERED, pursuant to sections 4(i), 303(r), and 403 of the Communications Act of 1934, 47 U.S.C. §§ 154(i), 303(r), and 403, that American Hospital Association request for blanket waiver to permit hospitals to use amateur radio as part of emergency preparedness drills is HEREBY DISMISSED.

27. IT IS FURTHER ORDERED pursuant to sections 4(i), 303(r), and 403 of the Communications Act of 1934, 47 U.S.C. §§ 154(i), 303(r), and 403, that Amateur Radio Policy Committee Petition for Rulemaking is HEREBY DISMISSED.

28. IT IS FURTHER ORDERED, pursuant to sections 4(i), 303(r), and 403 of the Communications Act of 1934, 47 U.S.C. §§ 154(i), 303(r), and 403, that this *Report and Order* is HEREBY ADOPTED.

---

[61] *See* 15 U.S.C. § 632.

[62] *See* 5 U.S.C. § 601(6).

[63] *See* 5 U.S.C. § 605(b).

[64] *See id.*

29. IT IS FURTHER ORDERED that the Commission's Consumer and Governmental Affairs Bureau, Reference Center, SHALL SEND a copy of this *Report and Order*, including the Final Regulatory Flexibility Analyses, to the Chief Counsel for Advocacy of the Small Business Administration.

FEDERAL COMMUNICATIONS COMMISSION

Marlene H. Dortch
Secretary

APPENDIX A

List of Commenters

Abbey, Russell (Abbey)
Anders, Roland A. (Anders)
Angelos, Christopher (Angelos)
Arkansas Department of Health (ARDH)
Arlington County Virginia Office of Emergency Management (ACVOEM)
American Radio Relay League (ARRL)
Association of Public Safety Communications Officials (APCO)
Atchley, Jr. George W. (Atchley)
Bagby, Erik M. (Bagby)
Baillie, Gordon (Baillie)
Barnett, Daniel (Barnett)
Barrett, Patrick (Barrett)
Baumgarte, Dennis (Baumgarte)
Bellar, Kirk (Bellar)
Bennington, R. Lowell R. (Bennington)
Beshlian, Paul (Beshlian)
Blackwell, Tom (Blackwell)
Blowsky, John (Blowsky)
Bone, Merle (Bone)
Bourne, Kenneth M. (Bourne)
Broadway, Gordon S. (Broadway)
Broshofske, Kenneth (Broshofske)
Brown, Douglas (Douglas Brown)
Brown, R. (R. Brown)
Burbridge, Bill (Burbridge)
Burningham, John S. (Burningham)
Burns, Bill (Burns)
California Public-Safety Radio Association (CAPSRA)
Carr, Lawrence W. (Carr)
Casselberry, Jeffery (Casselberry)
City of Daytona Beach (Daytona)
Clifton, Russ (Clifton)
Cody, Thomas J. (Cody)
Colston, Lloyd (Colston)
Connell, Robert (Connell)
Cooke, Mike (Cooke)
Corbaley, Leonard (Corbaley)
Courson, Paul (Courson)
Crosswell, Alan (Crosswell)
Dailey, Thomas C. (Dailey)
Dancey, Michael (Dancey)
Daniel, Jack (Daniel)
Davisson, Robert (Davisson)
DeKam, Douglas (DeKam)
Duckworth, James (Duckworth)

Dye, Jimmie W. (Dye)
Ellsworth, Sterling (Ellsworth)
Encalada, Armando (Encalada)
Fields, Thomas (Fields)
Fink, Denis C. (Fink)
Fishman, Bob (Fishman)
Forbes, Robert (Forbes)
Foreman, William (Foreman)
Frank, Ph.D., Harold H. (Frank)
Freitag, David B. (Freitag)
Frost, Mel (Frost)
Gadus, Joe (Gadus)
Geng, Karl (Geng)
George, Max M. (George)
Getman, Clyde J. (Getman)
Godfrey, John (Godfrey)
Gori, John (Gori)
Gosnell, Murell R. (Gosnell)
Gothelf, Alan (Gothelf)
Gourley, Joe (Gourley)
Greeno, Charles (Greeno)
Griffin, Jeffrey (Jeffrey Griffin)
Griffin, Larry (Larry Griffin)
Gross, Malvin Ryan (Gross)
Gundry, Alex (Gundry)
Hadley, George (Hadley)
Hamel, Patrick (Hamel)
Hansen, N. Michel (Hansen)
Harrington, Brian J. (Harrington)
Harrison, Lamond K. (Harrison)
Hashiro, Ron (Hashiro)
Headrick, Loyd C. (Headrick)
Hensley, Martin (Hensley)
Herr, Paul W. (Herr)
Hirsh, Craig (Hirsh)
Hoffman, Herb (Hoffman)
Holmes, Dolph (Holmes)
Holtz, Ronald (Holtz)
The Hospital & Healthsystem Association of Pennsylvania (HAP)
Huber, Dave (Huber)
Hudson, Dennis R. (Hudson)
Husher, Ray (Husher)
Jackson, Benjamin (Jackson)
Jarvi, Eric (Jarvi)
Johns, Bryan (Johns)
Johnson, James (Johnson)
Johnston, John B. (Johnston)
Josephson, David (Josephson)
Karpman, Michael M. (Karpman)
Keith, Joe (Keith)
Kimtantas, Charles (Kimtantas)

King, David (King)
Kirk, William (Kirk)
Kirley, Paul O. (Kirley)
Knight, Mike (Knight)
Larribeau, John (Larribeau)
Leggett, Nickolaus E. (Leggett)
Los Angeles County (Los Angeles)
Lothrop, Fred H.G. (Lothrop)
Lynch, Chief Jeffrey P. (Lynch)
Mackay, Tom (Mackay)
Marcel, John (Marcel)
May, Jacquelyn J. (Jacquelyn May)
May, James Matthew (James May)
McDowell, Glen (McDowell)
McVey, W. Lee (McVey)
Metropolitan Chicago Healthcare Council (MCHC)
Mitz, Andrew (Mitz)
Moell, April (Moell)
Montierth, Joe (Montierth)
Myers, Tim (Myers)
Nehrbass, Charles R. (Nehrbass)
Nelson, Kathleen (Kathleen Nelson)
Nelson, Brett (Brett Nelson)
Newell, Peter R. (Newell)
Newton, Richard (Newton)
Niemuth, William M. (Niemuth)
Noble, Andrew (Noble)
Oakley, Michael (Oakley)
Parker, Morris C. (Parker)
Parlini, Flash (Parlini)
Paterson, Jr., John M. (Paterson)
Payne, Robert (Payne)
Pechner, Michael (Pechner)
Peters, Timothy (Peters)
Philopena, James T. (Philopena)
Pielage, Henry W. (Pielage)
Platt, David C. (Platt)
Potter, Ronald (Potter)
Powell, William (Powell)
Ray, Richard L. (Richard Ray)
Ray, James M. (James Ray)
Reid, Don (Reid)
Richardson, Malcolm (Richardson)
Richmond, Gerald (Richmond)
Rickabaugh, Greg (Rickabaugh)
Rinaca, Phillip (Rinaca)
Russell, James (Russell)
Savegnago, Allen Kurt (Savegnago)
Sawyer, Gary (Sawyer)
Sawyer, Gary (Sawyer)
City of Seattle Office of Emergency Management, Seattle auxiliary Communications Service, and

Western Washington Medical Services Communications, Inc. (Seattle)
Siddon, Dewayne (Siddon)
Silicon Valley Regional Interoperability Project (SVRIP)
Simonowits, Gerald (Simonowits)
Simpson, Monte L. (Simpson)
Slattery, Timothy (Slattery)
Slye, Jr., William R. (Slye)
Snyder, Capt. Steve R. (Snyder)
Somers, Sarah (Somers)
Soptich, Lee (Soptich)
Squires, Caleb (Squires)
Stanford, Henry King (Stanford)
Stanley, John (Stanley)
Staples, Alan (Staples)
Stewart, Sr., William W. (William Stewart)
Stewart, Terry W. (Stewart)
Sweetman, Steve (Terry Sweetman)
Swift, John C. (Swift)
The Boeing Company (Boeing)
Thomas, Glenn (Thomas)
Timmerman, Benjamin R. (Timmerman)
Tortorella, Michael (Tortorella)
Traynor, Stephen (Traynor)
Turney, Bill (Turney)
Uhlir, Charles (Uhlir)
Vandermark, Christopher (Vandermark)
VandeWettering, Mark (VandeWettering)
VanWambeck, Stephen (VanWambeck)
Vordenbaum, Marilyn (Vordenbaum)
Wade, Martin D. (Wade)
Wade, Martin D. (Wade)
Wagoner, Bradford (Bradford Wagoner)
Wagoner, William L. (William Wagoner)
Wagoner, Charles (Charles Wagoner)
Washington State Department of Health (WADH)
Wathen, James (Wathen)
Watkins, John (Watkins)
Welton, John (Welton)
West, David (West)
West, Gordon (Gordon West)
Whedbee, James Edwin (Whedbee)
White, Shirley (White)
Williamson, Wayne Dee (Wayne Williamson)
Williamson, Martha Mary (Martha Williamson)
Williamson, Erik Wayne (Erik Williamson)
Williamson, Dee Wayne (Williamson)
Wilson, Gary (Wilson)
Wintersole, Mark (Wintersole)
Wireless Telecom & Public Safety (WTPS)
Wisehart, Christopher (Wisehart)
Witte, Robert (Witte)

Woodard, Thomas Lee (Woodard)
Young, Charles (Young)
Zalen, Janice (Zalen)

List of Reply Commenters

American Radio Relay League (ARRL)
Association of Public Safety Communications Officials (APCO)
Baremore, Kenneth R. (Baremore)
Blackwell, Tom (Blackwell)
The Boeing Company, (Boeing)
California Emergency Management Agency (CEMA)
County of Los Angeles (Los Angeles)
Crockett, John M. Jr. (Crockett)
Gothard, John F. (Gothard)
Guice, Bobbie (Guice)
Hashiro, Ron (Hashiro)
Hospital and Healthsystem Association of Pennsylvania (HAP)
Houlne, William (Houlne)
Intermountain Healthacare (Intermountain)
Ivens, Kevin (Ivens)
Jung, Clement (Jung)
Kaimimoku, Cynthia (Kaimimoku)
Little, Michael (Little)
Mariotti, Duane (Mariotti)
Masuda, Ruth (Masuda)
McVey, W. Lee (McVey)
Maryland Emergency Management Agency (MEMA)
Metropolitan Chicago Healthcare Council (MCHC)
National Public Safety Telecommunications Council (NPTC)
Oakley, Micheal (Oakley)
Peters, Timothy (Peters)
Rinaca, Phillip (Rinaca)
Sheppard, Mark (Sheppard)
Traynor, Stephen (Traynor)
Watson, Jr., Howard B. (Watson)
Wilkerson, Jr., Johnny L. (Wilkerson)
West, Karl J. (West)
West, Gordon (Gordon West)
Woodard, Thomas Lee (Woodard)

APPENDIX B

Final Rules

Part 97 of Chapter 1 of Title 47 of the Code of Federal Regulations is amended as follows:

The authority citation for part 97 continues to read as follows:

AUTHORITY: 48 Stat. 1066, 1082, as amended; 47 U.S.C. 154, 303. Interpret or apply 48 Stat. 1064-1068, 1081-1105, as amended; 47 U.S.C. 151-155, 301-609, unless otherwise noted.

1. Section 97.113 is amended by revising paragraph (a)(3), adding new paragraphs (a)(3)(i) and (a)(3)(ii), redesignating paragraphs (c) and (d) as new paragraphs (a)(3)(iii) and (a)(3)(iv) respectively, and redesignating paragraphs (e) and (f) as (c) and (d) respectively, to read as follows:

§ 97.113 Prohibited transmissions.

(a) * * *

(3) Communications in which the station licensee or control operator has a pecuniary interest, including communications on behalf of an employer, with the following exceptions:

(i) A station licensee or control station operator may participate on behalf of an employer in an emergency preparedness or disaster readiness test or drill, limited to the duration and scope of such test or drill, and operational testing immediately prior to such test or drill. Tests or drills that are not government-sponsored are limited to a total time of one hour per week; except that no more than twice in any calendar year, they may be conducted for a period not to exceed 72 hours.

(ii) An amateur operator may notify other amateur operators of the availability for sale or trade of apparatus normally used in an amateur station, provided that such activity is not conducted on a regular basis.

(iii) A control operator may accept compensation as an incident of a teaching position during periods of time when an amateur station is used by that teacher as a part of classroom instruction at an educational institution.

(iv) The control operator of a club station may accept compensation for the periods of time when the station is transmitting telegraphy practice or information bulletins, provided that the station transmits such telegraphy practice and bulletins for at least 40 hours per week; schedules operations on at least six amateur service MF and HF bands using reasonable measures to maximize coverage; where the schedule of normal operating times and frequencies is published at least 30 days in advance of the actual transmissions; and where the control operator does not accept any direct or indirect compensation for any other service as a control operator.

* * * * *

By Michael Tracy, KC1SX

QST Product Reviews— In Depth, In English

Our lead test engineer describes product review testing to help readers make the best use of this popular column.

So why do reviews? Some of the reasons are obvious, some not so obvious. Most folks want to get the best possible equipment for their hard-earned cash. Others might be satisfied if they find something that fits their needs as long as it doesn't have any serious problems.

In one form or another *QST* has been "reviewing" Amateur Radio equipment since the early 1930s. The first investigations were pretty basic, giving block diagrams and circuit descriptions. In 1975, Recent Equipment saw the addition of test results from the ARRL Lab, and the column was subsequently renamed Product Review.

In the pages that follow, the process of Product Review will be described, and the Lab test data will be explained in a manner that will aid in providing a better understanding of these large collections of numbers.

The Process

Selection

The Product Review Editor selects equipment for review, and selects an appropriate person to perform the review. The editor may choose to do the review himself or may select a writer knowledgeable in the field from among the licensed members of the Headquarters staff (with the exception of the Advertising Department), Technical Advisors and Contributing Editors.

Purchase

After an item is chosen, procurement must be made. To ensure that the equipment is as close to "typical" as possible, purchases are made from Amateur Radio dealers or indirectly by third parties. In effect, we purchase equipment the same way our members do. Indeed manufac-

Figure 1—ARRL Test Engineer Michael Tracy, KC1SX, testing IMD performance in ARRL Lab screen room.

turers are often not aware that a review is in process until the "wrap-up" (described later).

Laboratory Testing

When new equipment arrives, its first stop is in the ARRL Lab. The equipment is inspected for any possible shipping damage, inventoried for completeness, and then run through a series of performance tests (in most cases—some review items do not require any bench testing).

Hands-on Testing, Writing and Editing

After the Lab testing, the item is handed over (or shipped) to the designated *reviewer*, who is then responsible for putting it through its paces in real world situations. The reviewer is responsible for writing the actual review text. The Product Review Editor then edits the completed text in order to make it fit the available space and comply with *QST* style.

Afterward

Equipment that has been reviewed is generally auctioned off to members via the **prauctions** page on the ARRL Web site.

Lab Testing—Overview

Types of Testing

Although the types of equipment that generate the most interest are transceivers, receivers and amplifiers, the ARRL Lab often tests station accessories as well. These include items such as transverters, power supplies, SWR meters and just about anything else that can be tested on a bench. Antennas are not subject to Lab tests because the ARRL does not have the calibrated test range required to obtain proper gain and pattern figures.

Accessories and Specialty Items

The testing that is performed on accessories depends on the type of equipment. For example, SWR meters are checked for power accuracy and SWR, plus insertion loss, return loss (measures SWR of the meter input when the output is a proper load) and frequency range. These are all important for optimum operation.

Radio Equipment

Judging by inquiries to the ARRL Technical Information Service, transceivers create an enormous amount of interest. Of course, they are usually the first thing that comes to mind as soon as "the ticket" is on its way from the FCC. Some folks hold onto their first transceiver for decades; others trade rigs every few months. Most of us fall somewhere between these two extremes, but all of us seem to be interested in the new ones. Receivers also tend to create a lot of interest.

Lab Testing Up Close (and What the Numbers Really Mean)[1]

RECEIVER TESTING

Sensitivity

Sensitivity is a measure of a receiver's ability to make use of weak signals. One common measurement standard is called minimum discernible signal (MDS), although this is more aptly known as the receiver's *noise floor* because the human ear can often discern signals that are weaker.

The noise floor is the amount of power present in the receiver's internal noise, determined by measuring a signal level equal in power to that noise. The output of the receiver consists of the receiver's internal noise, plus the constant unmodulated tone from the signal generator. This is the "stick" by which all radios are measured for *QST*'s Product Review data tables. Typical noise floor figures for modern transceivers can be anywhere from –120 to –140 dBm. The term dBm refers to decibels relative to a milliwatt. If you think these are very small signals indeed, you are correct! Receiving a level of –120 dBm is somewhat akin to trying to view a 4 W night light at a distance of several miles without the aid of a telescope.

Unfortunately, it is impossible to duplicate "real world" conditions on the test bench—an approximation is all that can be achieved. To further complicate matters, real world conditions are different for everyone, so any attempt to duplicate a given set of conditions would only be useful to a fraction of hams. The best that can be hoped for is a consistent "yardstick" for making measurements that allow meaningful comparisons.

In the shack, the radio is connected to an antenna, and what you hear from the speaker is a combination of receiver noise and local noise (atmospheric and manmade). In some circumstances in HF and most in VHF, the receiver noise might dominate, but in the vast majority of cases, on HF the local noise predominates (even on a "quiet" band in winter). While atmospheric noise is very random (similar to the receiver internal noise), manmade noise sources are often pulse-type or otherwise very periodic in their characteristics.

The noise from the receiver that is heard by the ear is proportional to the bandwidth. Reducing the (effective or "noise") bandwidth from 500 Hz to 50 Hz will result in a 10 dB or ten times reduction in noise power. Narrow bandwidths can make a dramatic difference in how weak a signal can be copied by the ear. Most rigs do not have the capability to get that narrow, but for many to shift from a 2 kHz to a 500 Hz filter will make a noticeable improvement in the received signal to noise (S/N) for a CW signal. We use a 500 Hz filter for such measurements, when available.

Other types of sensitivity measurements include signal to noise (S/N), signal plus noise to noise (S+N)/N and signal plus noise and distortion to noise and distortion (SINAD). These are all ratios so they are measured in dB. For AM, sensitivity is often specified by manufacturers as 10 dB S/N, a level where the signal is 10 dB greater than the noise. In the Lab, we measure AM as (S+N)/N at a level of 10 dB so that all receivers can be readily compared.

On FM, the measurement standard is 12 dB SINAD. Although 12 dB might sound like a fairly high signal level, FM signals are difficult to discern with noise levels higher than this, so it is the level of minimum practical signal strength. This can be measured on a special instrument known as a SINADDER, but it can also be measured by looking at distortion on a sine-wave modulated signal because the noise is also distortion (relative to a constant-amplitude single-tone waveform).

Dynamic Range

Dynamic range is generally the difference between the weakest signal that can be perceived and the strongest signal that can be present without adversely affecting that weakest signal.

Specific to receivers and transceivers, dynamic range is the difference between the receiver's noise floor and the level of strong signals that are close in frequency yet outside the receiver's passband (therefore assumed to be undesired). While receive dynamic range is a critical issue to contest operating, it can be important even to casual weak-signal DXers if they have to share a crowded band with strong local stations. Stations with high gain antenna systems are also prone to dynamic range issues.

When problems do occur, a rig's attenuator can be of help. If a particular receiver has a noise floor of –140 dBm and the local noise level is –130 dBm, adding 10 dB of attenuation will not make any difference in the weakest signals that can be perceived, yet it will reduce problems from the interfering strong signals.

Actually, it should be noted that –140 is typical only of a rig with a preamp on. It is preferable to turn the preamp off prior to adding attenuation because the preamp adds some noise of its own as well as generating undesired products. Under circumstances when the band

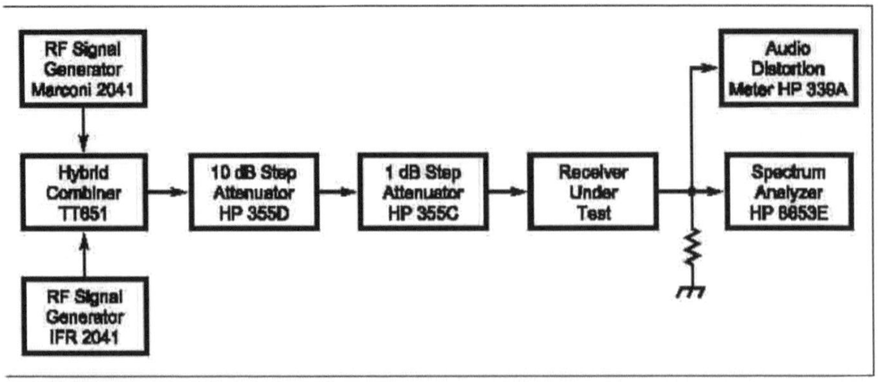

Figure 2—The test setup for measuring receiver dynamic range.

[1]Notes appear on page 36.

abounds with moderate signals (assuming they are ones you want to work), you can even increase the attenuation even more. A good example is operating the lower bands during the early portions of Field Day. Of course, it is usually better to have a rig with too much gain and capable of reduction rather than having not enough gain in the first place.

Blocking Dynamic Range

Blocking dynamic range (BDR) refers to a condition in which the weak signal is "blocked" or suppressed. You'll often hear this described as *desense* because the strong signal reduces the effective sensitivity of the receiver.

BDR as a lab measurement normally refers to the point at which the weak (presumed desired) signal is reduced by 1.0 dB ("blocked") by the presence of a strong (presumed undesired) signal at a frequency above or below the desired signal. The frequency difference between the two is the *spacing*. Thus, blocking dynamic range is a measure of the difference between the receiver's noise floor and the level of the signal that caused the blocking condition.

A measurement that is *noise-limited* is one in which the undesired blocking signal caused an increase in receiver noise output before the desense effect was observed. Usually, this is caused by interaction of the signal with the phase noise of the receiver's internal oscillators. It is often the case that a transceiver that has high transmit composite noise will be noise-limited on receive since the same oscillators are used for each. Some consider this to mean that a *real* BDR measurement cannot be made for that rig. The ARRL Lab considers that the effective blocking dynamic range on a noise-limited measurement is the point at which the noise increases by 1.0 dB. That point results in the same change in the signal to noise ratio as would occur had the desired signal decreased by 1.0 dB.

So, for a receiver where the noise floor is –140 dBm and the 20 kHz spacing blocking dynamic range is 125 dB, the level of signal that caused blocking effect would have been –15 dBm. To relate that to something that may be observed on a receiver, it is convenient to use S-units for discussion purposes. However, it should be noted that few transceivers follow the established S-meter standard. In that standard, S9 = –73 dBm (or 50 microvolts, for a 50 Ω system). Therefore, –15 dBm would be close to S9+60—quite a strong signal, but certainly a level that might be observed under the right conditions. Also, it should be mentioned that many radios do not have a blocking dynamic range that is that high.

Two-Tone Third-Order IMD Dynamic Range

Intermodulation describes the effect of two or more signals mixing (modulating) each other, if you will, thereby creating undesired signals on other frequencies. These signals are referred to as *intermodulation distortion* (IMD) products and they are most often created in the amplification or mixer stages of a receiver, although they can be generated in any non-linear element. In the ARRL Lab we simulate this with two carefully selected signals, as described below.

IMD dynamic range is the difference between the receiver's noise floor and the level of the unwanted signals that caused an undesired signal to appear right on the listening frequency. The process of mixing makes the largest of such signals appear at a frequency spacing equal to the difference of the two signals. For example, if the receiver is tuned to 14,020 kHz and there are strong signals at 14,040 and 14,060 kHz, a false signal may be heard because the second harmonic of 14,040 (28,080 kHz, generated in a nonlinear stage) beats with the 14,060 kHz signal to produce a difference signal at 14,020 kHz, right where we are trying to listen. Because the signal is the result of a product of a second order term and a first order term, it is referred to as a third order response. If the receiver were tuned to 14,080 kHz, it would also hear the other third order combination.

As with blocking dynamic range, IMD dynamic range can be noise-limited. In this case, the effect on the frequency that the receiver is tuned to is created entirely by the interaction of the nearest frequency strong signal and the receiver's phase noise. This results in a noise "signal" that is equal in strength to the receiver's noise floor. In this case, when the more distant signal is removed after the IMD noise is observed, then the noise would still be there. In the case of non-noise limited measurements, if you remove either signal the intermodulation ceases.

It is important to note that these lab measurements don't duplicate real-world conditions because unmodulated carriers are used for the measurements. On the air, there are usually many more than two undesired signals for the receiver to contend with. However, these tests provide an excellent means by which to compare different receivers.

Intercept Points (Third Order and Second Order)

Third-order intercept is related, as you might expect, to two-tone, third-order IMD. Now, if receivers behaved in an ideal fashion, the signals that you intend to listen to would produce a linear receiver response—that is, as the signal gets stronger, the output would get louder and as it gets weaker, the output would decrease, exactly in proportion. A 3 dB change (a doubling or halving) of the input signal power would produce the same 3 dB change in the output. Of course, real receivers don't behave quite this way. In fact, the whole purpose of automatic gain control (AGC) is to prevent changes in output with sudden input changes, helping to preserve the listener's hearing. Nonetheless, a significant portion of the receiver's response is indeed intended to be linear.

This applies only to desired signals within the passband of the receiver. Because IMD products are created by a non-linear mixing process, they change at a faster rate than the desired signal. As the undesired signals go up, the third-order distortion products also go up, but three times as fast. Likewise, when the undesired signals get weaker, the distortion products decrease three times as fast. Sharp readers will conclude that this response change is also linear—indeed that is so, but this line (if plotted) would have a slope three times the response plot of the desired signal. If these two responses were plotted on the same graph, the two lines would intersect at a point. This point is known as the third-order intercept. Actually, because the value stated is the input signal level, this is technically the third-order input intercept.

As stated earlier, real receivers are not linear over their whole input range. As a result, the third-order intercept can never be reached (or measured) because the receiver always goes into gain compression or desense before that can happen. For that reason, the third-order intercept is, strictly, a theoretical point. While its usefulness may not be immediately obvious, this figure gives a good indication of a receiver's overall strong signal performance.

The second-order intercept is similar to the third-order intercept. Second-order IMD products are produced directly from the sum and difference of the undesired signals. So while the third-order products are produced by signals that are near the desired frequency, the second-order products are often quite distant in frequency. For example, if a receiver is tuned to 14,020 kHz, then the frequency of two signals (note that there are many more possibilities) that would cause a second-order response at 14,020 are 6020 and 8000 kHz. The rate of change in the second-order products is twice that of the desired signal. The second-order intercept is then the point at which the second-order response plot would intersect the desired signal response.

IF and Image Rejection

As if the effects of multiple undesired signals were not bad enough, receivers also can experience problems created by the influence of external signals over frequencies that are intentionally present within the receiver. One such internal frequency is the receiver's first intermediate frequency (IF). In general-coverage HF receivers, this is usually a frequency higher than 30 MHz, such as 45 MHz. Even with robust filtering before the first conversion stage, some energy from strong external signals that coincide with the receiver's first IF can still find its way into the first mixer. To measure IF rejection in the lab, a signal generator set to the receiver's IF is connected to the antenna jack, and the generator output is increased until a signal appears at the receiver output that is equal to the receiver's noise floor. The difference between the noise floor and the generator level is the amount of rejection.

In many receivers, good IF rejection can be provided by sharp filter skirts at the RF stages. In wideband VHF and UHF receivers, however, particularly handheld units, the IF is often within the receiver's normal operating range or very close to it. On bands that are close to the IF, the rejection is often poor because of the modest rejection provided by the filter skirts at close frequencies.

Another example of the influence of external signals on internal ones is *image rejection*. One of the characteristics of mixers is that they produce many different products in addition to the intended one. Filtering following the mixer is intended to attenuate these undesired products, leaving only the desired IF signal. Some RF frequencies can produce images in the first mixer such that the images coincide with the IF and are therefore not attenuated after the mixing process. These signals are measured in the test of image rejection.

Testing image rejection is much the same as testing IF rejection—a signal at the image frequency is dialed up on the signal generator, and the level is adjusted for a noise floor signal on the output of the receiver. Because images are usually far removed from the tuned frequency, image rejection is often excellent, perhaps 80 to 100 dB or more. On the higher UHF bands, however, the image rejection in a handheld wideband receiver may be poor because of the very broad front-end filtering often used at those frequencies.

Other Tests (Audio Output, IF/AF BW, etc)

The tests described so far cover the "meat" of a receiver's performance, and they are usually given the most weight when comparing different models. Of course, there are other receiver performance issues that interest different folks, and these are covered in the comprehensive set of tests performed for *QST*'s Product Reviews. The audio output test gives information about the transceiver's audio performance—useful to know if you plan on using the receiver in a noisy environment. The IF/AF bandwidth test gives the net bandwidth of the receiver's cascaded IF and AF stages using its nominal filter widths. The squelch sensitivity test tells the strength of a signal that will "break through" the squelch at its minimum setting (called the threshold). The S-meter test notes the strength of a signal that indicates S9 on the receiver's S-meter. This reveals how different S-meters can be on various receivers.

TRANSMITTER TESTING
Power Output

Power output, the most straightforward of transmitter tests, gives an easily understood result. The aim in this test is simply to determine the actual power output from a transmitter in watts. While most MF/HF transceivers are designed for a nominal output of 100 W, they will sometimes exceed this figure by a few watts, or in some cases, fall just shy of the mark. Maximum output often varies from band to band as well.

Those who like to dabble in low power (QRP) operating from time to time will also want to know a transmitter's minimum output power. The ARRL Awards program defines QRP as 5 W or less power output. Many transceivers can be "throttled back" to less, but some exceed that level and that is useful knowledge for this type of operating.

Spectral Purity

FCC rules have strict requirements for spectral purity on the HF and VHF bands—these are outlined in *The ARRL's FCC Rule Book*,[2] and they are also described in detail in *The ARRL RFI Book*.[3] In addition to rules compliance, it is useful to know the amount of a transmitter's harmonic and spurious output to prevent interference to other radio services and other amateur bands—a chief reason that our allocations are generally harmonically related.

Two-Tone IMD

Transmit two-tone intermodulation distortion, or two-tone IMD, is a measure of spurious output close to the desired audio of a transmitter being operated in SSB mode. This spurious output is often created in the audio stages of a transceiver, but any amplification stage can contribute.

If you've ever heard someone causing "splatter," the noisy audio that extends beyond a normal 3 kHz nominal SSB bandwidth, then you have heard the effects of transmit IMD. Frequencies close to the transmit signal are affected the most, but depending on the amount of IMD, large portions of the band can suffer from one poor transmitter.

Carrier and Unwanted Sideband Suppression

One of the main benefits of single sideband operation is that the required frequency spectrum is greatly reduced compared to AM. It allows stations to operate close together without interfering with each other. This assumes that the reduction in the carrier and opposite sideband is sufficient to prevent interference. Thus, it pays to know the amount of suppression instead of just taking it for granted. The level of suppression is measured relative to the desired sideband. In the ARRL Lab, this is done by feeding a sine wave at a known audio frequency into the microphone input, and adjusting the amplitude level until the transceiver is operating at its rated output. Although having more suppression is almost always better, 45-50 dB or so is generally adequate.

Keying Waveform

The CW keying waveform can tell quite a bit about the way your transmitter will sound in someone else's receiver. The ARRL Lab test for this is performed using a custom-built keying generator (basically a precision timing circuit with a switching transistor output). The generator is set up to send a string of dits at a rate of 60 WPM, and the output of the very first dit and second dit are captured on a storage oscilloscope. Subsequent dits are usually identical to the second dit. This test shows whether there is any dit shortening in break-in (QSK) operation (usually there is some), it also shows the waveform shape (which can indicate a tendency to produce key clicks) and indicates the keying delay—the time from when the key is depressed until RF actually starts to appear.

The top trace in these photos is the voltage on the transceiver's key jack, as determined by the transceiver itself (since the keying generator does not put out any voltage). When the transceiver is key down, the voltage on this line will be close to zero (as it would be if you were using a straight key). When the transceiver is key up the voltage goes up to whatever value the transmitter's circuit produces while in receive. Sometimes this key line voltage can be oddly shaped (such as having a curved rise time on key up), but this is not of any consequence.

Turnaround Time Tests

The turnaround time test measures the delay between receive and transmit, and the delay between transmit and receive. This test is performed in the SSB mode (important for folks who like to operate digital modes), and in the FM mode (important for packet operators and in some cases for FM repeater operation). A transmit-to-receive delay of 35 ms or less in SSB indicates that a rig is suitable for digital operation. In FM, the receive-transmit delay determines the appropriate TNC settings for packet. If the delay (either T-R or R-T) on FM is long enough (200 ms or more), it starts to become noticeable to folks operating on repeaters— the T-R delay can cause loss of the first syllable (or part of it) of some words. The R-T delay can cause the loss of some syllables unless you remember to add a short pause between PTT and start of speaking. Long R-T delays can also lead to "doubling" in group conversations if other listeners are not aware of it.

Composite Transmitted Noise

In some receiver dynamic range measurements, you'll see a "noise-limited" figure, as discussed above. Often this is the result of an internal oscillator (such as the primary VFO) that is "noisy." All oscillators have some minor variations in their output that can be in either amplitude or frequency or both. This variation, which results in noise appearing close to the oscillator's intended frequency, is referred to as *phase noise* because it is manifested as short-term changes in the phase of the oscillation frequency.

Measuring the transmit phase noise can be done at any frequency by comparing to the output of a low noise signal generator. *QST* Product Reviews include a performance figure of composite transmitter noise. The majority of this is usually also the receiver's phase noise, but since other noise sources can also contribute, the name is a little different. If the noise level of a transmitter is high enough, it can even show up in a receiver that is close in frequency; however, the receiver's dynamic range performance is often affected at lower signal levels.

Expanded Testing (and reporting)

In the latter half of 1995, the ARRL Lab staff considered a number of ideas on how to give ARRL members more value without changing the way *QST* Product Reviews were presented. The result of this was the introduction of an expanded set of Lab tests, with the results to be included in special Expanded Test Result Reports. These are available on the ARRL Member's Web Pages (or by mail for those without Web access). The expanded reports include data on all the bands for which it is taken (*QST* reviews only report worst case figures), and includes some new tests that were not previously performed. In addition, some background on the test methods are given. More information on these expanded reports can be found in the April 1996 *QST* article, "Under the Microscope—The ARRL Laboratory's Expanded Test Result Report," by Dean Straw, N6BV. A copy of this article appears on the Product Reviews section of the Member's Pages. Because of their time-intensive nature, only some of the products that go through Product Review are selected for the expanded testing.

Hands-On Testing and Writing

After the ARRL Lab has put a piece of equipment through its paces on the bench, it goes to the reviewer. The reviewer must become familiar with the equipment by checking out all the features and functions in order to assess its ease of operation. Next, the reviewer will "put it through its paces" in real world situations, usually at a home station, to see how the equipment behaves in a practical sense. A reviewer must be thorough, and use the equipment in as wide a range of operating conditions as possible. Although the idea is to attempt to replicate the same situations that most readers will encounter there is, of course, a limit to the degree that this is possible. It is one of the reasons some Product Review items are evaluated by multiple reviewers.

Once a reviewer is finished with the new equipment, he or she must actually write about it. The reviewer must be thorough here, too, touching on all aspects of the equipment and documentation. Reviewers must be as objective as possible, avoiding the bias of personal preferences or opinion. At the same time, the reviewer may add some creativity and style (and anecdotal experiences) to make the review more readable than dry technical text.

Editing and Wrap-Up

The editing and wrap-up phases take place after the equipment has been completely evaluated. However well written, every Product Review must still undergo some amount of editing. Aside from typographical or grammatical correction, the text must also be double-checked for completeness and technical consistency.

Before the finished review is approved for publication, a copy is provided to the equipment manufacturer. This is done so that any technical errors or omissions that may have been missed in the earlier review stages can be corrected or issues resolved. Manufacturers do not have a free hand, however—only objective comments are considered for inclusion.

The last step before publication is the final editing—this is where the graphics, figures, tables and text all come together to form a "final" version of the review. This is the job of ARRL's Graphics, Production and Editorial staff (of course, they prepare *all* articles for *QST* and other publications).

What Happens Afterward

Equipment used for reviews is retained in the ARRL Lab for at least 30 days after publication of the review in *QST* to allow a retest if needed. It may then be retained by the ARRL, but most often the items are sold on the basis of competitive bids. A minimum bid is established, below current market price, and invitations to bid are published at **www.arrl.org/members-only/prodrev/prauctions**.

Where Do We Go From Here?

Over the past two decades, the Product Review column has continued to expand and improve, and testing in the ARRL Lab has followed suit. This process continues even today. As the ARRL Lab receives input on test methods from professionals in the field, we try to incorporate the latest measurement techniques while maintaining as consistent a process as possible to allow meaningful comparisons.

Notes
[1]For details of the ARRL Lab test procedures, see the ARRL Lab Test Procedures Manual at www.arrl.org/members-only/prodrev/testproc.pdf.
[2]*The ARRL FCC Rule Book*, Thirteenth Edition Chapter 4, pp 44-48. Available from ARRL dealers or the ARRL Bookstore for $12.95 plus shipping. Order number 9000. See **www.arrl.org/shop/** or call toll-free in the US 888-277-5289, or 860-594-0303.
[3]*The ARRL RFI Book*, Chapter 17, pp 9-11. Available from ARRL dealers or the ARRL Bookstore for $24.95 plus shipping. Order number 6834. See **www.arrl.org/shop/** or call toll-free in the US 888-277-5289, or 860-594-0303.

Michael Tracy, KC1SX, is an ARRL Test Engineer. He can be reached at mtracy@arrl.org.

ARRL Membership Benefits

QST Monthly Magazine

QST covers new trends and the latest technology, fiction, humor, news, club activities, rules and regulations, special events, and much more. Here is some of what you will find every month:

- Informative product reviews of the newest radios and accessories
- A monthly conventions and hamfest calendar
- A public service column that keeps you up to date on the public service efforts hams are providing around the country and shows you how you can join in this satisfying aspect of our hobby
- Eclectic Technology, a monthly column that covers emerging Amateur Radio and commercial technology
- A broad spectrum of articles in every issue ranging from challenging topics to straightforward, easy-to-understand projects

ARRL members also get preferred subscription rates for *QEX*, the ARRL Forum for Communications Experimenters.

Members-Only Web Services

- **QST Digital Edition**
  All ARRL members can access the online digital edition of *QST*. Enjoy enhanced content, convenient access and a more interactive experience. An app for *iOs* devices is also available.
- **QST Archive and Periodicals Search**
  Browse ARRL's extensive online *QST* archive. A searchable index for *QEX* and *NCJ* is also available.
- **Free E-Newsletters**
  Subscribe to a variety of ARRL e-newsletters and e-mail announcements: ham radio news, radio clubs, public service, contesting and more!
- **Product Review Archive**
  Search for, and download, *QST* Product Reviews published from 1980 to present.
- **E-Mail Forwarding Service**
  E-mail sent to your **arrl.net** address will be forwarded to any e-mail account you specify.
- **Customized ARRL.org home page**
  Customize your home page to see local ham radio events, clubs and news.
- **ARRL Member Directory**
  Connect with other ARRL members via a searchable online Member Directory. Share profiles, photos and more with members who have similar interests.

Technical Information Service (TIS)

Get answers on a variety of technical and operating topics through ARRL's Technical Information Service. Our experts can help you overcome hurdles and answer all your questions.

Member Benefit Programs and Discounts

- **ARRL "Special Risk" Ham Radio Equipment Insurance Plan**
  Insurance is available to protect you from loss or damage to your station, antennas and mobile equipment by lightning, theft, accident, fire, flood, tornado, and other national disasters.
- **MetLife® Auto, Home, Renters, Boaters, Fire Insurance and Banking Products**
  As an ARRL member you could enjoy up to a 10% discount on various insurance programs.
- **The ARRL Platinum Visa® Card**
  Show your ham radio pride with the ARRL Visa credit card. You earn great rewards and every purchase supports ARRL programs and services.

Outgoing QSL Service

Let us be your mail carrier and handle your overseas QSLing chores. The savings you accumulate through this service alone can pay your membership dues many times over.

Continuing Education

Take courses to help you prepare to pass your license exam, upgrade, learn more about Amateur Radio activities, or train for emergency communications or public service. ARRL also offers hundreds of books, CDs and videos on the technical, operating, and licensing facets of Amateur Radio.

Regulatory Information Branch

Reach out to our Regulatory Information Branch for information on FCC and regulatory questions; problems with antenna, tower and zoning restrictions; and reciprocal licensing procedures.

ARRL as an Advocate

ARRL supports legislation in Washington, D.C. that preserves and protects access to existing Amateur Radio frequencies as a natural resource for the enjoyment of all hams. As a member, you contribute to the efforts to preserve our privileges.

ARRL The national association for **AMATEUR RADIO®**

AMERICAN RADIO RELAY LEAGUE • 225 MAIN ST • NEWINGTON, CT, USA 06111-1494 • TELEPHONE 860-594-0200 • FAX 860-594-0259

www.arrl.org/join